Saving St Brigid's

Regina Lane

Bridin Books

First published in March 2014
Third edition published May 2016
Copyright © Regina Lane 2014

This book is copyright. Apart from any use permitted under the Copyright Act 1968 and subsequent amendments, no part of this book may be reproduced or transmitted in any form or by any means, electronic or mechanical, including photocopying, recording or by any information storage or retrieval system, without the prior written permission of the copyright owner and the publisher of this book. Every attempt has been made to locate the copyright holders for material quoted in this book. Any person or organisation that may have been overlooked or misattributed may contact the publisher.

This project has been assisted by the Australian Government through Department of Sustainability, Environment, Water, Population and Communities.

Bridin Books
6 Valiant Street
Abbotsford, 3067
Victoria Australia
info@bridinbooks.com.au
bridinbooks.com.au

Cover art by Teresa O'Brien
Cover photography by Wes Pryor and Teresa O'Brien
Family tree art by Teresa O'Brien
Map © Teresa O'Brien

Copy edited by Ian Sibley and Alex Kolasinski
Set in Garamond 11pt.
Layout Red Bilby Media
www.redbilby.com.au

A catalogue record for this book is available from
the National Library of Australia.

ISBN 978-0-9923433-4-7   (pb)

PRAISE FOR SAVING ST BRIGID'S

'This is one of those books that comes along once in the blue moon. The kind that arrives unheralded, without literary pedigree or fanfare, without glitz or commercial appeal. And it blows your socks off. No summary can do it justice.'
— *Sydney Morning Herald*

'Every now and then a book arrives out of left field and demands, by the sheer force of its presence, to be taken seriously. Saving St Brigid's is one of these books.'
— Fiona Capp, author of *My Blood Country*

'Written with considerable skill…this is not a book to be read in small doses…it is an entirely gripping read.'
— *The Irish Echo*

'A cliff-hanger, a race against time to save a church…an exciting and pacey read.'
— Rachael Kohn, 'The Spirit of Things', *ABC Radio National*

'Regina Lane's stunning account is like a glass of cool water, a refreshing reminder of what we lose when we forget where we belong… a remarkable story.'
— Scott Stephens, Religion and Ethics, *ABC*

'She (Regina) gives herself so generously in her writing that her book becomes a love story, touching all the moments of self-doubt, of ecstasy, of despair, of friendship, of the transfiguration of faces and places, and of exacting ordinariness that are the grammar of love.'
— *Eureka Street*

'Saving St Brigid's is a David and Goliath story about a group of passionate and determined locals who are determined to save their parish church in spite of the intransigence of Catholic Church officials…Regina Lane's excellent book does justice to the epic nature of this struggle.'
— *The New Daily*

'It is a fascinating, uplifting narrative about a community that successfully resisted such monolithic power and in the process empowered itself.'
— *Tintean Magazine*

'Regina Lane brings the spirit of the region's multi-faceted history alive through the tale of modern rebellion, and in doing so, creates her own culture of thought, which leaves a legacy of its own.'
— *Bluestone Magazine*

As I turned the pages of *Saving St Brigid's* my mind resonated with many of the deep-seated emotions – loss, anger, courage, perseverance, empowerment – contained within them. The book will inspire Irish readers in particular, who will recognise, in the searing saga of this wonderfully committed community, the raw struggles and stories of their widely scattered forbears. It will bring a welcome warmth to Irish hearts during the winter evenings of their green island.

All over the Western Catholic world today this painfully true story is being repeated. *Saving St Brigid's* provides an invaluable blueprint of hope for the future. It needs and deserves to be told in a confused, vulnerable and anxious age.

Reading this unique book stirred something in my soul. We all carry a 'St Brigid's' within us – a shrine to a just cause, a symbol of an aching vision, a commitment to a fierce desire for what is right and loving and beautiful. This sacred space resides in every human heart but, perhaps because of our temperament and history, it carries a particularly powerful echo in the Irish one.

You will be touched at many deep levels of memory and destiny as you give yourself to this courageous story.

Fr Daniel O'Leary

Part proceeds of the sale of this book will go to The Friends of St Brigid's Association Inc.

For my parents, *Loretta* and *Michael Lane*, who were, and always will be, the inspiration.

Aboriginal people are respectfully asked to note that names and photographs of deceased persons occur in this book.

Contents

Foreword by Mary Black
Prologue by Shane Howard

1	The last mass	1
2	'A new Ireland in the south'	9
3	Sweet sixteen	21
4	One of ten	35
5	Between love and fear	51
6	'You have my word'	71
7	Locked out	85
8	Power and pride	93
9	Going home	105
10	A ruling from Rome	117
11	On the market	127
12	Asking hard questions	139
13	The legal challenge	155
14	'Old and empty'	171
15	Saving St Brigid's	185
16	A black day	209
17	The race to the finish line	231
	Epilogue	241
	Afterword	249

Foreword

Mary Black

I started touring Australia in the late eighties. It was obvious from that first trip that there was a strong Irish diaspora throughout the country. I became all the more aware of this when I met Shane Howard, singer songwriter, who was my special guest on my Australian tour in 1992. Even though Shane was born and reared in Australia, his knowledge of Irish music and culture was akin to my own. We fast became friends. Though Shane was 3rd generation Irish and was raised on the other side of the world there were huge similarities between his upbringing and mine. Shane was not unusual in this. I soon learned that there was a whole community in south-west Victoria who had kept up their Irish heritage and faith, long after their ancestors first arrived on the famine ships 150 years before.

In 2006, I performed at the Port Fairy Folk Festival and Shane and his sister, Marcia, invited me over to Killarney to sing at a fundraising concert for St Brigid's. I was told that the Catholic Church was selling St Brigid's and that the local community had no say in the matter. I was appalled. Shane explained that the community had come together to try to fight the imminent sale.

I had always been struck by this area, not only by the landscape that reminded me of home, but the place names, the family names, even the faces could have been plucked from any town in rural Ireland.

Saving St Brigid's

This beautiful piece of Ireland in Australia had come about by the kind of chain migration I had heard about where, for instance, numerous families in West Kerry had gone to places like Chicago and Springfield, Mass., and developed whole new Irish communities.

The first time I walked through the doors of St Brigid's, it reminded me of my father's church and local hall on Rathlin Island, County Antrim and how important it is to the shrinking local community there.

It seemed so unfair that the Catholic Church was selling St Brigid's to the highest bidder with no thought for the community who had funded the building of this church – and whose money was used to maintain it and support the Catholic clergy – for over a hundred years.

I have been back to St Brigid's since 2006 and met many of the local people, including Regina's parents, Mick and Loretta, at those sessions at Killarney and Crossley. Each time, I see just how important St Brigid's is to keeping this small little rural community alive.

St Brigid's was built as a testament to the survival and strength of the Irish who settled in south-west Victoria. A hundred years later, their descendants fought an uphill battle against powerful vested interests to save their buildings, and hold onto the spirit of Ireland.

It is a delight to be a part of this wonderful story.

Prologue

Shane Howard

My family grew up in south-west Victoria, Australia. It's the same country as Regina Lane and her family's. We know how the dark chocolate-coloured soil underlies the luminous green velvet fields that roll down from the lakes of Tower Hill to the dunes and shores of the sometimes placid and sometimes tempestuous Southern Ocean. We know the same feeling of the stinging rain lashing your face in the wild winds and dark depths of winter. We know the vigorous sou-westerlies of spring that blow in from the Antarctic Circle, filling the sky with fast-moving clouds that create the play of sun and shadow on the hills and blow the winter away. We know the grip of summer sunburn and sea salt, potatoes and milk, benedictions and first communions, incense and the rich theatre of Irish Catholic ritual.

In this book Regina details her family's journey from their farming life in Ireland, through the desperate days of the emigration driven by Ireland's Great Famine, to farming in Australia and building a new life in a new land.

I know Regina's family story well. Her cultural history echoes my own. In fact when her parents, Mick and Loretta, returned to Ireland to trace and visit their ancestral lands, the ancestral Lane farm was neighboured by the Maddens. The Maddens were my ancestors, who came from the same area around Killaloe and Ballina in County Clare.

Saving St Brigid's

It's not surprising really. So many of the original Irish settlers in south-west Victoria would come from a particular area and would travel on the same boat. Chain migration would then follow as those who settled wrote back to Ireland and encouraged relations to follow. This is the story of so many of the Australians of Irish descent in this part of the small world.

Regina's story is a personal journey into the heart of her family culture and her Irish historical culture and what it means to keep that alive or try to give it meaning in an Australian landscape in the twenty-first century.

But the bigger questions of church and faith, colonisation and community occupy her mind as well and move from the fringes, to the centre stage of her thinking. Questions of justice arise, against the backdrop of a Catholic Church in crisis, reeling from the consequences of child sexual abuse.

The Lane family have been stalwarts of the local community since they first arrived here in the mid-nineteenth century. Regina's mum and dad have been pillars of the local Church community. Devout but not pious, they have been examples of the very best of what it means to live a Christian life. Regina's mother, Loretta, scrubbed and cleaned floors in the church and with her husband, Mick, helped maintain St Brigid's church and hall, perpetually. Loretta would do twenty good deeds for other people in a normal week and think nothing of it. She wouldn't make a big deal of it.

Regina's mother is a bridge between the world of my mother's generation and later generations. She carries so much of the long story and the social and historical map of the district in her head, in the same way as those older generations of women have done, since time immemorial, when they gathered in a huddle, at funerals and social gatherings, to draw and re-draw the relational map of the district.

Regina grew up in the thick of this deep well of Irish Catholicism and the never-ending talk and the manners and customs and old superstitions. That world, although it changes, still lives on in the digital age, for we are social beings and need each other to make our story and connect it together.

Prologue

In 1993, Mary Black popularised my song 'Flesh and Blood' in Ireland. It began for me a series of journeys to Ireland and beyond and a cultural awakening and a deepening sense of my ancestry and my own indigineity. Aboriginal Australia had awoken that curiosity in me, in the early 1980s.

When I returned to live in Killarney, south-west Victoria in 1998, I was delighted to discover that there was a fellow called Tommy Carty running traditional Irish music sesiuns in Warrnambool, Port Fairy and the Killarney Hotel. There were wild nights too in John O'Toole's Shed which was decorated with much of the religious paraphernalia that had come from the decommissioned St John's church in Dennington, including the old altar that served as a bar. Some great Irish musicians have graced the St Brigid's church and hall in the intervening years: Mossie Scanlon, Jackie Daly, Steve Cooney, Seamus Begley, Brian Kennedy, John Spillane, Liam O'Maonlai, Martin O'Connor and Mary Black, who has been a generous and ongoing supporter of the campaign to save St Brigid's.

In 2000, at the encouragement of Phillip Moore, my wife Teresa O'Brien and I convened a meeting of the Australian Irish Association of South West Victoria, in Killarney, and called together many of the elders of the old families of the district. We asked those old people what they wanted and they were unanimous in wanting their Australian-Irish story told and remembered. It was this imprimatur that sanctioned much of the drive of the campaign to save St Brigid's.

Teresa was elected secretary of The Friends of St Brigid's and took a central role in the organisation of the campaign to save St Brigid's church and the adjoining hall from passing into private ownership.

The campaign wasn't easy. There was a human cost. The campaign took a huge toll on so many of those involved. It placed a great strain on families and had the capacity to divide the community.

I was in Ireland, in Kildare, at St Brigid's Well in the crucial twenty-four hours before the sale that would decide the future of the St Brigid's precinct. I met with the Brigidines there. Prayers were offered. Promises were made to bring the eternal flame of St Brigid from Kildare to Crossley, if the church was saved, to light our own eternal flame. The symbolism was powerful. The fear of losing our community property was real.

We, the descendants, felt that we owed it to our ancestors to keep the precinct in the care and ownership of the community.

This was our sacred ground. If we couldn't protect our own heritage then all our history counted for nothing. We would be culturally bereft and adrift, without an anchor point. This was a spiritual home for our old people and our young people and we had to show them that we cared. We were also deeply aware that Irish history is littered with heroic failures.

At one level, this is just a little local story. But as the brilliant Irish poet Patrick Kavanagh says in his poem 'Epic', when a local feud over land appeared insignificant against the emerging tide of World War II, 'the Munich bother', as he called it,

. . . Homer's ghost came whispering to my mind
He said: I made the Iliad from such
A local row. Gods make their own importance.

Regina has wrapped all of this local history and culture and struggle up into the loving bundle of words that comprise this book; and the story transcends 'a local row' to ask the bigger questions about justice and culture, faith and community, and the importance of the spirit of place.

CHAPTER ONE

The last mass

It was one of those hot, clear summer days. The ocean shimmered bright blue in the sun. Wooden spud boxes were aligned by the fence posts, waiting for the harvest to begin. Jets of water fanned across the paddocks, with the rhythmic sound of the 'click, click' of the irrigators that had lulled me to sleep as a child. Hand-painted signs lined the highway: 'Spuds: $10 for 10 kgs'. A high-pitched child's voice in my head yelled out 'S-a-l-e!', and I smiled at the memory of us kids running for our lives down the lane, whenever a car pulled up at the corner to buy a sack of spuds.

I turned right off the highway at the old Killarney store. No longer a corner store, the sign on the wall tells the story – 'Antiques and Collectables', those things we no longer have use for; the discarded, forgotten things of old. How fitting, I thought darkly, for the day that lay ahead, as I looked up to that grand old red-brick church on the hill.

In the shadows beneath, nestles an iconic landscape. When you look at Tower Hill, you get the feeling you're looking at a painting, as if you've seen it before. That's probably because you have. Eugene von Guérard, one of Australia's most important painters of the colonial era, was fascinated by the crater lakes of Victoria's volcanic Western District, and his painting, called *Tower Hill*, is one of his most famous. I call it home.

I was not surprised to see the car park was full as I pulled up at the far end under the old cypress trees near the tennis court, looking back down over the Southern Ocean. Walking across the cracked asphalt and yellow daisies in the churchyard, everything looked as it always had. There's comfort in that, they say. But things had changed.

I entered through the foyer at the front, the wooden panelled opaque glass doors pegged back, the brown tiles swept and polished one last time. The aroma of my childhood hit me, a musty mix of candle wax, furniture polish and freshly vacuumed carpet. It felt strange to walk across to the far side of the church, and I found myself doing what I always had as a kid and walked in a straight line along the fawn-coloured tiles that trimmed the edges of the church and ran down the centre aisle like tram tracks. The Lane family only ever sat on the left side of the church when one of our girls had got married. On a normal Sunday morning we sat on the right side, in the second row, behind Val Mugavin and Lorraine Gavin, and in front of Des and Jim Gleeson. But this wasn't a normal Sunday.

It crossed my mind that I could have better dressed for the occasion, as I looked down the two aisles of twenty pews, packed end to end, familiar faces looking back at me. I squeezed in behind Mum and Dad alongside the McElgunn family. I craned my head to look around the congregation, considered terribly rude when we were kids, always earning us one of 'those looks' from Mum. That was the problem sitting at the front; you could never see who else was there. I loved it on the odd occasion we went to mass in Warrnambool, when we sat at the back of the church, and got to check out all the people who snuck in the back door late. We were never late to mass at Crossley. Mum would make sure of that. Except for the time when we girls had been arguing in the back seat about who would do the reading at 8:30 am mass. We crashed our orange station wagon into a cow which had swaggered onto the road and Liz and I smirked to ourselves at having got out of doing the reading. We'd have to be dead before we could actually miss Sunday mass altogether – two hours later we were sitting in our usual seat at nearby Infant Jesus Church, Koroit.

I was glad no one asked me to read today. I couldn't have held it together. I sat there through the First and Second Reading, looking up to the wooden pulpit, the Gospel resting on slats where the priest often leaned an elbow as he sermonised, with the slow dawning that I would never sit here in these pews again. Behind the pulpit stood the statue of Jesus, one hand raised to show the nail pierced through his palm, the other holding back his red cloak to reveal his bloody, fiery Sacred Heart. I smiled to myself, thinking of the picture that adorned the wall above Mum and Dad's bed, a wedding present which we tried to dismantle and hide many times when Mum and Dad were away, but which somehow always found its way back. No parent I know these days would keep such a gruesome image in their house, let alone above their bed. On the opposite wall, Jesus hung on the cross, a grey and bloodied body, his hands and feet nailed to the cross, a thorny crown jammed onto his head. I remembered a time when I'd never known how humans could inflict such torture or pain on others and how listening to the Gospels at St Brigid's, of Jesus walking on water and rising from the dead, I believed that if you only prayed long and hard enough, anything could be overcome. I felt a twinge of sadness, thinking of the candle burning on Mum's altar at home. She'd had her fair share of words with God in the past few weeks, but it hadn't changed much.

When the priest stood to say the Gospel, no altar boys flanked the pulpit holding candles. There were no altar boys left at all at Crossley, and no time to invite an old altar boy to do the job. There were no flowers, the organ sat silently in the corner. There was no slide show of St Brigid's rich history, or a special booklet printed to mark the occasion. The decision to close St Brigid's had been made hastily and deliberately so, it seemed. Not even enough time to invite the many priests and nuns who had long histories and great love of St Brigid's. Not even the Bishop attended.

I watched Dad bow his head when Father Bryant started his homily. He knew what was coming. I followed the lines of logic that he spoke and felt my blood boil. It sounded like a defence hearing, he in the witness stand, desperately making excuses to respond to the arguments my dad had so painstakingly laid out to the Church hierarchy. He sounded anxious, eager to get it over with, this day he'd waited for so long. It was unfortunate, but such is life, was the general tone of his homily. Churches cost money to maintain, he reminded the congregation, as if we had no comprehension. We can't keep them open: not enough people attend church on Sunday.

We sat there, heads bowed, guilty as charged.

Saving St Brigid's

I wanted to stand and speak out. I wanted to protest, to have my own Martin Luther King moment, the words of protest to flow eloquently from my mouth, inspiring the people to rise around me and demand that we, the people, have our voice heard. Rehearsing the facts in my head, as carefully researched and recorded by my father, and respectfully presented to the diocese, I felt my heart beating so loudly I wondered if the people around me could hear it. The saliva in my mouth dried up, and I sat on my palms to wipe the sweat from them. I thought I could do it.

I didn't.

Stupid, you fool. He's a priest and he's made up his mind. He has the might and the power of the Catholic Church behind him. None of us have the right to speak against him. That much is clear.

I don't even have a damn handkerchief, I cursed myself as I brushed away tears from my face, and forced down the lump in my throat, so I could shake hands in the sign of peace. I watched as Dad pushed the wheelchair of my ninety-four-year-old grandmother, the oldest person in the church, down the aisle in the offertory procession. My mother and my brother Patrick, and his baby boy, Thomas, carried the bread, water and wine to be consecrated by the priest. Four generations of Lanes, spanning the lifetime of St Brigid's. My family offered their gifts, and bowed their heads, before Father Bryant standing on the polished wooden step, at the front of the church. I could feel my Dad's pain in that moment of subservience. How had it come to this?

At Communion, I watched the procession of people filing towards the altar: Barbara and Peter Madden, Val Mugavin, Tich Kelly; all familiar faces of my childhood. There were other faces, too. People who I couldn't name, but looked like somebody I know, or should know. I noticed the swollen eyes, the look of shock on people's faces, as if they had just lost something they didn't realise they had. I longed to hear my mum's voice in a familiar hymn – 'The Lord is my Shepherd' was my favourite, but there was no such warmth on this occasion. Only silence and a stone look from the priest when he offered the body of Christ. I kneeled on the hard wooden pew, my knees feeling the pain that we dared not complain about as children. I said a prayer that was both an apology and a plea. I watched as each middle-aged parishioner who passed by my grandmother, sitting in her wheelchair, greeted her with a kiss on the cheek and a pat on her wrinkly old hand. Her head sunk into her chest, but she raised it in acknowledgement of each greeting and I saw both tears and smiles in her eyes. She might have left the farm in Killarney thirty years ago, but Connie Lane wasn't forgotten in these parts.

The statue of St Brigid, the patron saint of Ireland, after whom my parents chose my second name, had stood for nearly one hundred years, in the corner on the right, above the pulpit overlooking the church. A woman of the land, she held a staff in one hand, and a miniature brown church in the other. My grandmother, parked beside the statue, was wheeled out of the way, and two men lifted the heavy statue down from the column on which it stood and carried it out of the church, like a coffin bound for its grave. There was a mood of disbelief in the air, like at a funeral when the deceased has passed suddenly, taken before their time.

We were informed that the church was being decommissioned, and Lorraine Gavin and Pat Mugavin folded up the altar cloths. In her day, my Nana had scrubbed the priests' garments and the altar cloths on the old wash board, and starched them till they could nearly stand straight on their own. It was too much for poor old Nana, and she put her head in her hands and cried. Dad slumped his back a little and I could tell from behind that he was crying too. For all the times I've sat with my dad at a funeral, I can't ever remember seeing him cry. It was more than I could take, and I didn't even bother to hide my own tears as I watched a piece of my faith, my family story and our local history stripped away before me.

Father Bryant didn't show any emotion, as he explained the church was now a church no longer. We must leave the building immediately so the doors could be locked. Frank O'Brien, sitting ashen-faced, had the unenviable task of locking the doors one last time. There was no procession to end the mass; Father Bryant looked uncomfortable as he left the altar quickly and quietly, into the sacristy at the right of the church. No one paid attention to his orders, and people milled around, taking photos of the stations of the cross that lined the church walls, reading the plaques underneath commemorating the families who had donated them. We creaked open the doors to the old dusty confessional boxes, long since abandoned. My sisters and I milled around the altar we had hidden behind as kids when Mum did the church flowers on Saturdays. We lined up on the pew where the altar boys sat, rang the bells one last time, ran our hands over the marbled alcove where the water and wine sat in their crystal glasses. We knew every nook and cranny, we'd picked out the melted candle wax from every brass candleholder and polished them until we could see our own reflections. We'd raced each other down the aisle with feather dusters, counting out aloud the number of pews. St Brigid's wasn't just a place we went on Sundays. Going back to St Brigid's was like going home. We certainly took better care of it, it seemed!

My sister looked at me with real sadness in her eyes. 'Where are we going to have Mum and Dad's funerals?' It was a morbid, almost silly thing to ask. A question I could not answer. I looked over at Nana in her wheelchair. She looked like she was asleep. 'Where are we going to have Nana's funeral?' I replied. Only a few years ago, Nana had pulled Mum aside at a funeral at Crossley and told her she wanted it to be known where her funeral should be. It went without saying. I wondered what she was thinking, now that her wish could not be fulfilled.

But the day wasn't all sadness. The sun was shining and six hundred people had turned out with their picnic hampers. I watched Mum and Dad among the crowd, their light hearted manner disguising the slap in the face they'd received only two weeks earlier. As people moved outside and across the yard into the hall, the nagging voice inside my head from mass returned.

'You can't let him get away with it,' it said. Liz was as fired up as I was. We wanted answers. We approached Father Bryant in the foyer.

'Father Bryant, can we have a word?'

He looked up, surprised, threatened maybe.

Liz kept her voice soft, even. 'We just need to know how it came to this.'

He stepped back, looking us down. 'Your father wrote a letter to the Bishop. He went over my head,' he said accusingly. 'My lawyers have had a look at that letter. I suggest your father should do the same.'

'I guess Dad felt that he hadn't been given much choice, that people hadn't had a chance to have their say,' I said quietly.

'I spoke to people,' he said.

THE LAST MASS

'I don't think that's what he meant,' I stammered. 'There wasn't any community consultation...' I trailed off, realising that now a city girl, I wasn't in much of a position to state the case.

He seized upon that fact. 'You don't live here,' he spat out, his face reddening, sweat beads gathering on his forehead.

'Yeah, you're right, I don't. But there's a reason I came here today. And same for all those people out there too,' I said, nodding at the crowds outside.

I told him I'd listened to his sermon about how people should renew their faith and return to the Church and that I found it hard to accept in light of what had happened here. I explained to him that in three days' time I had to stand in front of three hundred young Catholics and encourage them to follow Church teaching and work towards social justice. It was a body of teaching I believed in and adhered to in my work, and yet it felt like it'd been forgotten here today, I said weakly.

Father Bryant is a tall, heavy man. He stepped backwards up onto the step which led into the sacristy. He was red in the face and sweating profusely. He pointed his finger down at my sister and me, and delivered the words that defined my understanding of the Catholic Church from that day forward.

'The Church is not a democracy. *I* am the power here.'

There was nothing more to be said. Liz and I stepped backwards out the door of the church, speechless. We couldn't tell Mum and Dad what had just happened. In their minds, it wasn't right to stand up to a priest like that. And we could see them, smiling and socialising with cup and saucer in hand.

I took off to the tennis court and climbed the rusted, rickety old umpire's chair, which looked out above the sandstone wall to the potato fields below. Some of them had been sown, a bed of dark green foliage, in perfectly neat lines, revealing the dark chocolate-coloured volcanic Tower Hill soil. Up close, you can see the white flower, sometimes pink, showing the harvest is soon to begin. It struck me that many harvests ago, it took a fungal disease that ruined a potato crop in Ireland in 1845, which was the very reason I was here today. The very reason St Brigid's was here today.

If our ancestors could survive a famine, make their way to these shores on overcrowded, disease-ridden boats, overcome poverty and oppression in a new land, and instil in their children the faith, strength and foresight to build a church, then the least I could do was try to help save it.

CHAPTER TWO*

'A new Ireland in the South'

They built themselves a new Ireland in the South…
It's as like the original as the beautiful clime will permit…
Killarney looks like an Irish village picked up and dumped here.
The stone walls along the road, the boxthorn hedges, the squat little houses right on the road, all whitewashed and made of big stones, the capped and shawled old women sitting at the door, and the pleasant jovial brogue of Tipperary and Cork.

Nathan Spielvogel, 1913

Rounding the bend at O'Toole's dairy, between Warrnambool and Port Fairy, the road stretches out in a long straight race, parallel to the coast line. The locals call it the 'mad mile'. At the far end looms Tower Hill, a prehistoric landmark of this vast ancient land. Twenty-five thousand years ago, hot magma came into contact with water, causing the magma to fragment violently. Combustion from the heat erupted and caused an explosion that shook the earth for miles. Gas and steam fed the explosion so that lava poured from the volcano like water from a fountain. Ash and debris rained over the surrounding countryside, burning the trees and killing all the wildlife in its path.

Today, the trees are green and abundant, the land thick with vegetation and the sounds of the birds and animals that inhabit this place can be heard from far away. It's hard to believe, in the fresh, crisp, clean

*This chapter draws heavily on the research and writings of historian Dr Helen Doyle.

air, that a place so magnificent in all its beauty could have once wreaked such havoc. To step from the busy highway into Tower Hill State Game Reserve is to step into another world. Far from the hustle and bustle, the silence hits one like a cold splash of water. The fresh, cool breeze on the cheek, the softness of the rich earth underfoot, the singing of the birds in the trees, the water shimmering in the sunset – every sense is stimulated by its awesome splendour.

There's something about this place, something ghostly ancient. The layers of volcanic material on the crater wall are like the growth rings in the trunk of a tree – each line a marker of the years that have passed since the violent explosion. The tree stumps that protrude from the wetlands remind us of the destruction the first white settlers imposed, as they cleared and cultivated the land for firewood and grazing.

Each time I drive over that hill towards home, my breath catches in my throat, my chest tightens a little. Beneath, in the green fields that roll down the hill, is the familiar and comforting view of our family home, where my sisters and brothers and I were raised, and still call home.

When I was in year twelve at school in Warrnambool, I studied 'The Search for Meaning' in religion. Asking myself the big questions about how we came to be here, I was studying conflicting theories of creationism. At the same time, I studied Australian history. I read a chapter of *The Fatal Shore* by Robert Hughes in class. Shocked, I took it home and devoured the whole thing in a weekend, sitting on the front porch, looking up at Tower Hill, a natural monument that defines the ancient history of this land. That's when I began climbing to the top of the hill, to look out to the sea, and wondering about the Aboriginal people that had lived on this land, the tribal clans of the MoonwerGunditj, TarererGunditj and KoroitGunditj people. From that clan, Koroit was named – the town on the northern side of Tower Hill, where I attended primary school and we often went to shop and to mass. The term refers to the 'smoky, hot ground' of the volcano and means 'belonging to'. I felt deep sadness and a sense of irony too when I learned this, for a people decimated by disease, alcohol abuse and killings under the same oppressors' reign that my Irish ancestors had fled.

Ours, too, was an ancient culture whose identity and spirituality was deeply embedded in the land. To the east of Tower Hill, the Celtic cross is dotted over the final resting places of our ancestors, whose journey began thousands of miles across the ocean. Beneath one of those crosses lie my great-great-grandmother and grandfather, Rebecca and Batholomew Lyons. Bartholomew was born in County Clare, but Rebecca was born in Australia after her parents, Luke and Sarah O'Brien, left County Galway in June 1841. The Ireland they left was an agricultural society ravaged by conflict between the Protestants, who owned 90 per cent of the land, and the Catholics, who leased it in small parcels of five acres each if they were lucky; but were landless if they were not. Bitterness and resentment festered between the Catholics and Protestants, and was handed down from generation to generation. Presumably because of regulations limiting the number of children, Luke and Sarah left their six children behind in Ireland when they took the £19 assisted passage to Australia under the Bounty Immigrant Scheme. We don't know what happened to them while their parents were gone, but in 1848, the six children were bought out to Australia through the efforts of the 'immigrant's friend', Caroline Chisholm. Their names are mentioned in her biography, as they were the largest family on board the *Sir Edward Parry*, among the 75 other children on board. Having given birth to eight more children in Australia, the O'Brien family were finally reunited. That same year, Rebecca was born. She and Bartholomew were married and went on to have four children: two boys who died as little babies, one day apart; and two daughters, Margaret and Sarah – my Nana's mother.

The Ireland of the late 1840s descended into famine, a starvation that would last at least four years and see the death of some one million people, changing the face of Ireland's demographic, political and cultural landscape. Galway, where Luke and Sarah came from, was one of the hardest-hit areas, with villages strewn with dead bodies, lying unburied for days. For the million more who boarded the 'coffin ships', praying to reach their destination, the trauma of famine would forever be imprinted in their minds and the stories of survival were passed down through the generations. Those who came to the Port Fairy, Killarney, Crossley and Koroit areas were from some of the worst-affected areas in Ireland, the south-west counties of Clare, Cork, Limerick and Tipperary. They came to Australia in desperation as a beaten people, with little but the will to survive.

Thomas Lane, my great-great-grandfather, who also lies at rest in Tower Hill cemetery, arrived from County Clare in 1854 at the young age of 21 and made his way to central Victoria, like so many of the Irish who came to Australia in the 1850s, dreaming of a road out of poverty paved with gold. Like most of the Irish, he arrived too late, after the gold had all but been found, when the goldfields had become scenes of great struggle between the gold miners, who rebelled against the imposition of expensive licensing fees, and the brutal way in which the British police enforced them. Though not all the protestors were Irish, there's no doubt they played a significant role in bringing those struggles to a climax on Eureka Hill. The Irish fought hard to ensure that the social structures of the old world would not be replicated here in the new, and in doing so, they had an enduring impact on the values that Australians hold dear – equity and egalitarianism, and the notion of a 'fair go'. While Thomas might not have sworn the Eureka Oath at that formative moment in Australia's democratic history, I can imagine that he too must have carried the memory of the poor and persecuted of Ireland in him and shared the desire 'to fight to defend our rights and liberties', a principle of protest that made its way down through the generations.

Thomas eventually moved to the area generally known as Tower Hill, in south-west Victoria, and settled on its western bank at Killarney, a green and pleasant land by the sea. Higher on the western bank of Tower Hill, three miles from Koroit, sat another thriving village called Crossley. The name 'Crossley' was thought to have been chosen by the influential Irish nationalist expatriate politician Charles Gavan Duffy, a self-declared 'Irish rebel to the backbone'. He had been elected to parliament on the votes of the Irish farmers in the district and famously championed the Irish cause for land reform in Australia, based on his direct experience of famine, the tenant rights movement and the nationalist rebellion in Ireland. He later became premier of Victoria.

The rich volcanic soil surrounding Tower Hill had attracted Irish farmers since the early 1840s when two Protestant Irishmen, William

'A NEW IRELAND IN THE SOUTH'

Rutledge and James Atkinson, established themselves as landlords. According to historian Patrick O'Farrell, the first farmers were brought out from Ireland at the expense of Rutledge and believed to be evicted Irish tenants. They leased out small plots to Irish immigrants as had been done in Ireland. Soon they were turning high yields of the humble potato, earning Tower Hill quite the reputation in the colony, the soil like 'nowhere else in Australia' – reason enough for Rutledge to double the rent on the Farnham Survey, which ran along the coast line, to £6 an acre. He imposed the Irish con-acre leasing system, where tenants leased strips of land on an annual basis, and were compelled to sow and harvest a crop by the contract date, lest they lose their tenancy, says Dr Helen Doyle. Farming is a fickle business at the best of times, so dependent on the forces of Mother Nature. Adding the potential for unscrupulous landlords and exploitation in sectarian Ireland, where the con-acre system was used almost exclusively for growing potatoes, it's no wonder that coupled with the potato blight, many historians attribute this system as one of the factors responsible for the great famine in Ireland. Despite the fertility of the soil and relative 'good times', the tenant farmers of Killarney, Victoria, must have been anxious not to see a repeat of history. More than anything, they wanted to own their own land.

Perhaps it was the cultivated strip fields, or maybe it was the whitewashed cottages designed in the Irish way, the peasant dress or the Irish brogue. Whatever it was, visitors in the nineteenth century remarked, more than anywhere else in Victoria it seems, on the resemblance of the area to that found in Ireland. A journalist visiting the township of Killarney in 1866 commented on both the similarity in appearance of the 'peasantry' and the 'hovels' they lived in with that of the 'Green Isle' where they came from.

Because of the rich agricultural land and the familiar farming practices, farmers began to prosper and were soon hiring Irish labourers from the port at Portland, fifty miles to the west, who had obtained passage after hearing how well their friends and relatives were doing in Australia. The prospect that they might save up and buy their own land propelled the chain migration, unlike in Ireland, where no such opportunity existed. By 1901, the county of Villiers in south-west Victoria was home to an Irish-born presence of 50 per cent of the total population of those born in the British Isles, who had mostly come from the south-west counties of Clare, Cork, Limerick and Tipperary. This number of Irish-born was 23 per cent higher than the national average, making it the highest concentration and as Clem Lloyd wrote in 1976, 'arguably the most Irish part of Australia'. Several historians of the Irish in Australia, including Patrick O'Farrell, Chris McConville, James Jupp and Helen Doyle, have since recognised the region as the most important area of Irish settlement in Victoria.

This was a society not ruled by the penal laws of the old country, but there's no doubt that the hangover of sectarianism was most definitely felt in this part of Australia. To be Irish in nineteenth-century Victoria was to know what it was to feel inferior, ridiculed and discriminated against. This only served to strengthen the assertion of Irish national identity, by a community united in their effort to ensure the tyrannical laws they had left behind were consigned to history. The land reform movement was perhaps the best expression of this. In Killarney, Rutledge was nicknamed 'Terrible Billy', says O'Farrell, perhaps for his contempt for the opinions of his tenants by denouncing the Duffy Land Act of 1862, calling free land selection 'rebellious' and 'seditious'. Since these tenants had voted Duffy into power – on his promise that he would 'make possession of the land as universal as possible' – it is no surprise that Rutledge earned the nickname. On the death of Rutledge in 1876, the Farnham Survey became available as freehold, and many of the Irish tenants were able for the first time to purchase their land.

My great-great-grandfather, Thomas Lane, was one of them. Though he had come seeking gold and found none, he laboured hard to own his own property and carve out a modest life for himself and his wife Catherine O'Shannessy, their two sons Thomas and Daniel, and daughter Mary. Thomas' story was a common tale of endurance and survival, of the sons and daughters of Ireland who set sail from a country plagued by famine and crossed the seas to a foreign land, where they defied the dominant Protestant culture and battled to uphold their faith and identity. Finally, they could dream of success and prosperity for their children, and a place in which to give thanks to God.

Thirty-five years later, in 1914, his son, Dan Lane, would share this dream at the top of the hill, at the opening mass of St Brigid's church, Crossley.

On the one hand, given the high concentration of Irish people, it is no surprise that possibly the first Catholic mass to be celebrated in the whole of the Western District of Victoria was in Rocks Road, Killarney, in 1848. While this claim has not been proven, it remains impressive that a church-school operated in Rocks Road at least as early as 1850. On the other hand, one might have expected, if anywhere, that the bustling port of Belfast would have hosted such an occasion, but it feels appropriate that the first Catholic mass in the Western District should be held among the potato fields. Today, in free, secular Australia, it is hard to imagine how, for those people used to defending their right to practise their culture and religion in Ireland, it must have felt in 1848 to walk those country roads to mass after the long journey they had made in search of peace and freedom. As refugees of the great famine, they must have relished the moment to pray in that little schoolhouse, stamping their unique brand of Irish Catholicism on the Western District.

Though the first mass might be of interest to us today, it was their stand for their right to Catholic education that was of broad, even national, interest at the time.

After the closure of a poorly built government school at Bridge End, near Crossley, the government purchased a replacement site on 'elevated ground' from a local farmer named Henry Ritchie. They then merged the government school at Bridge End with the Catholic school in Rocks Road. This meant the large Catholic population at Tower Hill no longer had a school to call their own. For a community inherently opposed to secular education, one can only imagine the discontent this must have caused. They had not come here only to live under the same cloak of oppression they had suffered back home.

Two months after the opening of the Crossley State School, in January 1878, undoubtedly well aware of the plight of his people, the Catholic priest Father O'Dowd shrewdly purchased a new site for a Catholic school right beside the new state school at Crossley. In a sign of triumph, if not defiance, the Catholic community built a combined Catholic church-school building on the site right beside the Crossley State School. Built at a cost of £1500, it was to become part of the Koroit parish. This building still stands and is now known as St Brigid's hall. This followed the passing of the Education Act of 1872, which stated that the new 'state' schools be 'free, secular and compulsory' and saw the withdrawal of state aid from denominational schools. This riled the local Catholic community, aggrieved that their taxes were used to build secular schools but they now received no government support for their own. Controversy flared and St Brigid's school played a key role in the debate. It is not hard to see why. St Brigid's posed a fairly unique scenario – on one side of the fence, 15 children were attending the Crossley State School – all eligible for government aid. On the other, 220 children were attending the Catholic school – *none* of them eligible for state aid. A branch of the Catholic Education Defence Association was formed in St Brigid's hall, in a meeting that attracted three-quarters of the local population.

Their united front clearly worked. By keeping their students enrolled in the Catholic school, they eventually assured the closure of the state school. The Catholic school later purchased the neighbouring state school site to accommodate its large of numbers of children. In December 1878, the Bishop of Ballarat, Michael O'Connor, congratulated the people on their action. This was a great victory for the Catholic community, on a scale unparalleled in other parts of Australia. For people accustomed to being outcast and inferior, it was a vigorous affirmation of their unique Irish Catholic identity.

Famine and oppression had shaped the worldview of Irish Catholics, who were as loyal to their Church as they were to the motherland. The right to practise their faith and educate their children in that faith was held precious and signified a sense of social and spiritual unity. The loyalty of this Catholic community was well recognised and remarked upon at the time, says Helen Doyle, who cites early historians' commentary to highlight just how 'distinctively Catholic' the area was – the fact that both masses on a Sunday were severely overcrowded is testament to this, as is the fact that many students from Crossley went on to join a religious order. The Koroit parish is well known throughout Australia because of the abnormally high number of priests and religious who came from there. Many took their vocations and stayed within the diocese of Ballarat; many of the women joined the Sisters of the Good Samaritan who had taught them at St Brigid's. My father could name at least ten priests, without thinking too hard, that came from Crossley.

The Koroit parish was unique for another important reason, and not just because it was the holiday retreat for bishops from around Victoria. In 1886, the Koroit parish was given the unique status of being made a 'Mensal' parish. Derived from the Latin word 'mensa', which means 'table', it was the responsibility of the Mensal parish 'to provide for the bishop's table'. The parish priest would receive a stipend to administer the parish on behalf of the Bishop, giving the Bishop access to revenue to carry out his duties as bishop of the Diocese. The Koroit parish therefore remained under the jurisdiction of the bishop; the priest being his administrator.

It is not hard to see why, back in 1886, they chose the Koroit parish, the place of the first Catholic mass in the Western District and home of the highest concentration of Irish in Australia. It is no overstatement to call this parish the 'cradle of Catholicism' in Victoria, if not Australia.

But the school hall was much more than a place for mass and education. Like any community hall, it was used for a range of community functions. Crossley stands out because it was also the site of some significant political meetings, where locals expressed support, firstly for the cause of Home Rule back in Ireland, and then later to stand against conscription in Australia. In this, they found their leader, the Irish expatriate Daniel Mannix – one of the most influential figures in Australian history. He is said to be related to a local family and to have been personally known by many of the locals in Killarney and Crossley who also hailed from his home county of Cork, in Ireland. There had been a long tradition of bishops holidaying at the Mensal parish of Koroit. Archbishop Mannix was one of them, and he was made more than welcome by the locals. According to Helen Doyle, the story goes that he composed his famous anti-conscription speech, delivered in September 1916, while walking along Killarney beach. It was their allegiance to Mannix that encouraged the local population to stage the strongest anti-conscription demonstration in all of Victoria.

Saving St Brigid's

In 1916, as the referendum on conscription approached, the Melbourne *Argus* newspaper had been accusing this Irish-Australian community of disloyalty and neutrality. No doubt the locals were passionate in their opinion on the subject. Their history demanded it of them, so much so that on an October evening in 1916, when the Liberal Member for Wannon, A.S. Rodgers, fronted an audience at St Brigid's hall, his voice was drowned out by the protesting crowd. Precipitating the much more famous 'Warwick egg incident' in Queensland, when an egg was thrown at Prime Minister Billy Hughes by anti-conscriptionists, the locals at Crossley threw eggs through the windows from outside. Under the headline 'Under Heavy Shell Fire', the *Argus* explained that several eggs landed on Rodgers as well as on the attendant police, forcing him to retreat. Apparently a lynch mob waited outside. The truth of this claim is doubtful; however, the Irish position was clear. There were no recruits to the British cause here.

The 1916 referendum results said it all. While the rest of Victoria, including the Wannon electorate, voted in favour of conscription, the Killarney booth was most definitely against: 195 votes to zero.

With the Gallipoli centenary celebrations approaching, the RSL recently enquired locally as to where the war memorial is. Unlike almost all small towns across the Western District, who pride themselves on their war memorials and avenues of honour, in Crossley, Killarney and Tower Hill there is none. In those times, direct experience of oppression in Ireland meant that *disloyalty* to the Empire was worn as a badge of honour. The 'Irish as rebel' might be a wildly exaggerated stereotype, but when it came to some of the biggest issues in Australian history – the education debate and conscription – the facts spoke eloquently: the Irish weren't afraid to stand up for themselves.

This was indeed a strong, proud assertive community, who had survived and prospered. They agreed they wanted to replace their existing church–school building with a larger church building. A committee was formed and my great-grandfather Dan Lane, president of the local council and a respected community leader, announced to the Bishop of Ballarat: 'We have decided to build a church. Let us build a good one; one that we can

'A NEW IRELAND IN THE SOUTH'

proudly hand down to our children as a legacy.'

The land, alongside the standing church–school building, was donated by local farmer William Dwyer. St Brigid's was designed by the well-known Catholic Church architect Augustus Andrew Fritsch; at 80 feet by 39 feet in the Romanesque style, it was noted to be 'something quite original in the Western District'. The furnishings of the church were described as being 'on a sumptuous scale' and the red bricks were transported by rail to Crossley railway station and carted by local men to the building site. A photo was published in the Catholic *Advocate* in September 1913, showing the local farmers, including my great-grandfather, wearing overalls with tools in hand, working on the new church. It was not just the hard labour they gave, but they had indebted themselves to £6250 as a community, to raise St Brigid's majestic roof.

The Irish had prevailed in Australia, and this grand church on the hill embodied the strong, assertive character of their Irish Catholic faith. They dedicated their church to the patron saint of Ireland, St Brigid of Kildare, who is venerated as the champion of Ireland's rural poor, peacemaker and carer of the earth. It would have been a proud day on that last Sunday in June 1914, when they walked up the hill to Crossley. People have always exclaimed over the interior and the acoustics at St Brigid's church, so it is not hard to imagine the awe the people must have felt when they sang 'Gloria' together in chorus in that magnificent building. A guard of honour was formed for the Bishop of Ballarat, Bishop Higgins, and Archbishop Mannix, who gave a stirring address on 'how unjustly Catholics were treated by the authorities of this State' and encouraged them to 'never lay down their arms until that injustice was redressed'.

He 'congratulated the people of Crossley upon their generosity and self-sacrifice, and he prayed that God's blessing and the blessing of St Brigid would rest upon them, their children, and [their] children's children'.

Almost a hundred years later, as the 'children's children' of those people of Crossley, we felt heavily indebted to their generosity and self-sacrifice and the legacy that they left us – in our hearts, in our minds and in the sacred place that they built.

SAVING ST BRIGID'S

Chapter Three

'Sweet Sixteen'

My mother, Loretta Lane (nee Maloney), was born at the Warrnambool Base Hospital on 10 October 1939, the year war broke out. The daughter of Eva and Jim Maloney, she had five brothers and two sisters. She grew up in Dennington, a township founded because it was the major crossing over the Merri River, which linked the townships of Port Fairy and Warrnambool.

Four days later, and fourteen miles down the mad mile, my father, Michael Lane, was born, the last baby to be born at the Koroit District Hospital. At only four pounds weight, his aunty Phyllis, a spinster with no children herself, told his mother, 'It'd be charity to knock him on the head. It'll be a battle to raise him up.'

Dad was taken home to Rock's Road, Killarney, and lived in an old farmhouse tucked in behind the sand dunes, on what was called the Farnham Survey, owned by the Irish Protestant, William Rutledge, down the road from the site of the original St Brigid's school. The third-born of Connie and Jack Lane, they went on to have four more children, a total of two girls and five boys. As his father, Dan Lane, had been before him, Jack was a potato farmer, much like everybody in Killarney. Jack ploughed the fields by horse, and Connie walked after him, a bag of spuds around her neck, sowing seed. Dad remembers as a little boy, dressed up in coat and boots on a cold wintry day, watching his father grading onions. They also grew cabbages and sold them to the Government, to be canned and sent to the troops at war. He remembers being petrified as a four-year-old when a bomber flew overhead, after a Japanese submarine had been found in Portland harbour. 'I thought the war was here,' he said, but life went on much the same. Unlike his great-grandfather before him in Ireland, he didn't have to worry about going hungry. 'We had plenty of vegetables on the farm. But we needed coupons for tea, flour and sugar, because of wartime rationing. Mum used to barter our veggies and butter for extra supplies. Or she bought it on the black.' And of course, they had their own milk from the dairy.

It was these farms that provided the need for the Farnham Butter Factory in Dennington, also owned by Rutledge, built in 1899, which later became the Nestle's factory. Almost everyone in Dennington worked at the Nestle's factory, on the banks of the Merri River, including my Mum's father, Jim Maloney, 'Pop' as we knew him, 'the old man' as he was known to his kids. Jim was the son of James 'Snowy' Maloney, born in 1877 after his parents Michael Maloney and Honorah Mason migrated to Dennington from Limerick (or Clare, depending on who you ask). Snowy married Mary Jane Stafford in 1905, and they had four children; Pop was the youngest. When Pop was only four years old, his mother passed away. From reading the death certificate, it appears she took her own life, while heavily pregnant with twins. Snowy Maloney was known for his love of the drink and spent his fair share of time in the Dennington lockup, an old sandstone building out the back of the old police station. It didn't stop him remarrying, adding a further five sons to his brood. The family of nine lived in a small house on the corner of Tylden and Errard streets, on the Princes Highway. It was a hard life; they had to fight to survive, eating eels from the Merri River, rabbits from the fields, the odd chook and home-grown veggies. The Maloney boys were known to be pretty wild, good for the fight, but the first to lend a hand when needed. They were hard workers who knew how to make a bob or two. Their problem was the affliction of the Irish – they just drank it away.

Pop left school at eleven, and like everyone else went to work at the Nestle's milk factory. He went on to become a great carpenter. He married my grandmother Eva Martin in 1932, a Methodist girl who'd been raised on share farms in the Colac, Cressy and Beac areas. She converted to Catholicism when she married. Things went well in the early years of their marriage. Pop was in good work, and their house wasn't a house to be ashamed of, even if it only had one bedroom for Nana and Pop. Mum slept in a room no bigger than a jail cell, where the wood box and the washing was kept. Mum's eldest sister slept on the verandah; Pop walled it in for her when she got Sherman's disease. He also built a sleep-out for the boys, which held a double and three-quarter bed, where Mum's five brothers slept.

Pop might have been a great carpenter, but like his father, he was also a great drinker, which had a big impact on their family life. Mum envied the other kids at school whose families lit candles and said the rosary at home at night. During the Month of the Holy Rosary, the nuns scolded those kids who didn't say the rosary at night. Mum explained that being a Methodist, her mum didn't know the words. 'Your father's a Catholic,' the nuns would scoff at her, but Mum couldn't very well argue that he wasn't in the state to be saying prayers come evening time. Mum would go home crying, scared of getting a belting from the nuns, so Nana gathered up the kids to pray the rosary in the sleep out. When Pop came home full, Nana explained they were saying the rosary and he should join in. Kneeling at the end of the bed, it wasn't long before Pop was snoring. Mum wasn't bothered; she proudly went off to school the next day announcing that her family *also* said the rosary in Our Lady's month.

In Killarney, Dad rode the three and a half miles to St Brigid's Crossley, as a five-year-old, for his first day of school. In the line to register on that first day, outside the old school, now the Crossley Hall supper room, a fight broke out, and one of the kids was injured. From then on, Dad kept an eye out for the troublemaker who started it, Dan Kelly, or Tich, as he came to be known to us. One day Dad decided he'd had enough of school, and when he pretended to be asleep, his mother had to drag him out of bed and dress him, before putting him in their grey 1939 Chevrolet car and driving him half the way to Crossley. He wouldn't get away with it that easily, because at Blackwood Lane she sat him on his bike to ride the rest of the way. Nana wasn't a person to be reckoned with. But neither was Dad. After she drove off, he turned around and rode all the way back home. 'I won that one. I didn't go to school that day. I was a pretty determined little bugger,' says Dad with a grin.

The Lanes went to mass at St Brigid's every Sunday. As dairy farmers, they often missed the half past eight Mass, and instead went to the half past ten service. This meant they didn't go to Communion; they had to fast from midnight the night before, and half past ten was too long for dairy farmers to go without food in the belly. Dad made his first Communion at St Brigid's, filing up the aisle, looking all pious and holy with his hands clasped in prayer, as the nuns had instructed. Taught by the Good Samaritan Sisters, they were made to practise their singing every day in St Brigid's church, standing in the choir loft singing 'Hail Redeemer King Divine'. At midday, it took two kids to ring the Angelus bell, as they did in Ireland every lunch and dinner time. On hearing the bells, farmers in the fields of Killarney would traditionally down their tools and pray the Angelus prayer, a prayer about the Angel of the Lord, the words of which Dad has never forgotten.

When the nuns weren't looking, there was always a fight on in the paddock behind the tennis court where their horses ran loose during the day while school was in. The Lenehans were a tough lot. Ray, one of the younger ones, had been at Dad to take him on. Dad wasn't too keen on the idea, he was only half Dad's height, and he felt like a bully, but Ray wouldn't let up, so eventually Dad gave in. It didn't last long; Dad flattened him, and so had to stand up to his older brother, Pat Lenehan. Pat was quick on his toes and ducked and weaved and avoided all Dad's punches. They got in trouble with the nuns, were made to shake hands and promised never to fight again. 'We'd always been mates. It was just a game to see who was the toughest.' I think Dad could live with losing that game.

St Brigid's school only went up to grade eight, so Dad finished his schooling in 1953. Tich Kelly had already left earlier in the year, the day of his fourteenth birthday, to work on the farm. He looked like he was having a great time of it. Dad remembers Tich rode his horse and cart past St Brigid's every morning on his way to the milk depot, laughing and singing out to us 'poor mugs still left at school'. Dad, Pat Lenehan and Peter Madden all finished their schooling at St Brigid's; the others,

'SWEET SIXTEEN'

the likes of Gerry O'Brien, went on to the Christian Brothers College (CBC), in Warrnambool. Dad sat the scholarship exam for CBC, but failed the maths component badly. 'My parents thought I was dumb and there was no point sending me on to school, so they sent me home to work on the farm.' He was the only boy in the family that didn't go to CBC in Warrnambool. He'd had a slow start at school: in the first year or two he was close to bottom of the class. But by his final year, he was in the top two or three. One of the nuns took him aside and told him he *must* continue with his education, that she thought he had a vocation. Dad nodded, got on his Shetland pony and rode home; finished school at fourteen years old. On coming home from school, Dad rode the Shetland pony to round up the cattle, and drive them up the lane to the highway and lock them in the dairy yard, before riding home for afternoon tea. Almost forty years later, with his tenth child just born, Dad bumped into that same nun in Melbourne. He'd returned to school at age 45 to finish his VCE, and went on to complete a Social Work degree at Melbourne University. 'You were right about the vocation,' he informed her. He told her about his ten children and his return to study. 'It just wasn't quite the vocation you had in mind,' he laughed.

Mum, too, was fourteen when she left school. The drink had got the better of Pop, driving the family into debt, and so they packed up the three youngest children and moved to South Australia, leaving Mum and her brothers, Pat, Max and Geoff, to fend for themselves. It was all my Nana could think to do, to pull her husband away from the drink, and the debt. 'I have to do this. I know you'll be alright, Loretta, you'll get through,' she told Mum. When I asked how Nana put up with him, Mum says simply, 'She loved him. We all did,' as her eyes welled up with tears. 'He was a good man,' Mum always said. 'He just wasn't very good to himself'. Despite her father's vices, Mum always had a soft spot for him, and laughs when she remembers how quick he was to shoo the kids off to confessions if they'd committed a sin, like not getting to mass on Sunday, though Pop rarely managed to get there himself.

In today's language, Mum and her older brothers became street kids, asking around Dennington for a roof over their heads. Back then, it wasn't so unusual. Mum knocked on the door of Stan and Agnes Dalton, the couple who owned the Dennington shop across the road from the Nestle's factory. She stayed a couple of nights with them, and they offered her a job. If it wasn't for them, Mum says, she'd never have got through. They became like second parents to Mum, and an enduring influence throughout her life. They helped her to see the good in her father. 'It was the drink, Loretta, but a finer man you never would find,' Stan assured her.

It was a hot summer that first summer Dad found himself working like a man, spending long days on the back of the spud digger, paddling his fourteen-year-old legs to fold the long stalks through the rotating prongs. In February, his uncle Bill Richie became ill with jaundice, and Dad went to Crossley to milk his thirty cows for him, alongside his aunt Edie. Dad rounded up the cows one morning while watching his brother John, and all the school kids from Crossley, catching the train from the old Crossley station to Hamilton, to see Queen Elizabeth in her first visit to Australia. Dad wasn't allowed to go and knew he was missing out. He worked for the Richies for three or four months; his payment was a pair of new boots. He went home in July, and learned how to cut seed potatoes. They had no shed then: his father taught him how to slice a potato into four to six pieces for planting seed under a piece of tarp on a rainy day. It took Dad all day to cut a bag of seed that first day. The next day he cut two, but went on to cut ten bags a day.

In 1948 Jack joined in a partnership with his brothers, Danny and Pat, called Lane Brothers Killarney. They bought a farm of 88 acres in Andersons Road, Tower Hill. Dad's uncle Pat pulled out of the partnership in 1954; Jack and Dan carried on. At night time, Dad and his brother Frank and his cousins would brand spud bags with a cake of black nugget, stretching out the bags and wetting the cake with water. They would brand up to 300 bags a night with 'JJ & DJ Lane, Killarney', the name of one of the leading potato growers in the area. The Lanes grew 120 acres of spuds, a lot for those days. They were the first farmers to use a modern harvester and every farmer in the district came down to have a look at the 'Queen Mary', as it was nicknamed. The Lanes also did a roaring trade in onions, transporting them across the border to Albury. That is, until 'the onion wars' broke out.

'SWEET SIXTEEN'

The Onion Board controlled all the onions grown in Victoria and weren't happy about the interstate trade. Vigilantes went around the roads, slashing bags, trying to seize the onions to prevent them being transported across the state. Things came to a head one day when Jack, Pat Madden and Teddy Gleeson set off in convoy, with a police escort and the necessary travel permits in hand, and were chased by the onion board representatives. On a hill just outside Colac, the vigilantes climbed aboard and began throwing the bags of onions off the truck. The police intervened and the onions were seized. Jack, Pat and Teddy took the onion board all the way to the Supreme Court. Probably influenced by his father, Dan, who'd spent 40 years in local government, Jack knew the law, and wasn't afraid to stand by it. So Jack stood in the Supreme Court, holding up Section 92 of the Australian Constitution, stating his right to trade across the border. Together with Pat and Teddy, they were victorious. I can only imagine how proud the young fifteen-year-old Mick must have been of his father – Dad has taken a keen interest in matters of law and politics ever since.

From December through April each year, the Lanes had twelve men sleeping in their long shed down the backyard. The men only came to the house to bathe, and Connie cooked and washed for them. Most of them were Irish, working through the winter in the central highlands and spud picking in Killarney through the summer. They worked, drank and fought hard. One of them, Mick Lyons, claiming he was born on St Patrick's day, asked for the day off and got drunk for three or four days afterwards. Mick Green would get drunk at the Killarney pub every night, come home, light the fire, and play the mouth organ all night. The other workers always complained, and one night one of the other blokes fired a shot through the wall to shut him up. Another picker, Vincent O'Leary, came into the house one day, asking for a bath. He said he was going to Geelong to get married. He cleaned himself up and went off to Geelong. About six months later, the police knocked on the door and presented a picture of him. The weekend he left, he went to Geelong, and broke into a jeweller's shop. They never did know if he got married or not.

The Lane brothers, Jack and Danny, bought another 74 acres down

Andersons Road in Tower Hill from the Estate of Digger Lane, where I grew up, and planted the whole lot. It was a good year: they were selling at a record price of £50 a tonne. They normally went for around £5 or £6 a tonne. They paid for the farm in the first year. On advice from their accountants, they split the partnership; Danny took Anderson's farm of 88 acres, Jack took Digger's farm of 74 acres. Dad was sixteen years old when he and his brother Frank went into partnership with their father. They were paid £2000 for their wages, for that year and about three years after. By that time, Dad and Frank used the £2000 to buy their way into the partnership, which included their share of the machinery too. 'I was only sixteen when it began, so I was just doing what I was told really,' says Dad.

Mum worked at the Dennington shop, while boarding with different families in the neighborhood. It was her father's Catholicism and her mother's strict religious devotion that gave Mum her strong faith. She took herself off to church at least every Sunday, more often if she could get there. Mass was the one thing she could rely upon. The Eucharist became the central part of her life and remains so to this day. When I was fourteen, complaining about going to church, Mum would remind me of how faith carried her through when she had no home to go to. Undoubtedly a cheeky little brat; I'd retort that I didn't have to pray for such things, I did have a home to go to! 'Never take anything for granted,' she warned. 'You should thank God for the roof over your head.' And I'd go off to mass to give thanks for what I didn't properly appreciate.

It was through Agnes Dalton and the many Nestle's workers who had passed through the door of the Dennington shop that Mum first heard of the Crossley dances. The excitement and anticipation of the Crossley dances became one of those mysteries of grown-up life that Mum couldn't wait to discover. For a shilling, people caught the bus from Warrnambool, stopping at Dennington, on the way to Crossley. The Daltons did some of the catering and Mum would help load the cakes and slices onto the bus. Her friends spent their days side-by-side at St Anne's College or working at Nestle's. For Mum, living and working in the shop all day, her only social outlet was talking to the factory workers who came into the shop and hanging off every word they said about the Crossley dances.

She couldn't wait for her time to come.

'SWEET SIXTEEN'

Dad had been to a few dances since he was fourteen to help his mother in the kitchen. Connie was president of the Catholic Women's League and one of a small group of women who went from house to house to collect legs of mutton and beef to make their legendary steak paste, corn beef and mock chicken sandwiches (derived from tomato, onion and seasoning – the poor man's version of the real thing). It was Dad's job to work the heavy bread slicer, slicing freshly baked bread specially delivered to Crossley on Sundays. Otherwise he'd stand in the corner and watch the dancing, or look over his father's shoulder while he played cards with the men in what was called the 'young men's room'.

At the time, Mum's older brother, Pat, was dating Dad's older sister, Helen. One Sunday afternoon, Pat took Mum for a drive out to Killarney to see his girlfriend and left Mum sitting in the car for an hour. Dad was wearing his grass-stained footy shorts, grubby knees and a black beret, kicking the footy to himself on the front lawn. They were both too shy to talk.

Before long, Helen asked my grandmother if she could take her little brother to the Crossley dances; that way she could stay out later, dancing with Pat. So as a chaperone to his big sister, Dad found himself in the Crossley hall, eyeing off a certain young Loretta Maloney, also being chaperoned, by her big brother Pat.

At sixteen years old and at her first dance, Mum was beside herself with excitement when she noticed Dad and that big, thick head of black hair she remembered from that day in the car, on the front lawn in Killarney.

Dad plucked up the courage to ask her to dance, but didn't really get the words out, Mum tells me. He was way too shy for that. Just nudged her foot with his. Given that his mother could any minute poke her head out of the little service window from the kitchen, and with his older sister dancing with Mum's older brother, it was no wonder he was nervous!

'It was a big thing to ask a girl to dance,' Dad explained. 'I didn't want to make a fool of myself.' Luckily, he'd had some lessons at the Crossley Hall, through the Catholic Young Men's Society, and he knew the moves.

Mum was impressed. So much so, it wasn't long before she asked him to be her debutante partner. They attended debutante practice every week, and every other ball in the district. But it was Crossley they kept returning to, on a Sunday night, the most important night of the week.

They can't explain what it was that was so special about Crossley. Undoubtedly it had something to do with the band, which really set Crossley apart. Swinkles' Orchestra was named after the pianist, Peter Swinkles, a Dutchman who played music by ear. Over lunch on Sundays, the radio played 'The Hit Parade', the top twelve latest hits. That night at Crossley, one of the girls would sing the song to Mr Swinkles, who would pick it up straight away and play to the adoring crowd. Bizarrely, it was that old hall out on the hill that was known for being the first with the latest.

Other smaller country halls like Kirskstall and Illowa, moved their Catholic balls to the much larger Crossley Hall. Sometimes, Crossley played host to nine in one year. The highlight was the fifteenth of August, the Feast of the Assumption ball. Being a holy day of obligation, everyone went to Mass that morning. The farmers took a public holiday, and went to town to buy a new suit or bowtie for the ball. People travelled from fifty miles away to Crossley. They came from across the Western District, as far away as Hamilton and Terang, even Colac, Portland and Heywood. Mum and Dad looked forward to the fifteenth of August ball all year; Mum spent months talking to the Nestle's girls about what they would wear. With little money, she often had to wear the same dress, but borrowed a cummerbund or hair band to make up for it. If she could afford it, she would buy some cheap material and the Haberfield girls in Dennington would whip her up a dress on the Sunday afternoon.

Mum remembers the year her brother Maxie returned from Port Augusta, just in time for the ball. He and Uncle Pat had been gone looking for work; they say they slept in their suitcase. Mum loved her brothers dearly, so I can imagine her response when Max surprised her at the front door. She swung it open so hard that she banged her friend in the head, leaving the poor girl with a colourful bruise on her head for the big night. And then there was the year when Dad came down with the flu and spent the night lying in bed, looking up at the lights at Crossley, missing out on the biggest night of the year, while Mum went down the highway on the bus, wishing her tall dark handsome man was there to take her hand.

As they did for Mum, the dances became Dad's central social outlet. Working at home on the farm all day, he loved catching up with the boys from school. Like the Lenehan boys, who were known for throwing an eel or chook in the window to scare the girls. The girls would scream that there was a snake on the floor, and the joke never wore thin. Like their school days, the Crossley dances also played host to a good fight or two. Because it was out in the country, without the police presence they had in town, there were always a few troublemakers, mostly from Warrnambool, who came looking for a fight. The locals were quick to defend their turf, and with such large families, they were never without backup. Like the time one of the Farley boys got picked on. Gerry Farley took on three blokes at the one time flattening one of them whilst standing on another and holding the third at arm's length. Meanwhile his brothers were doing their best with the others; Mick Farley stood toe to toe with a bloke and fought for ten minutes. The troublemakers had met their match, and didn't show their heads around Crossley after that.

All this, and not a drop of alcohol was drunk in the Crossley hall. Well, at least not that anyone ever saw. Certainly the women didn't drink. In those days, no one was allowed a drink within 200 yards of a dance hall. So the men would drive their cars down the hill to enjoy a legal drink. Otherwise they'd just open up the car boot in the yard, if they were feeling brave. But not when John Matthey was near, the strictest of policemen who used to go around all the cars, shining his torch in, looking for the contraband. If getting your grog confiscated wasn't bad enough, knowing that John Matthey had an overflowing fridge at home was cause enough to drink quickly in the Crossley yard.

If it wasn't the policeman, it was the parish priest shining his torch in the dark, to make sure there were no young couples misbehaving in the back seat. He didn't hang about much after 10 pm, so once he was gone the young lovers would head straight back outside. Father John O'Farrell, fresh off the boat from Ireland, wore big thick black glasses, and assigned to his first parish, he wasn't particularly well liked, especially when he tried to stop the dances at Crossley and run a dance in Koroit, instructing all the

Young Christian Workers members that they must attend. They did, and only thirty people stayed behind at Crossley that night. They didn't miss much, the Koroit dances never came close to the magic of Crossley, and a week later things were back in full swing at St Brigid's hall.

When Mum was seventeen, she had to move to Melbourne to take care of her sister who had had a bad car accident. Between caring for her sister and her day job nannying, Mum still found the time to pen many a letter back home to Dad. Full time in the family partnership, Dad too had his hands full. Despite the obstacles and considerable distance, their relationship withstood the test, and they kept the flame alive.

And then came the day that put Dad to the test in a way he'll never forget.

On the highway at 'Diggers', while his brother Frank ploughed the paddock, Dad was building a new fence with his father. They built them to last in those days and in the exertion of digging three feet into the earth and then manoeuvring the heavy timber post, Dad at first thought his father was letting up for a bit as he slowly walked back a few metres to 'sight' the post to ensure the fence was straight. But his father was wobbly on his feet, walking off in the opposite direction, staggering right into the path of the oncoming tractor. Dad caught eyes with his brother's confused look as he grabbed for the steering wheel, and he called out to his father.

'Dad! Dad, what are you doing?!'

His dad was having a heart attack. The boys rushed to his aid; struggling to get him on their backs they knew they had to get him to a doctor. But Jack declared that he hadn't made his will yet. Business always came first! With Jack still groggy and disorientated, they rushed him home. He got changed, his shirt half unbuttoned, his braces accidentally buttoned onto his shirt. Jack was a determined man and ordered Frank to take him to Port Fairy to make his will. Before he got in the car, he came over and looked Dad straight in the eye, gasping for words. Dad thought his father was going to die then and there.

'Mick, I want you to look after the farm. You're a good farmer. I need you to take care of it. And your mother. I want you to look after your mother.'

'SWEET SIXTEEN'

So as a seventeen-year-old, Dad felt the weight of the farm and his family on his shoulders, a responsibility he honoured until the day his mother died more than fifty years later.

With Jack in hospital, Dad and Frank came home to finish the fencing on the highway. It is important to get the boundary fences right and Dad was worried about doing a proper job. Michael and Frank Mugavin arrived with a truck full of fencing gear to lend a hand, as any good farmer did in a crisis, knowing two young men were at it on their own. Michael Mugavin drove the tractor, pulling the wire to create the suspension between him and the heavy iron bar that Dad was holding with all his body strength to keep the spool of wire in place. Only a day earlier, Dad had wondered why his father was relenting under the strain of the hard labour. On this day, Michael Mugavin looked back over his shoulder, pausing to see if Dad had the strength to keep the iron bar and spool of wire upright against the tension caused by the tractor.

The next time he looked back, Dad was on the ground. Unconscious, he lay there with barbed wire ripped through his trousers, his forearms and knuckles in shreds. Not sure what had just happened, the Mugavin men drove him to the Koroit hospital, thinking he had passed out from the blood loss. It was in fact Dad's first epileptic fit, although on that day it went undiagnosed. When it comes to epilepsy, they say that if your first seizure was not caused by an obvious blow to the head, then it is just as likely caused by an intolerable level of stress in the brain.

Clearly, the scare of his father's heart attack, and the responsibility it now bestowed on him, was more than a seventeen-year-old could take. Still, after they bandaged up his wounds, Dad went home and finished the fence.

It would be another year, and a near fatal fit while driving Mum down Toorak Road, South Yarra, before Dad was diagnosed at the Alfred hospital with the condition that would define their early married life. Mum and Dad were married at twenty-two years of age, in May of 1962, at St Joseph's Church in Warrnambool. When her father took ill before the wedding, it was left to her brother Pat to give her away. Mum got dressed at her parents' house so she could kiss her father before she left. Mum and Dad moved into the house at 'Diggers' at Lane's Lane, which faces out to the ocean and is just down the highway from Tower Hill Lake. Mum lived in our house for eight years before she stepped foot inside the Reserve. Back then, people didn't live in the area for the sea views and nature walks. The houses were built facing the road, not the ocean, for there wasn't time to sit around and admire the view. Even if you had a window that faced the ocean, cypress trees and boxthorn hedges – to protect from the ferocious Southern Ocean winds – blocked the view.

When Grandad Lane had his second heart attack, he was told by his doctor he would die if he had a third. He was a tough man, a proud one too, and avoided the doctor at all costs. Dad says his father often sewed up his own hand with a needle and cotton after an accident. He survived nine heart attacks. After one of them, Dad sat by his bed in hospital. His father had been ordered to lie flat on his back and not move. He was sitting up chatting, but would quickly lie down again, before he got a shooing from the nurses. After the sixth attack, he was allowed to go home, only if he had complete bed rest, under strict instruction he should not do any work whatsoever. Marie Bushell nursed him in hospital and nearly drove off the road with fright the next day, when she drove through Killarney and saw Jack Lane on his tractor ploughing the fields. He was a fit man; Dad reckons he's never seen anyone work harder than his father, Jack. He died fourteen years after his first heart attack, at 61 years old – Dad was only 33.

In the last years before Granddad died, Dad ran the whole farm at Killarney and Tower Hill. Up at 6 am for milking, and depending on which fence or irrigation pipe needed to be fixed or moved, he often wasn't home again until 9 o'clock at night. With the demands of a growing family to care for, it was no wonder Mum never got to visiting Tower Hill!

Epilepsy was a heavy burden in their lives. The seizures were relatively infrequent, but the stress it caused never ceased. He needed to be two years free of a seizure to be able to drive again; he kept falling short by just a few months. It wasn't easy being a farmer without a licence; he ploughed fields all day long, but relied on Mum to drive him down the highway from one paddock to another. He counted every one of the five years, five months and five days before he got it back.

Chapter Four

One of ten

Angela was born eleven months after Mum and Dad were married. Robert, seventeen months later. They remember life at Tower Hill before there was hot running water, a television or even a flush toilet. They worked on the farm, though they weren't big enough to drive the tractor; Robert would work the pedals and Angela would steer. They were the only two of us old enough to milk in the dairy morning and night, before it was sold.

After Robert came Monica, followed fourteen months later by Catherine. Eighteen months later, Bernard was born, then Patrick, Mary-Ellen and Elizabeth. I was the baby of the family, born in 1980. We were all raised at Lane's Lane, Tower Hill, in a house that expanded as our family did. Angela did her HSC while rocking me to sleep, in the bedroom where the six of us girls slept. When I grew out of the cot, Liz and I top and tailed for years it must have been, because I clearly remember the night she fell out of our top bunk and hit her head on the chest of drawers below, without waking up! When I was little our uncle built on a couple of extra bedrooms, and we spent every Saturday with our cousins having acorn fights and building tree houses in the cypress hedge that ran down the side of our house. We didn't have much in the way of toys or books or games, but it wasn't like we knew much different, at least in the early days. When someone in the family got a bicycle, we took turns riding it, the rest of us running down the lane alongside to keep up. The paddocks were our playground; we climbed the haystack, rode the motorbike, built go karts and swam at Killarney beach. We were never bored, we weren't allowed to be, because there was always work to be done, and from a young age we all knew how to boil a pot of spuds and fry up a pan of sausages. We made games out of folding washing and cleaning the house and never started the day without making our own beds.

Our social lives revolved around the Catholic Church, of course. Once a month on a Sunday, we went to Shamrock House, the big bluestone building that was once a pub, at the Crossley crossroads. It was then owned by the Salesian Order of Don Bosco and run by the most gentle of souls, the much loved Father Murphy. The first Sunday of the month was 'twelve star day' for kids (which had something to do with the big gold spiky thing behind the altar where God lives, I thought). Mass started at midday. We loved it, not least because it meant we could stay in our pj's for the morning (while Mum and Dad went to mass at St Brigid's), but also because mass in the cosy little carpeted chapel with the log-fire at Shamrock only ever went for half the time it did at big old freezing St Brigid's. There was no kneeling on wooden slats. Or homilies that went on for hours. When Father Murphy talked, he used our names and made the places of the Bible easy to picture in our mind's eye. He asked us questions, fed our curiosity and always left us with a little thought for the day, a challenge, or a new way of thinking about our little world.

On 'twelve star day' all the kids from around the district would bring their lunch after mass, and the afternoon was spent playing organised games, like musical chairs and 'the priest of the parish'. As well as a maze of rooms to run and hide in, there were also a swimming pool and three giant trampolines at Shamrock. It was great fun.

Shamrock House was both a campsite for disadvantaged families from Melbourne (that's where disadvantaged people came from, I thought), and also a refuge for the down-and-out (who with their jolly red faces never seemed that 'down' to me). Because we didn't really go on family holidays, when Father Murphy set off on his annual September holiday, in his big old blue bus full of people from all walks of life, Liz and I were only too happy to climb on board. Unlike all those 'disadvantaged' kids, who, unbelievably, lived 'on top of each other', in 'the flats' in Melbourne, Liz and I sat gleefully on the bus, with a hole burning in our pockets from the $100 note Mum had solemnly given each of us, wiping our faces with a dribble of spittle on her lipstick-stained handkerchief as she kissed us goodbye. 'Now don't ya's be showing the other kids now will ya's?' she would warn as we ran off to the bus.

I've never felt so rich in all my life. Nor have I ever had so much fun. We drove all day and all night, and stayed in shearer's quarters in the desert in Mungo National Park, in caravans on the Murray and on some of the most beautiful beaches in New South Wales. If it hadn't been for Father Murphy, I'd not have such a love of the Australian landscape. Nor would I have had anything to compare to the Gold Coast. That's where all the kids at school went on their family holidays. So, in my show-and-tell, I was careful to leave out the bit about having to attend daily mass along the way. That hardly compared to Dreamworld, now did it?

The softly spoken, gentle-natured Father Murphy was a great friend of our family, and a great role model to me. To drive past the now privately owned Shamrock House today, is to smile at the memory of the adventure of my happy, colourful Catholic childhood, and a man that probably influenced my life more than I realise.

Angela and Robert were the only two to go to school at St Brigid's, driven by Mum every day and taught by the Good Samaritans. This was the time of the tail end of the Second Vatican Council, a time of great change in the Catholic Church, which saw mass switch from Latin to English and nuns disrobe their full, bulky old habits and veils. St Brigid's school was closed in 1971, with a closing ceremony and a full day of celebrations to mark the moment. There's a great photo of Dad and his school mates, Tich Kelly, Jim Madden, Brian Lane and the like, sitting on a horse and cart, all dressed up in school shirts and shorts and braces, just like their school days. Former students came from everywhere to mark the moment, many of them priests and nuns. It was the honour of Jim Gleeson, the first to be married at St Brigid's in 1914 and the eldest person in the district, to lock the doors of the old school for the last time.

Angela, Robert and Monica all started catching the bus to St Patrick's primary in Koroit, on the other side of Tower Hill Lake from our house. The closure of St Brigid's school affected the whole community. No longer were Mum and Dad meeting other parents on a daily basis when they dropped the kids off, and attending school concerts in the Crossley hall. The old time dances were no longer either, the arrival of rock and roll, television and the end of the 'six o'clock swill' saw to their demise. Pubs were open late and had jukeboxes and entertainment; there was no need to travel away from town for a night out. By the seventies, Mum had given birth to seven children at St John of God hospital, and when it looked like it was going bankrupt, they joined a committee to fight and save the hospital. Like their own parents, they were heavily committed to community life. Mum was quick to join the mothers club, as much for a social outlet as anything else, and became an active member of St Patrick's primary. During my time at St Pat's, Mum was on the school board, the mothers club and volunteered at the Senior Citizens club and in the Year of the Family, the same year her mother died, Mum decided to organise a reunion for past mothers of St Patrick's primary. Held on the Feast of the Assumption, the fifteenth of August, it was a successful fundraiser as well as bringing together a hundred mums from a long time past.

With Mum's extensive involvement, it goes without saying that the parish priest was a regular in our household. I have fond memories of Fr Downes, who, with his deep Irish brogue, always addressed me by my first and second name. 'Regina Brigid!' his voice would boom down the phone. When he moved to Robinvale, Mum and Dad took us on a family holiday to stay in his presbytery. Again, we thought this was fabulous, sneaking around all those rooms, eating mandarins straight from the trees, and slipping into bed, between stiff white sheets that were never so stiff or white at home.

Then there was Father O'Connell, who wasn't as jovial as Father Downs, never with a hair out of place on his perfectly placed comb-over. Father O'Connell used to drop into our household so often that our favourite trick to play on Mum, as she stepped out of the shower giving orders, or was 'blowing her top' at one of us, was to yell from the kitchen 'Father O'Connell's at the backdoor'. 'He's not?!' she'd bark strongly, without confidence. We thought it was hilarious. It wasn't often that we could have it over Mum. If Father O'Connell really *was* at the back door, it didn't matter what other emergency needed to be attended to, we kids ran and cleared the washing off the couch, scrambled around for some Salada biscuits and Kraft singles, and a tea cup with a matching saucer, that wasn't chipped. This was no easy feat, but he was the parish priest. Only the best would do. He would light a cigarette and sit in our lounge-room chain-smoking, pouring out his problems, or those of the parish, onto Mum and Dad. We didn't mind when he came to visit; it meant that we could slink off to our rooms and escape whatever jobs Mum had planned for us.

I remember the arrival of Father Linehan. It didn't take him long to learn that the people of Crossley had a mind of their own. At his first mass, he walked out onto the altar and down to the bottom step, folding his arms and fixing his gaze firmly on the people at the back of the church.

'I'm not starting until everyone fills up the front seats,' he declared.

His arms firmly folded, his gaze steady and strong, he waited.

People shifted in their seats. Someone coughed. But no one moved.

'Well, I'm not moving!' bellowed Plunger Lenehan from the very back row.

I stifled a giggle as Mum gave me one of 'those' looks.

Mr Lenehan folded his arms and eyeballed the priest from the back of the church.

There was a long silence.

After what felt like minutes, Father Linehan threw his hands in the air, sighed, spun around on his heel, and got on with the mass.

The second mass was his second lesson. His sermon that day had been about 'opening your ears and your eyes' to the holy spirit. After the homily, he gestured to the altar boy to get him something from the sacristy. The altar boy wasn't paying attention, off in another world, staring at the roof. Father Linehan went red in the face, flailing his arms around, as he gesticulated wildly to the boy.

'See that's an example of what happens when you don't use your eyes or your ears,' he said in frustration.

At the end of mass, after Father had read out the announcements, he called for feedback or comments from the congregation. It was an unusual chance for dialogue in a building that was only accustomed to hearing the rote call and response of priest and parishioner.

'Yes, I've got something to say,' came a voice from the back row. 'I think you should offer that altar boy an apology,' called out Les Lenehan.

'An apology? What for?'

'You know what for.'

'What do you mean?'

'You owe that boy an apology,' Les repeated. His tone of voice said that he wasn't to be reckoned with. It wasn't quite the response Father Linehan had expected when he'd graciously opened the floor for comment. To avoid the embarrassment of admitting his error, he suggested they continue the conversation after mass.

Father Linehan never called for feedback from the congregation at St Brigid's after that.

After mass, Mum and Dad would look over at the ailing hall, cobwebs covering the windows, and feel racked by sadness and some guilt, too, that they'd let the old ones down by letting the place go. But Mum had decided that after her youngest was through primary school, she'd go and do some voluntary work at Lyndoch nursing home, where she was a regular visitor to see her mother, who lived out her years there. Her best plans were waylaid when in November 1987 Mum got a little surprise. At forty-seven years old, Mum discovered she was pregnant. With five young adult children living and working away, and four at various stages of primary and secondary school, it was a shock to the system to think about changing nappies again. Busy organising Monica's twenty-first birthday in the spud shed at home, Mum kept it from us younger ones for fear we would spill the beans to the guests before time. The day after the twenty-first, with all my siblings sitting around the room, Mum shared her news with us kids.

'I'm having a baby.'

It was unbelievable. And I said so. 'I don't believe you,' I said, looking at the funny expressions on my elder brothers' and sisters' faces. They all cracked up laughing; I guess they didn't believe Mum either at first!

I was over the moon! I was going to have a younger brother or sister! As far as I could tell, that was all there was to think about – a baby to play with. I had no comprehension of the health risks, the increased odds of things going wrong, and thought nothing much of Mum's regular visits to the doctor and early hospital admittance before her due date. When Dad came home one Thursday in April and told us we were allowed to take the next day off school, because Mum was having an operation to have the baby, I remember wishing they could wait another day, so I could go to school to submit my footy tips! Little did I know that Mum's natural pregnancy as a 47-year-old was more than a little out of the ordinary in those days, and I was the only one taking it lightly.

My little brother, Michael James Junior, was born on 15 April 1988, two days before Angela, my eldest sister's, twenty-fifth birthday. He was a perfectly healthy, happy baby. Waking up from a general anaesthetic, Mum wasn't convinced. We giggled at her lying in bed, stroking her newborn baby boy, saying 'isn't she beautiful', calling him 'Grace Mairead' and repeatedly asking Dad if 'she' had Down syndrome. I had no idea what she was talking about but thought it was hilariously funny.

I'll never forget the excitement of that day – the nuns at St John of God fussed around us, feeding us biscuits and soft drink and Dad shouted us pies and milkshakes at a coffee shop. (This was about as much of a first as getting a new baby brother!) Angela made the hurried flight back from Darwin, Robert from Melbourne, and by nightfall we'd drawn quite a crowd at Macy's Hotel to wet the baby's head. At home, the phone never stopped ringing, back at school all the mums and teachers were eager to hear the updates, and a few weeks later, Liz and I spent a whole day sticking 200 baby cards into scrapbooks.

Our little baby slipped into line amid the business of life at Tower Hill – school canteen, uni exams, young romance and wedding plans for Robert in December of that year. Mum used to say the only real time she had to herself with her little baby at that point was when she was breastfeeding!

All his life Dad had dreamt of study, and only a couple of years before Michael was born did Dad share his ambition with Mum. In the midst of a rural recession Dad knew that the farm wasn't going to keep them fed, and lots of other jobs, like driving trucks or working at a factory, were off limits for a man with epilepsy. More than anything, Dad wanted a qualification.

He explained to Mum that it would be hard for them. 'Our lives have always been bloody hard,' Mum laughed. She supported him all the way.

Dad went to TAFE in Warrnambool and completed year eleven in two weeks. After a conversation with the legal teacher, who saw Dad's intellect and passion for political and legal matters, he offered Dad the opportunity to sit the year twelve legal exam – the following day, that was. Dad took home the text, read the prescribed chapters and sat the exam. He passed with flying colours, and was awarded his VCE before the year was out. That same teacher suggested he go on to tertiary study. He had little idea what to study, only knowing that he loved the social sciences, and so he enrolled in an Arts degree at Deakin Uni, in Warrnambool. He was then accepted into a Bachelor of Social Work at Melbourne Uni, travelling to Geelong one day a week for lectures, in between working the spud harvester at home.

All the while, Mum was still heavily committed at St Patrick's, Koroit. But before Michael was a year old, Mum lost two of her close friends, who she'd danced with at Crossley, and decided that she had to do something about the Crossley hall. The school had been demolished not without objection five years earlier, and the hall was in such a bad state, it was headed for the same fate. Mum decided they should have a 'Back to Crossley' ball to get everybody back, one last time, as a finale to the place she loved so much. She'd always felt an obligation to the older women, Connie Lane and the like, who'd worked so hard collecting food and fundraising, and taking care of the supper when Mum was going to the dances. They went to see the parish priest, who told them they were crazy; he doubted anyone would turn up. Mum promised him that if they cleaned the old place, the people would come. He repeated that he thought she was crazy, but didn't stand in her way.

I remember as a child, walking into the old hall for the first time. Bird shit and hay from one end of the hall to the other, was piled as high as my father's six-foot frame. Mum and Dad had a working bee of their own before they dared asked anybody else to join them. We used rakes to get rid of the rubbish and sprayed it out with pressure hoses. They knew if people saw it in the original state, they'd think they were crazy too. But it wasn't too long before others joined, and a committee was formed. I remember my dad high on the scaffolding, fixing the holes in the roof and erecting new spouting. It made me feel like I was in my own Enid Blyton classic, having discovered our own run-down old farmhouse to restore, a whole playground of places to run and hide, through the fake door on the stage, and down the steps into the bar room. We were eight and nine year old kids, but we weren't immune to the work. We swept, mopped, polished, sanded and stained the floors, replaced old windows, hung new curtains. The old place was coming back to life and so, it seemed, was the surrounding community.

They knew for it to be a success they must have the music of the times. It was the Swinkles band that had made the dances at Crossley in their day, and it was never going to be the same without them. With no clue what to do to solve that one, Mum and Dad went off to Melbourne for a nephew's twenty-first. There they were introduced to a young man called Peter Swinkles. When they enquired, they discovered that yes, he was the son of *the* Peter Swinkles. They couldn't believe their luck! The next day he took Mum and Dad straight out to see his father, who remembered well the great 'tall and the short' couple, my six-foot-something Dad and five foot-nothing Mum. He went to his room and found the notebook with all the music he'd played way back in the 1950s at Crossley. He was more than happy to come to the party. He cobbled together his band, who were so excited to come back to Crossley, they didn't want any more payment than what they'd been paid back in the fifties and sixties - one pound ten shillings each.

So 26 January 1990 came around, the old piano was tuned up and sawdust was sprinkled on the floor. We kids lined up the bar with soft drink; no alcohol was ever allowed at the Crossley dances. All the old women - Nana Lane, Mrs Shanley and Bridgi Madden - were ferried out, and lined up on the old red cinema chairs in the supper room, just like they always had. Mum coordinated the kitchen effort, faithfully following Nana's well-loved old sandwich-spread recipes of mock chicken and steak paste. A bus came out from Warrnambool, and men and women in their fifties who'd not been out here for thirty years streamed through the door, mouths wide open. 'Are you one of Mick and Loretta's?' they'd exclaim, hugging and kissing us, and lavishing Mum and Dad with their praise. Liz and I pored over the visitors' book: the comments said our parents were heroes and deserved gold medals. We thought they were famous. The Lenehan boys kept up the tradition of the 'wild dances at Crossley' and threw a chook through the window to shrieks and laughter. Nobody could believe what good nick the old place was in, and they all started asking about hiring the hall for their next family function. 'We thought it was the end, but it was really only the beginning,' said Mum, with a weary smile.

No one was more surprised than Father Linehan. He was awestruck by the turnout of 500 plus; he admitted he thought it was an impossible dream, and had to pop down to check. He couldn't get away, there were so many people to talk to. Mum and Dad made $1500 profit from the night, and handed it straight over to Father Linehan. The money was used to paint the sanctuary of the church a brilliant magenta red colour, giving the whole place a new lease on life. A meeting was held to vote on the future of the hall. It was unanimous. The committee got busy, Dad began applying for grants and before long, small amounts were flowing in, enough to laminate the benchtops here, a new toilet system there, a new tank outside. Looking back, the improvements Mum and Dad invested so much into at St Brigid's were badly needed at home. We didn't have drinking water running to our kitchen sink until midway through the nineties. We collected buckets of fresh water from a tank at the back door. Every Christmas when everyone was home, our toilet system blocked up, and chipped benchtops and second-hand cupboard doors that swung off their hinges were just a part of life at Tower Hill.

By the time I was a teenager, I'd almost had enough of Crossley. I'd stay at my best friend's house, across the paddock, and jealously take note of her brand-name sneakers and matching doona cover set, and wonder why Mum and Dad could always afford to put money on the church collection plate when we knew that bills at home were never paid on time and they scratched to put food on the table. When Mum won the Moyne Shire Australian of the Year award in 1995, and she appeared on the front page of the *The Warrnambool Standard* with 'Tower Hill's Lifeline', I thought it was some acknowledgement of what we kids put up with. But even then, when they listed the myriad things Mum did for the community, it sounded simple and straightforward and had no resemblance to the chaos of our daily lives. The newspaper could hardly capture the phone that never stopped ringing, the endless 'to do' lists, and conveyor belt of scones, tubs of curried egg and dozens of bags of sandwiches that were cut in our kitchen, out the door to another funeral or fundraiser before we could get our hands on them. Or how many times a week we heard the back door slam and the car start as Mum yelled out, 'I'm just running up to Crossley'. People often ask what life was like growing up as one of ten children, as if it was the most stressful endurance test one could survive. I shouldn't speak for Mum, but I think the ten of us was the easy bit. If I was ever brave enough to complain, Mum would be quick to come back with 'You only get out of community what you put into it'. Yeah, yeah, I thought, quite convinced that when I grew up, I wouldn't have need for my community, and would happily sit behind the picket fence and potter around my own backyard.

Amid all this, Dad managed to finish his Bachelor of Social Work at Melbourne University. As it happened, he graduated on the same day my brother Bernie, number five in the clan, graduated with his own Arts/Teaching degree. *The Warrnambool Standard* ran a picture, and before we knew it, we were at Wilson Hall at Melbourne Uni on graduation day, posing for a full family photo for *The Age* newspaper with Dad and Bernie in their cloaks and hats, two-year-old Michael sitting on Dad's knee. 'Michael picks brains instead of spuds' was the headline. It was exciting, and we were all so proud of Dad, who battled away for ten years to fulfil a dream he'd held ever since that nun told him he should pursue his education. In a way, the hardest part was yet to come. Entering the workforce well into his fifties, Dad struggled to find work, first at home and then anywhere even close to it. There were many late nights and long, time-consuming applications, interviews, and more interviews, followed by anxious waits beside the phone. We learned to predict the result based on the mood in the house when we walked in the door after school. Eventually Dad got his first break, a year-long contract in Hamilton, where he stayed the night, most of the week. I was in year eight. Dad went wherever he could get work through the rest of my secondary schooling, sometimes in Melbourne, down to Gippsland, a six-month stint in Port Augusta in South Australia. All the while he lived in hospital residencies; he came home when he could, and a few times we joined him for a family 'holiday'. After so many years of battling to get his epilepsy under control, and then working so hard to get his Social Work degree, it didn't seem fair that his age and lack of formal experience worked against him on so many occasions, forcing him so far from home.

In 1999, the year Father Bryant arrived, I moved out of home to start my own Arts degree at Melbourne University, following a tradition of Angela, then Dad and then Bernie. Dad was away working in Port Augusta at the time.

'I'm looking forward to meeting this famous Michael Lane. I've heard so much about him,' said Father Bryant when he met Mum. It goes without saying that she held him in the highest regard, as she did with all men of the cloth, by virtue of the white collar they wore around their neck. Mum expected she and Dad would soon have the relationship of mutual trust, respect and support that had characterised their relationship with previous priests, all the way back to Father Paddy Bowen who married them. By 2002, only fourteen-year-old Michael was left at home when Dad was offered a permanent job in Taree, New South Wales. Mum and Dad were sixty-three by this stage and, after much indecision, decided to take the offer. We all thought that them getting away and extracting themselves from their responsibilities, especially at Crossley, would be good for them. Monica and her husband and children had just moved back to Warrnambool after fourteen years making a life in Melbourne. They were more than happy to move in at Tower Hill, and take on caring for Michael for a couple of years. The timing wasn't lost on Mum, it tore her apart to leave Michael without his parents at fourteen, the same age she was when her own parents left. This was different, though: Michael was in his own bedroom, in his own house, cared for by his own family. She needn't have worried.

We hardly recognised Mum and Dad when we went to New South Wales to visit. They drove us around the area, to beaches they'd walked on and picnic spots they'd visited. Forever a tea drinker, Mum even took me out to coffee and cake, and told us of movies she and Dad had seen.

One of Ten

We thought it was beautiful but hilariously funny to watch. Those were the things other people did, not Mum and Dad. Mum and Dad worked and fundraised, scratched and saved at home, and lived their lives around and for other people. It was a rare treat to see them behaving like a young romantic couple, with only each other to worry about. The warmer New South Wales weather was also doing favours for Mum's bad back, ruined, no doubt, from years on her hands and knees polishing the floor at St Brigid's. In recent years, it had deteriorated badly, there were times when Mum was unable to walk, and crawled to the bathroom, the pain was so bad. But beach walks and warm weather wouldn't keep them there. Michael was entering into VCE, and Mum had promised herself that she'd be there for him, in the way that she was for all of us. This had nothing to do with her academic experience, she always said she had nothing to offer when it came to our school work and left that for Dad to advise. But Mum did what she does best: keeping the fires burning, making endless cups of tea, baking scones, and waking us every morning with a glass of orange juice to get us going for the day. Clearly, she couldn't let Michael go without. Mum returned home in time for Michael to start year eleven. Dad stayed on to work in Taree.

It was back in 2003, not long after Mum and Dad had first left, when Father Bryant called for parishioners interested in the future of St Brigid's Church in Crossley to put their name forward to go onto a committee. My brother Patrick, living in Tower Hill, put his name forward. No meeting was called.

Two years later, in October 2005, while living in New South Wales, Mum and Dad happened to be back in Crossley. Father Bryant called a meeting of interested parishioners together into the sacristy after Mass. Dad and four women met with Father Bryant, who told the group that the parish had lost money every year for the past five years, because of declining church numbers, and said that the church might have to close.

There was no doubt that church attendance was in decline, as it was all over the Western world, but there was no evidence that Crossley should be the first to go. To the contrary, St Brigid's had the capacity to draw bigger crowds; Christmas Eve mass at St Brigid's had traditionally drawn as many as 500 people, until Father Bryant put an end to it.

Because of its beauty, St Brigid's has always been a very popular church for young brides, particularly those whose own parents and grandparents had been married there. But Father Bryant repeatedly refused to be the celebrant, which wouldn't necessarily preclude a wedding, except that neither would he give the permission required for another priest to come in and say the mass. When Liz went to see Fr Bryant to ask if she could be married at St Brigid's, she was told, in no uncertain terms, that 'St Brigid's isn't open for weddings anymore'. Liz tried to explain our family history with the church, and how much it would mean to her. He brushed off her arguments and before long, Liz surprised herself by getting emotional at the realisation the church she always assumed she'd marry in, wasn't available.

In the end, Father Bryant caved, saying 'I can't stand a crying woman'. Later, he would tell Dad that marrying Liz at St Brigid's was the biggest regret in his life.

But it wasn't just weddings which were not allowed. Families in grief, whose parents and grandparents had made lifelong commitments to St Brigid's, were told that they wouldn't be allowed to send off their loved one from their beloved church.

The day of Mum and Dad's visit in 2005 was, coincidently, census day, the day heads are counted for the church books. Eighty-five people were at mass that day at Crossley. Because Father Bryant had said so in the sacristy, 8:30 am mass was no longer, and moved to Koroit. Soon after, Mum and Dad attended mass in Koroit. There were only 45 people there.

Dad objected to the proposed plans for St Brigid's closure, arguing that surely other options should be pursued, and closure was a last resort. Father Bryant did not listen to what he had to say. Dad returned to New South Wales and sat down to pen a letter to the Bishop.

Four days after that little meeting in the sacristy, Father Bryant finally called together the group of interested parishioners he'd formed two years earlier. As a committee member, my brother Patrick attended, and though uninvited, so did Shane Howard, the musician and a local of Killarney. He was the Chair of the Australian Irish Association of South West Victoria, which formed at the Killarney pub in 2000. The meeting was attended by many of the older residents of the area who were asked what they most wanted the association to achieve. Resoundingly, the elders asked that their story and the story of their people be documented and remembered.

There is a degree of sadness and a sense of loss in regard to the decommissioning of St Brigid's church. Such is the long memory of Births, Deaths, Marriages, Midnight Christmas Mass and regular Masses in St Brigid's. Such is the measure of our changing times, Shane wrote in the letter. *St Brigid's has become an iconic image of the unique Irish Catholic culture that existed in Killarney, Koroit, Tower Hill and Crossley since our families travelled from Ireland and settled here after the Great Famine. Many are still farming and living in the area today. The church and hall are central to many stories, memories and significant events in the lives of the many generations, now far and wide, whose ancestry in Australia connects them back to this area.*

It was in this letter that Shane first mooted that St Brigid's be used to establish an Australian-Irish cultural and historical centre. The letter was tabled, Father Bryant noted it and said it had to be considered, before proceeding at this, their first meeting to discuss the future of St Brigid's, to announce that 'a decision has already been made, and the church is to be closed and decommissioned in December this year'. There were objections from parishioners at what an inappropriate time of year it was for such a big occasion, and how little time it allowed for planning. Father Bryant extended the date until 8 January 2006. A decision regarding the sale of the buildings, tennis courts and land would be made later, he said.

SAVING ST BRIGID'S

^ Nana and Pop: Eva and Jim Maloney

^ Grandad and Nana: Jack and Connie Lane

^ Loretta on her Communion day, at St John's Church, Dennington

^ Loretta and her baby brother, Doug

^ The Maloney brothers: (left to right) Doug, Ray, Geoff, Max and Pat

^ The Lane kids riding down Rocks Road, (left to right) Helen, Michael and Frank

^ Michael, at St Brigid's, Crossley

^ Jack Lane, and three of his children: (left to right) Michael, Helen, and Frank

^ Loretta and her bridesmaid

^ Michael (second from left) and his mates

^ Michael and Loretta on their honeymoon

^ Michael and Loretta, on their honeymoon, 1962

^ 26th May 1962, wedding day, St Joseph's Church, (left to right), Jack and Connie Lane, Michael and Loretta Lane, Eva and Pat Maloney

^ Michael and Loretta, 26 May 1962

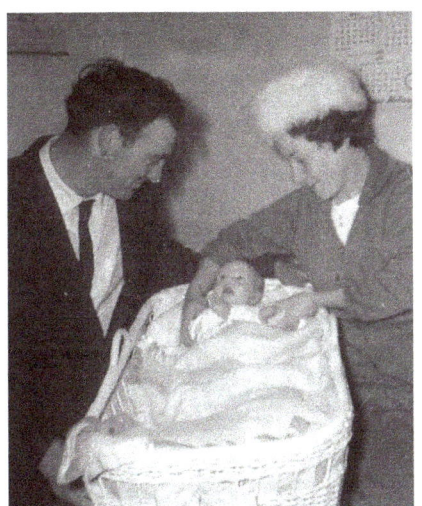

^ Michael and Loretta and their first baby, Angela, born 17 April 1963

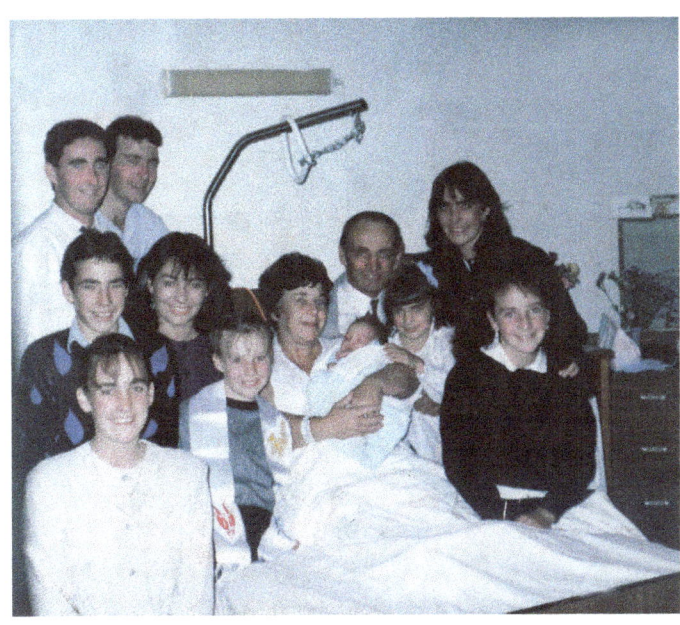

^ Loretta and Michael and their tenth baby, Michael Jnr, born 15 April 1988

^ Four children in under five years: Angela, Robert, Monica and baby Catherine

^ Mum and baby Patrick, (left to right back row) Robert, Angela, (left to right, front row) Monica, Bernard and Catherine

^ Christmas Day at Tower Hill, 1970s

^ Dad, Regina (left) and Liz (right) hard at work at home

^ (Left to right) Angela, Robert, Monica, Catherine, Bernie

^ (Left to right) Liz, Bernie, and Mary-Ellen walking down the lane to catch the school bus

^ Our family on my Confirmation day, Crossley Hall, 1992

^ Michael Jnr, Crossley Hall, Mum in the background

^ Mary-Ellen, Regina and Liz at the Maloney family reunion, Crossley Hall, 1982

^ 'Tower Hill's Lifeline', said the *Warrnambool Standard* headline. Mum wins the Moyne Shire Australia Day award for her services to the community, 1995.

^ 'Michael picks brains instead of spuds', *The Age*, March 1993. Dad graduates from Melbourne University on the same day as his fifth child, Bernie. Little Michael holds both their degrees.

^ The Lane family at Liz and Sam's wedding at St Brigid's Crossley, 8 January 2005, one year exactly before it was closed. (Left to right) Regina, Michael, Mary-Ellen, Patrick, Monica, Mum, the groom Sam and the bride Liz, Dad, Robert, Catherine and Angela

Chapter Five

Between love and fear

My father worked hard all his life,
He was a good husband and Mum was a good wife,
Just honest, hardworking people,
All they had was their faith and their family.

After the last mass, I drove back to Melbourne, listening over and over to Marcia Howard's song 'Wild and Free', depicting her childhood in Dennington; a childhood much like my own. I sobbed my heart out; it seemed so unjust that our people could believe so faithfully, that a humble little community could muster the strength and foresight to build a church and for generations our families gave all we could, and yet there was no place for us to have our say when it came to deciding its future.

I didn't just grow up in the Catholic Church; it had shaped my life choices, my political preferences and my career too. In my final year at university, I'd just returned from a couple of months backpacking around South-East Asia when I decided to get on a bus and go to Woomera Detention Centre in the Easter of 2002, to welcome the persecuted who had survived the torture and trauma of life in Afghanistan and Iraq, but also life in detention under the Howard government after the arrival of the *Tampa*. It was not the bloodshed and violence I witnessed that most shocked me – it was society's ignorance and apathy that I found most confronting on my return. Angry and frustrated, and increasingly disturbed by the gross human rights violations on Australian soil, I had trouble sleeping and had recurring nightmares about those pleading, desperate faces. On one particular morning, I woke after another nightmare with tears in my eyes. As my dream faded from my memory, I recognised the desperate, pleading faces. Locked behind the razor wire fence were my mother, my father, my brothers and sisters, my nieces and nephews. They were pleading for my help, pleading for freedom. In my dream, I felt useless, helpless. Just like the lived experience, I simply stood at the fence crying, repeating 'I'm sorry'. That dream taught me volumes about what I learned at Woomera.

After the dream, I decided I had to do something. I took up an internship with the Catholic Commission for Justice, Development and Peace, researching and interviewing refugees. A few months later, I landed my first professional job. The Brigidine Sisters offered me a position travelling around their secondary schools to educate and empower their students to take action towards a more just society. The learning and empowerment went both ways. My days at the convent office, next door to the Brigidine Asylum Seeker Centre, provided both a shocking insight into how the most defenseless lose out when it comes to vote-winning politics, and an inspiring lesson into the small but significant victories for humanity, when there are people who are prepared to actively oppose such injustices. The Brigidine Sisters were such people. Retired from teaching, they devoted their lives to supporting asylum seekers in detention and in the community. Gentle and compassionate, they attended to their basic human needs, but also, strong and determined, they stood up to fight inhumane ministerial decisions and high-court challenges. In this, they were guided by their patroness, St Brigid, 'Mary of the Gael', who as pagan Celtic goddess was a woman of the land, attuned to the seasons and elements of nature, and in whose honour a perpetual fire has burned in Ireland since pre-Christian times, when they invoked Brigid's spirit to protect their homes and herds from evil spirits. It was St Brigid the Christian nun, who scholars say pioneered monastic life in Ireland and is said to have been the first Christian bishop in Ireland, which I knew from a childhood of Sundays looking up at her statue, a church in the palm of one hand, a staff in the other. But it was her legacy as a strong, compassionate, earthly woman who stood for peace, justice and equality, that was the greatest inspiration to me in my early twenties, a time when Church and religion might have otherwise fallen away from my life altogether.

During my time at the Brigidines, I was offered a second job, at the Catholic archdiocese where I'd interned a year prior. In the great Catholic tradition of upholding workers' rights, I was deliberately titled 'social justice worker' and learned the ropes of campaigning, researching and writing, lobbying and public speaking. I spent my life in my little Toyota Corolla travelling around Victoria, speaking in school assemblies and Sunday mass, about reconciliation with Indigenous Australia, refugee rights, global poverty and the emerging challenge of climate change. I learned much greater respect for my Church, and a great tradition of social teaching that directed popes and bishops through history to speak out on behalf of the planet, the poor and the marginalised. Though I certainly didn't agree with everything the Church stood for, I found a place where I felt I was genuinely making a contribution to the greater good.

But I still always felt something of a fraud that I wasn't a 'real' Catholic, because I didn't attend church on Sundays. I tried, but beyond the familiar and comforting rituals, I just didn't get much out of it really. I heard sermons that were so focused on notions of what it means to be a 'good' Catholic that the real message of Christ seemed somewhat blurry, forgotten even. I always felt like there was a massive disconnect between the challenge of injustices in our world, and my daily work, and the preaching that I heard in Mass on Sunday. Yet, I was often introduced as 'one of ten', and felt seen to be a good, wholesome, church-going Catholic. Of course, that was just my own perception. Though I do remember after one talk I gave, being questioned on which parish I belonged to. I blushed. 'I don't really belong to any parish, I go to all different churches,' I stammered, convincing myself it was only half a lie, that I had tried out mass at a few different places. But my Catholic guilt increased with every day I walked past St Patrick's cathedral, on my way into the office, until one day I confessed the truth to my boss. He cracked up laughing. 'Half the people you work with are LC's, Regina.'

'LC's?' I said meekly, blushing furiously.

'Lapsed Catholics.'

He explained how our Catholic upbringing instilled the sense of justice and the drive to act upon it, but it was a double-edged sword for the Church. The privilege of Catholic education our forebears fought so hard for, taught us to critically question and think for ourselves. Our questions were often not heard, and when they were, the answers were often unacceptable to a new generation of enquiring, critical thinkers, who saw the hypocrisy in the Church positions on issues that affected their lives, as well as the growing concern over a Church hierarchy doing its best to avoid, deny and cover up the explosion of allegations of clergy sex abuse.

I wrestled with these issues as I continued with my work. In 2005 I moved out of the Archdiocese but not the Church altogether. I became the coordinator of a small Catholic organisation, set up by the nuns and brothers who were leaders of their Orders, to advocate on social-justice issues based on the principles of Catholic social teaching. I had my work cut out for me. The Howard Government had just won control of the Senate, and under the twin mantra of greater economic growth and improved national security, they hastily drove through a raft of legislation to wind back 100 years of worker's rights, take away our time-honoured civil and political rights, and transform the culturally and politically vibrant landscape of our universities into the more elitist user-pays system that generations before us fought so hard to avoid. These were turbulent, if not downright depressing, times to work in social justice.

So engrossed in the politics of the day, by Christmas 2005, I had barely heard a thing about the closing of St Brigid's. I knew nothing of the letter that Dad had sent to the Bishop of Ballarat outlining, over seven pages, his objections to the hurried closure of St Brigid's. Under separate headings Dad discussed the distinguished role St Brigid's historically played in the Catholic Church in south west Victoria, in providing the pathway for a significant number of priests, nuns and brothers who had taken up vocations after an upbringing at St Brigid's. He outlined his belief that St Brigid's hall was worthy of listing in the National Trust and should be preserved. He outlined our family involvement, listed all the grants he'd successfully received over the years, a recent application he'd made, and shared his feelings about the decision to close the church. He shared his view that people had not been adequately consulted and no facts or figures had been provided to justify the decision. He opened a discussion on what effect shifting demographic and social trends had had on falling church attendance and the impact on declining numbers of priests. He explained the opposition from the parish priest many had in seeking to get married at St Brigid's and how people were disallowed from having funerals at St Brigid's. He questioned if a deliberate attempt had been made to wind down activities at St Brigid's.

It was refreshing to read my dad's words acknowledging how this approach had alienated my generation from wanting to attend mass. We'd never had these conversations with Mum and Dad. Mass on Sundays is the first duty of being Catholic. When we were kids, Sunday mass was a no excuses event. The only Sundays I remember not having to go to mass were the Sundays after a family wedding – two masses in one weekend was taking it a bit too far, we successfully argued. When we were teenagers, staying the weekends at the homes of friends in Warrnambool, we would always take ourselves off down to St Joseph's to attend mass, even if it was just to pick up a bulletin to prove that we'd been. When I first moved out of home at eighteen, I'd just spent three days partying at the student village where I lived, when Mum rang. I hadn't even met my flatmate, when she woke me to tell me my mother was on the phone. 'How is it?' Mum asked. I filled her in, trying to hide my hangover.

'Why aren't you at mass?'

'Mum! I've only been gone three days, I don't even know where the church is!'

'Well, you found the pub alright by the sound of it!'

It's been a long time since Mum has asked if I'd been to mass, but as far as she knew, we all did our duties on Sundays. We didn't tell them otherwise; it was easier left that way.

The tone of Dad's letter was disarming, noting down these facts of life, and posing them as challenges that he himself was willing to help achieve action to overcome. It was a letter of hope, seeking reconciliation and renewal towards a new kind of Church, but it was far from revolutionary.

My parents are conservative Catholics; they might have had a lot of practice in grassroots community development, but they weren't setting out to change the status quo. Dad was not picking a fight with the way the Church ran its affairs. He even noted that the Church was no democracy, accepting the fact. He simply wanted things to be done the right way. It didn't seem like much to ask really.

Dad noted how demographic and social and economic trends had changed the landscape of our district, but ventured that centralisation was not the answer, suggesting that survival for the Catholic Church rested with re-engaging at the local level. This was the stuff I talked about on a daily basis in my working life, when I was out and about trying to mobilise and motivate people to take action. People are more willing to contribute and feel more ownership among a smaller group. More people in larger, more centralised churches only creates the opposite effect. Dad expressed his belief that the closure of St Brigid's was the worst possible option for the Church and would only serve to alienate more people, compounding the anger, bitterness and disappointment the parish already felt. He predicted that it would not achieve the intended effect of driving people to Koroit Infant Jesus for mass, but instead drive people to Warrnambool, or worse, to give up going altogether. He said he felt it was a betrayal of the priests and religious who'd gone before at St Brigid's, and our forefathers, who'd worked so hard to build and maintain it. He finished by offering his skills and experience as a social worker, at no cost to the parish, to work with the community to reconcile and rebuild the parish and pleaded that the Bishop intervene to have the decision deferred for twelve months, until a thorough investigation be considered.

The Bishop wrote a three line letter in response, acknowledging receipt of Dad's letter, four days before Christmas.

The next day Dad received a phone call from Father Bryant, who'd just received Dad's letter, forwarded direct from the Bishop – a letter that was never intended for Father Bryant to read. So much for confidentiality. It's no wonder the perpetrators of sex-abuse crimes in the Catholic Church got away with it, if their superiors followed the same protocol and simply forwarded on the complaint, unbeknown to the poor victim.

Father Bryant didn't sound happy about the letter and Dad 'going over his head', as if Dad had simply set out to undermine his authority. Dad explained how he'd felt his objections had been ignored previously and he felt an appeal to the Bishop was the obvious next step. He let Father Bryant know that he'd tried to inform him about his letter at the previous Saturday night's mass.

'This isn't personal. I don't agree with the decision you've made, and how you've gone about it, but I'm not opposed to you personally,' Dad said, trying to keep focus on the issue itself.

'It's personal alright. You're the prick who wrote to the Bishop! Of course it's personal,' Father Bryant responded. 'You'll be hearing from my solicitors, I intend to take action against you for slander. I suggest you should consult your own solicitor.'

Dad was near speechless. He gently offered to get in the car and go visit immediately, so that the matter could be discussed properly.

'It's three days before Christmas. I'm busy,' Father Bryant snapped back.

Dad offered that he could visit after Christmas. 'It's too late for that now. I suggest you would be better to start counting your pennies because you're going to need them.'

Dad was stunned. He explained that he was disappointed at how the decision had been made, with a lack of consultation. Father Bryant retorted that he had set up a committee – two years earlier. Dad quietly reminded him that it had only met once, only to be told that a decision had already been made.

'I didn't get around to it. It wasn't deliberate. That's just how it happened.'

Dad asked why a special appeal for funds had not been called for, as was common practice at church. Father Bryant admitted he hadn't got around to that either, but he planned to, in June of the following year. By that time St Brigid's would be mothballed.

He went on to explain that he'd made the decision to stop weddings and funerals at Crossley; and marrying Liz, who had to fight tooth and nail for the right to marry in our church earlier that year, was one of his greatest regrets.

But it was his last comment that most riled us.

'My mother has contributed a priest to the Church. What sons have *you* contributed?'

Questioning my parent's contribution to the Catholic Church was a cheap shot, but it hit where it hurt. We were completely shocked. We grew up seeing priests as holy men, incapable of foul language or behaving badly like the rest of us. My parents had worked so hard to build and rebuild community all their lives, and had paid personally for their efforts. I'd only ever heard people, especially priests, use respect, and kind and affectionate words when they spoke to or about my parents. Mum and Dad were at a loss to know what to do next.

My brother Robert happened to drop in at Tower Hill just after the phone call. He was heavily involved on the board of his own parish council, and had numerous contacts in the Ballarat diocese. He got in touch with a nun who knew that the Bishop was due to consult with Father Bryant in January. She advised Dad to record the conversation and send it to the Bishop, this time marked 'private and confidential'. The first I really heard of this whole affair was at our family Christmas dinner, a few days before Christmas. Amid the eating and drinking and children playing, I wandered past a bedroom to find my eldest sister Angela bashing away at the computer, with Monica and Mary Ellen throwing in their contributions, to make the Bishop understand both the seriousness and the ridiculousness of the situation before it was too late.

St Brigid's last mass was scheduled for just two weeks time.

Dad outlined the conversation that had taken place, expressed his concern about Father Bryant's irrational behaviour, and reaffirmed his commitment to the Catholic Church and support of priests and the priesthood, which Mum and Dad have always faithfully done, both informally and financially. He finished off spelling out his Catholic credentials lest the Bishop not understand that Dad was indeed 'a good Catholic', not the troublemaker Father Bryant had insinuated. He wanted the Bishop to know that he deserved a hearing, that he 'held the faith' and was on their side.

Your Lordship, I am now 66 years of age. Together with my wife I have raised and educated 10 children through the primary and secondary Catholic school system. Three have continued their Catholic tertiary education and are now teachers in the Catholic system. Two others have been actively involved school board members for years at their local Catholic primary schools in their parishes, my son has been a member and leader of a Parish Council, and one daughter, after employment at the Melbourne Archdiocese, is now the National Coordinator of an organisation led by Catholic religious orders. Furthermore, I currently have 14 grandchildren attending school in the primary and secondary Catholic school system. I have always been a supporter of my Catholic church, and have been very disturbed to be subjected to such attempts to bully, threaten and intimidate me. These efforts have only served to strengthen my resolve to seek a just and fair solution to the issue.

This time, there was no response.

Two weeks later, and three days after the last mass, I found myself driving to Ballarat, to a national Marist Brother Catholic Youth Justice Festival as the guest speaker. I had the opening and closing slot. The Bishop of Ballarat was a special guest. I'd spent weeks preparing my two forty-minute presentations, and though I should have been focused on the job ahead, I could hardly stop crying my eyes out all the way down the western highway from Melbourne. My outpouring of grief over St Brigid's closure surprised even me. I couldn't decide what prompted it. It wasn't like I was in regular attendance at St Brigid's. Perhaps it was the obvious fact that I'd now lost the opportunity to follow in the footsteps of my sisters and get married at St Brigid's. But more than anything I felt aggrieved that an injustice had just taken place, and I felt completely powerless to do anything about it.

And so it goes in times of loss, I was only now coming to fully appreciate my family's close connection to St Brigid's. The part of the world where I grew up was often described as having 'a rich history'. Just as that phrase was starting to bear meaning it felt like it had been ripped away, before anyone could ask another question. The church will now be 'decommissioned', we were informed, without being informed what exactly this meant. As we understood it, a decommissioning meant that it is officially no longer a Catholic Church, a ritual where a religious relic is taken from beneath the altar where it was placed at its opening, and commissioning, in 1914. However, this ritual did not happen in our presence at the final mass, and we were under some understanding that a bishop was required to perform such a duty.

Emotional and confused, I arrived at Ballarat for the welcome drinks for guest speakers and special guests on the first night. After chatting with the organisers, I hesitantly made my way to see the Bishop, a man I'd seen but not met before. Not much taller than myself at five foot, he is completely bald, with a rounded face. Introducing myself, I explained how my father had recently written a letter to him. 'I know who you are,' he said indifferently, without warmth or recognition. I chatted politely, about the last mass, what a big day it was, careful not to be critical in front of a man of his standing. I felt awkward, desperately trying to regain some professionalism and distance myself from the tears I'd wiped away as I pulled into the car park earlier. I met the other guest speaker, a Bishop Kevin Dowling from South Africa, a tall, thin man with a broad smile and a warm nature. We chatted briefly about his work with HIV AIDS sufferers but I was unable to focus my attention, acutely aware the man who had the power to redirect the future of St Brigid's was in the room. He kept his distance.

The next morning, I delivered a speech written around the theme of the festival; 'What is?' As requested, I delivered an overview of the current major challenges facing Australia. Starting where the students were at, I talked about the first time I learned about Australia's black history, of dispossession, stolen children and diminished culture, and how despite some progress, there was much unfinished business to be taken care of. I suggested how this failure to own up to our past directly influenced our draconian refugee policies and enabled politicians to turn back leaky boats and lock up innocent people. I talked about the failure of our government to act on climate change and to do its fair share when it came to overseas aid.

My speech was long and detailed, but well received by the students and young people, as well as the bishops, religious and lay schoolteachers. The Bishop of Port Pirie, himself actively involved with the refugees in the desert of South Australia, commented that 'The Catholic Church needs more intelligent young women like you'. Relieved to have my first speech out of the way, I appreciated the sentiment but couldn't rid that uneasy feeling, or get that song out of my head. 'All they had was their faith and their family.' This festival was designed to unpack and discuss social justice challenges, and yet I had a nagging feeling that I now had a new one to add to my list. But as an employee of a Catholic organisation, addressing a room full of Catholics, I could hardly say what I was really thinking.

Bishop Kevin from South Africa had clearly been through that process before and decided otherwise. He was Bishop of a diocese where 94 percent of his parishioners were infected with HIV AIDS. His stories left me agape at the sheer challenge he faced. The humanitarian challenge seemed the more manageable bit; it was fighting the Catholic Church position on condoms that left him most wearied and disillusioned. At the bishops' conference in Rome, he'd spoken out strongly, suggesting that the Church would save more lives in Africa if it repealed its prohibition of the use of condoms, than it would by insisting that Catholics not use them. He shared this message, albeit more subtly, in his address to the young people on the first night in Ballarat. He reminded the audience that the Catholic Church must face up to these challenges if it was to remain true and relevant in today's age. Listening to his stories and watching his slideshow, his pictures divided between the themes of hope and despair, I wasn't the only one in the room with tears in my eyes. But it wasn't just the people of South Africa for whom I was crying. Just like I'd said in my speech earlier about when I first read the Bringing Them Home Report, I was also crying for myself. Back then, the revelation of injustice had obligated me to act, and I felt a sense of lost innocence, knowing that my view of my country was forever changed. In that darkened marquee in Ballarat, I had the same feeling about the Catholic Church, my Church, and I was beginning to feel obligated to act.

Afterwards I sought out Bishop Kevin in the hall where teenagers were singing and dancing and I told him my story of three days prior at the last mass, again the tears welling. I felt utterly pathetic at my reaction to an injustice that paled in comparison to his daily challenges of life and death. He listened intently. 'You shouldn't feel like that. An injustice is an injustice, no matter where it happens and how many people are affected.

Keep speaking the truth, Regina,' he said and gave me a hug. He reminded me of the quote I planned to use in my final presentation on Friday, by Martin Luther King. 'Injustice anywhere is a threat to justice everywhere.'

I ran workshops and participated in group activities, but my mind was on Mum and Dad. In a break, I rang home. I'd heard Dad sound flat before, depressed even. But not beaten. As we debriefed on the last mass of a week ago, his was the voice of defeat. He'd done all he could. And he'd got nowhere.

I told him the Bishop was here, and I still had my final speech to say 'What Now?', a motivational piece explaining my own journey through life actively fighting for social justice. I was meant to share my own experiences, feelings and challenges. But I could hardly say what I really felt.

'Why not?' Dad asked.

'Dad, there's like five Bishops here. I can't.'

'But it's your story. They asked to hear your story. St Brigid's is part of your story.'

'I can't, Dad. I could lose my job.'

'But Gina, this *is* your job, isn't it?'

I was silent as the weight of that crucible moment bore down on me.

'Can you put Mum on?'

'I think you should say something, love,' her voice weary and sad. Sitting under an old willow tree in the school grounds I saw a white car drive through the gates. It was the Bishop.

I couldn't believe what I was hearing, really. My parents might have worked hard in the community, but they weren't outspoken types. Never before would they have encouraged me to even think about speaking out against the Church hierarchy. But now they just wanted the truth to be told. I got off the phone feeling I had little choice. 'Always speak the truth,' Bishop Kevin's voice rang in my ears. I went off to Reconciliation, a ceremony where the priest absolves the congregation of their sins, silently offered up to God. Bishop Kevin was the lead celebrant. In his homily, he took the notion of individual sin and turned it on its head, instilling in us the idea I can best recall in the words of English philosopher Edmund

Burke, that 'evil triumphs when good people do nothing'. Bishop Kevin urged us to 'open our eyes and ears', and explained that Reconciliation was not about sin and guilt, but about the need to seek truth and work towards justice. He talked about the twin driving emotions of love and fear, and how fear could only be overcome with love. Sitting cross-legged on the floor, among a sea of silent students in the candlelit marquee, a picture of Mother Mary on the wall, his words burned right through me.

'Always search for and speak the truth,' he urged again. I was convinced he was speaking directly to me.

After the ceremony of Reconciliation, the priests and bishops set themselves up for individual confession. I went back to my room and lay on my bed, staring at the ceiling, my heart pounding. I rang Dad.

'I'll do it,' I said.

'What time is it?'

'I dunno. It's about ten o'clock, isn't it?' I said, looking out the window.

'No, your speech. What time is it tomorrow?'

'At 9 am. Why?'

'I'll see you there'

Home was two hours away. I told him he didn't need to.

'I'll be there,' he said firmly.

I got up and went back to the marquee. Poking my head inside the tent of flickering candles, I saw a handful of priests, their long white robes flowing, sitting in different corners of the room, their figures reflected in contorted shadows on the white marquee walls, in quiet conversation with young students who listened intently and then bowed their heads for God's blessing. In the middle of the room was an altar in tribute to Mother Mary, a huge framed portrait surrounded by candles and burning incense. At its foot knelt a young blonde girl, her hands clasped in prayer, a pair of white opal rosary beads strung through her fingers, her lips murmuring words I couldn't hear, but knew well. 'Hail Mary, full of grace, the Lord is with thee.' I watched her for a few minutes, as she reeled off the joyful mysteries, praying to the Virgin Mary for the salvation I wasn't sure I believed in. The whole scene caused me to take a step back, making me feel strangely like I was watching an unfamiliar ritual in a foreign country.

Saving St Brigid's

I took a deep breath and waited to see Bishop Kevin, also dressed, against his will, in a priestly white robe. He'd preferred to have worn jeans and a t-shirt, he told me. When Jesus was going about his work, he didn't dress differently, he had said with a wry grin. I sat down on the chair opposite, and told him I had no confession to make, but that I had some things to say. I said how I felt his homily tore through me, that I had things I wanted to say tomorrow that my parents thought needed to be said. But I was full of fear, I told him. Of what, I wasn't exactly sure. He told me I had a choice to make, between love and fear. He wished me luck, and I went back to my room, a whole new speech to write. I sat at a little desk in that old bluestone boarding school through the dark night, reliving my childhood memories and trying to find the words as to why St Brigid's had helped shaped my life. After a while, it started flowing, but I fussed over the tone, the language, careful to be respectful and sensitive. I turned out the light at 4 am and slept heavily for three hours.

At 9 am, as I stood by the stage in the humid marquee, wiping my sweaty palms on my three-quarter pants, I vaguely heard some housekeeping announcements about moving parked cars from outside the school chapel. Number plates were being reeled off, but I wasn't paying attention. All I could concentrate on was my heartbeat pounding loudly in my ears. I stood on my toes, searching for my dad, in the back row. And then I was introduced back to the stage.

I'm often asked why I got involved in social justice. I'm never really quite sure how to answer that. It's not that straightforward. And most people don't have a few days to listen. I don't think I could ever really put my finger on it. The need to be active, to participate, to want to make a difference, feels like it's always been there.

Yet last Sunday I think I got my answer. I grew up in a place called Tower Hill, in south west Victoria. It has a strong Irish Catholic tradition; needless to say I grew up on a potato farm. With five sisters and four brothers, I was the ninth of ten children. My parents did it tough, they worked bloody hard, and though us kids knew how to go without, there were four things that were never in short supply. Love, family, faith and community.

Bishop Connors was sitting right in front of me, in the third row. At this point, he closed his eyes. I wondered what he was thinking.

Last Sunday I attended the closing mass of St Brigid's Catholic Church and historic hall at Crossley. The church that my great-grandfather built, where my grandmother sang in the choir, the church and school my father rode his horse to, the hall where my parents met and danced and fell in love. The church where my elder sister celebrated her first communion, the church where my five sisters were married, where my nieces and nephews were christened. I had planned to marry there one day; my grandmother wants her funeral there. It was in honour of St Brigid, and that church, that Mum and Dad took my second name. St Brigid's wasn't just a place where we went every Sunday morning at 8.30 for mass, it was a cornerstone of our community.

It wasn't the first time I'd stood in front of such a large audience. Never before did I feel I had their full attention. Today I could feel it. Three hundred pairs of eyes were on me. The woman in the second row looked like she might burst into tears.

It was a place where people met each week and caught up with their neighbours, talked about their lives, their children, the weather and when their spud crop would be harvested. The hall was a place we had Christmas parties, wedding receptions, and play groups. The tennis courts were where we played in the stinking heat, my feet burning through my sneakers, as I tried my hand at becoming a pro and failed, but learned a few things about teamwork and leadership. After tennis Mum would bring us up frozen bottles of cordial and we'd join her in the cool quiet of the church as she arranged the flowers, singing church hymns, while we ran up and down the aisles or scared each other in the dark and dusty confessional boxes, until we were yelled at and made to polish vases. It was a place where I watched my parents become leaders in a community, when they resurrected a dilapidated hall and a flagging community. My parents worked hard at that place, bloody hard, so we kids grew up always helping out at working bees, cleaning, painting, mopping floors, mowing the church grounds. In my teenage years, it was a place where I cursed my parents under my breath, making me go to church, making me spend Saturday afternoons doing church flowers. So over it I was, I clearly remember vowing to Mum, that 'when I grow up, I'm never going to do what you're doing, living your life for the community like this'. I looked around at my friend's perfect homes and gardens and vowed that I would only ever worry about my own backyard.

Saving St Brigid's

My mother always said, 'You only get out of community what you put back into it.' At 15, I was quite convinced that I had no need for my community, so I was happy to withdraw my services!

I watched Bishop Connors with his eyes closed and wondered if he could see the scenes of my childhood that were so vivid in my mind.

I guess somewhere deep inside, I was always aware that this place was special to me, to my family and to our story. But just like anything, you don't realise its importance until it's gone. On Sunday, apparently due to falling mass attendances, the final mass was celebrated in the church. The final luncheon was had in the hall. I drove down to Crossley from Melbourne on Sunday morning. As I walked into the church, my mother and father were standing tall and proud, in the front row, and as I looked around at the 600 familiar faces that turned up to say goodbye, I felt an overwhelming sense of my place. I realised then, that just as the potter moulds the clay, God, through my parents and that sacred place, had moulded me. I knew who I was, where I'd come from, I knew then what had made me the person that I am today. At Crossley, the seed had been sown. In some sense, that place taught me everything I know or feel about community, about participation, about being active and working hard, about justice, about welcoming the stranger - it taught me about people.

By now I could see the tears being wiped away. I didn't expect that, and it made me wonder if I should keep going. Bishop Connors still hadn't opened his eyes. I wondered if he was praying.

Some of you might know Shane Howard, a local man, Irish descent, but well renowned musician and story teller of indigenous, Australian and Irish history, who said poetically after the closure, 'this was our dreaming place'. I agreed. It was a place where we found our spiritual connection, where we could believe, where we could dream.

At the closing of the mass, the statue of St Brigid was taken down. I watched my 93 year-old grandmother, sitting in a wheelchair, break down in tears. My father standing, rubbing her shoulders, broke down too. I'll never forget that. Sitting there, with four generations of my family, I realised the rich heritage I had inherited, and gave thanks for a place that had given me so much. I cried and felt profound grief that I would not be able to share that place with my own children.

My voice broke and for a moment I couldn't contain myself. I stood back from the lectern and looked away, trying to blink back the tears. A young girl leaped up from the front row and gave me a hug. I took a deep breath. I knew I was treading on dangerous ground. Four bishops wearing black sat in a row in front of me. When I opened my mouth, I surprised myself by how strong and determined my voice sounded.

But I also felt immense hurt and anger. Whilst the closure was said to be the falling attendance at mass, the decision to close the church was made with next to no community consultation. No facts or figures were provided to justify the closure. I believe this is an issue of social justice. How can the church speak on issues of social justice when the people that make up the church community are denied the right to make decisions that affect their lives? This raises the very principles of Catholic social teaching, of subsidiarity, of dignity, of participation, of the common good, that I learnt at St Brigid's, and that I've striven to uphold in my work. The closure rocked the foundations of belief on which I have committed myself. Martin Luther King said: 'Injustice anywhere is a threat to justice everywhere'. I believe in that. I expressed disappointment to the parish priest that these principles were not upheld, and he replied that 'the church isn't a democracy, I am the power here'.

I heard the collective drawing in of breath and the sound of shock and disapproval. At the end of the row, in the second aisle, a young guy I knew, a friend of a friend, in his first year in the seminary, was watching me with such intensity my eyes were drawn back to his every time I scanned the room. I wondered what he was thinking. At the back of the audience, a group of young artistic types, tasked with creatively responding to my speech, were whispering to each other with wild hand-gestures. I wondered how on earth they might act it out. After my first presentation, they portrayed an asylum seeker reaching through the doorway, to the taunts of racist comments and then to the voices of kindness and compassion that I'd shared in my speech. It had been quite confronting to watch my lived experiences acted out before me like that.

SAVING ST BRIGID'S

What now? My what now is to start again at Crossley. It's to do my utmost to protect the heritage that has been handed down to me, and go home and fight so that the buildings of St Brigid's church and hall are not lost to the community today, or for future generations. Who knows? Maybe one day my children will find their spiritual connection there, will go there to believe and to dream.

I went on with my speech, sharing other stories and experiences of injustice in Australia and probing the audience to consider their own power in making the choice between love and fear. I finished by telling the audience about how I made that choice in honour of my father, for making me the person I am today. The audience rose to their feet and clapped loudly. There was cheering and whistling, as I tearfully made my way down the aisle to the back of the marquee, into Dad's tearful embrace. Booming over the loudspeakers, the ethereal sounds of the didgeridoo rose up above the applause as I recognised a tune I knew and loved.

Out here nothing changes
Not in a hurry anyway
You can feel the endlessness
With the coming of the light of day
Talk about a chosen place
They want to sell it in a marketplace.

The young Seminarian came to speak to Dad and me. 'You really gave me something to think about up there,' he said, his eyes filled with deep concern. He was from outback South Australia, and was used to the seldom visit of a priest; the parishioners sharing the role of 'saying mass' amongst themselves. Dad agreed that such a future would have to become the way of things for the Catholic Church. It was an option that hadn't been explored for St Brigid's.

Round about the dawn of time
Dreaming all began
Proud people come
Livin' in a promised land

Between Love and Fear

Running from a heart of darkness
Searching for a heart of light

A shy young Aboriginal bloke, also from an outback community in the Northern Territory, came over with his mate. 'I'm not Catholic, so I don't get that bit,' he said, 'but what you said up there, about your place . . . and your people . . .' he trailed off, without looking me in the eye. I nodded, tears welling. Our life experience was so different, but as they say, the things that bind are stronger than the things that divide. I felt like hugging him, as Shane Howard's voice carried across the yard.

Standin' on the shore one day
Saw the white sails in the sun
Wasn't long before they felt that sting
White man, white law, white gun
Don't tell me that it's justified
Cause somewhere, someone lied.
Someone lied.
Think it's called genocide

Now you're standin' on solid rock
Standin' on sacred ground,
Livin' on borrowed time,
And the winds of change
Are blowin' down the line.

The young actors started their performance, using four doorways painted red that had acted as props throughout the festival for various speakers and performances. Four actors came along, and sizing up the door, as if they might want to enter, hesitantly opened a door each, looking through to the other side, and then closing it again, leaning on it, thinking. Then they opened it again, slowly, but with a little more confidence. They slammed it quickly. Then they opened it, quickly, as if they knew who was standing behind, and closed it again, frightened. They opened, and closed, louder and louder for what felt like minutes, throwing all their body weight behind their effort. Their furrowed brows and pursed lips showed their frustration, their anger. They opened and slammed until their bodies felt against the closed doors like rag dolls, exhausted. They collapsed on the floor, and the room was silent. And then they stood up slowly, one by one. They dusted off their pants, regained their footing, and shook the strain out of their bodies. This time when they opened the doors, they found a hand that was reaching out for them. And when they took the hand, they walked through, their faces full of tentative hope and relief. They reappeared smiling together at the front of the stage, hand in hand, a sign of strength and unity. They couldn't have reflected my emotional turmoil more perfectly, even if they finished with smiles that I couldn't muster. Though I spoke of it, I'm not sure that I really believed myself that there was much hope when it came to the future of St Brigid's. Certainly there were few hands presenting themselves. Or so I thought.

Chapter Six

'You have my word'

Dad didn't drive all the way to Ballarat just to see me. There was somebody he wanted to speak to. That somebody didn't look particularly keen to see Dad. Bishop Connors made his way over to us, introducing himself to Dad. Outside the marquee, people milling all around, a Marist brother handed the three of us a plastic cup of water. We got straight down to it, asking why he hadn't been invited to St Brigid's decommissioning mass. He looked slightly confused, as if he hadn't been informed it was on. He asked what had taken place. Dad patiently and respectfully explained to him the proceeding of the Mass and asked why his Lordship wasn't there.

'I get invited to lots of closing Masses. I can't be at all of them,' the Bishop said without hiding his annoyance at our questioning.

'We appreciate that,' Dad said softly. 'But we understood that a church had to be decommissioned by a Bishop.'

'Well, yes, I would normally attend,' he said, sounding out the words. 'But Father Bryant has made the decision to stop Masses at Crossley, and so I wouldn't expect to be invited.'

'You mean St Brigid's hasn't been decommissioned?'

'As far as I'm aware, the Mass you attended was the last mass Father Bryant is prepared to say.'

What was he talking about? I raised an eyebrow at Dad.

'But he told us it was a decommissioning. He told us we must leave the building quickly, and we were not allowed back inside.' Shut up and let Dad talk, I told myself.

Dad asked again, and had the Bishop confirm again, that St Brigid's hadn't in fact been decommissioned. It was still a Catholic church after all. Thank God.

Dad insisted on his written request that our parish be offered the opportunity for a full review of the situation, so that people could participate in decision-making about the future. The Bishop didn't deny his request, but wasn't exactly forthcoming with offers either. He acknowledged that consultation wasn't Father Bryant's strong point.

'I think we need an independent mediator to come to lead a community discussion,' I said.

Bishop Connors turned his attention to Dad to respond. 'I'll see what I can arrange, now I really must go,' he said handing Dad his plastic cup as he turned on his heel and left.

Dad was pleased. 'Well, that's good news.'

'Good news? He hasn't got a bloody clue! What the hell is going on here? How could he not know that one of his priests was closing down a church?'

'Well, it's still a Catholic church. It's not decommissioned,' Dad said with a satisfied smile.

'So Father Bryant's lied to us from the altar? What a joke!'

I left Dad to join in the next round of workshops. Exhausted, I went back to my room to lie down. Outside the school chapel, guests milled around in evening wear and suits, while a bridal couple posed for photos. My dusty old car, its back window pasted with stickers to save the forests and the refugees, was parked right outside the chapel's main doors. 'Woops,' I grinned to myself, remembering the announcement that was made just prior to my taking to the stage, an announcement about moving cars and number plates. I had heard, but not listened. I laughed to myself, feeling the fog of my exhaustion lift, and hoped I'd be forgiven.

Back in Melbourne, I got busy writing letters too. The Bishop had told us St Brigid's was still a Catholic church. Now was the time to insist on some open dialogue in the parish. Firstly, I apologised to him, if I made him feel uncomfortable by sharing my personal story like that. I did feel bad about it. I can't imagine he enjoyed sitting there listening to me cry my eyes out. Especially if I was reacting to something that hadn't actually happened yet.

It was of great surprise to me that you were unaware of the closure of St Brigid's on the 8th January. It appears to me from what you have said that St Brigid's church has not been officially decommissioned. I believe it is vitally important for the 600 or so people who attended, and the wider community (many of whom were unaware of the closing), that the status of St Brigid's as a Catholic church be promptly and clearly explained.

The *Moyne Gazette* of 1 January 2006, reported that Father Bryant was quoted as saying 'I haven't formally put anything to the Bishop as yet'. I explained in my letter the confusion this created. The article went on to say that Father Bryant 'has yet to begin the formal process of applying to the Bishop for the alienation of the Church, which he said, must occur before a sale takes place'. This was good news for us, because it meant the Bishop, as much in the dark as he seemed, was the person in the position of power to call the shots. I sought his confirmation that our parish needed a proper consultation process, and asked for information as to when and how this would occur. Lastly, I asked for his affirmation that the buildings would not be sold until an adequate process of community consultation had taken place. A week later, I got my reply.

I regret that my brief meeting with you and your father did not allow for a more measured consideration of all the factors that have led to the situation where Father Bryant has decided that he is no longer willing to celebrate mass, at least on a regular basis.

I regret that he hardly gave us the time of day, I thought with annoyance, but consoled myself with the fact that there it was, in writing. St Brigid's hadn't been decommissioned. I let out a sigh of relief. Well, that was that then. Father Bryant had made a mess of things. Surely the Bishop would do his job and sort it out.

Saving St Brigid's

The Bishop went on:

He regrets the manner in which he spoke to your father after I provided Father Bryant with a copy of the letter that your father had sent to me in December 2005. He also agrees that the style of consultation with the parishioners that he used in coming to the decision to discontinue the celebration of mass in Saint Brigid's church was less than satisfactory.

This was good. Great, in fact. It was a John Howard kind of apology, but it was acknowledgment nonetheless. And it was pretty clear that Father Bryant was acting without the permission or even knowledge of the Bishop. The Bishop was on our side. And finally clarification as to whether or not the Bishop knew of Fr Bryant's plans: *It is a fact that I was not invited to attend the celebration of what Father Bryant deemed to be the final celebration of the Eucharist in St Brigid's church.* He went on to explain that priestly capacity was stretched to the limit, a comment we'd heard a few times now, but I still felt was hardly an excuse for closing the church with a few weeks notice so no one has time to ask questions. Was I that naïve to think that a more sensible and mutually beneficial approach for the Catholic Church would be to sit down with its parishioners and discuss these challenges, rather than hold them up as weak excuses for poor process and behaviour?

But it was the last comment that showed he'd not taken on board a thing we said in Ballarat. *The church at Crossley is a very short distance from the church at Koroit. The maintenance of buildings that are very seldom used is also a factor that must be carefully noted by those who would wish to see them used on a regular basis, and at the same time be provided with appropriate insurance cover.*

The argument that people should simply drive on to Koroit to attend mass on Sundays entirely missed the point. Infant Jesus church might only be five kilometres away, but it might as well be on the other side of the state for long-time parishioners of Crossley, Killarney and Tower Hill. We're not in the horse and buggy era anymore. It wasn't a question of travelling the distance. It was a matter of community identity and ownership – concepts that the Bishop had failed to register. He had also ignored some very good reasons as to why St Brigid's Crossley was less used than before, that when a parish priest refuses to allow people to marry, christen their babies or bury their loved ones in a church they feel at home in, they are less likely to return to church on Sunday.

The last assertion, that church buildings cost the parish a lot to maintain, was also hard to swallow, given that all the maintenance for the past twenty years for the Crossley hall had been fundraised and coordinated by my parents. Beyond paying insurance costs, we knew nothing of other expenses the parish was covering. Sighting such figures was proving ridiculously hard work. The argument that St Brigid's was a financial burden on the parish seemed rather hollow. But I wasn't altogether unhappy with his letter, since he closed with an assurance I hadn't expected.

I assure you, that I shall not give approval for the alienation of the property owned by the Parish of Koroit at Crossley until I am convinced that such a decision has the approval of the overwhelming majority of the parishioners.

In December that might have felt like an insurmountable task, but by the time I received the letter at the end of January, we weren't the only ones who didn't approve.

A week after St Brigid's was closed a surprising advertisement appeared in the *Warrnambool Standard* newspaper. I shared a ride with my sister Angela from Melbourne home for the meeting on a Monday night, wondering who on earth had initiated it. We pulled up at the Blackwood Centre in Koroit's desolate main street at 7 pm. Even the Commercial Hotel next door seemed to be dead quiet. Mum and Dad, Mary-Ellen and Liz were the only ones there. A sky-blue station wagon pulled up, and a young woman, not much older than me, got out. She was wearing a patchwork skirt over corduroy pants, an earring through her nose, and her hair pulled back by a crochet hair band.

'Expecting many?' Dad asked by way of greeting.

'Haven't got a clue,' she replied, opening a bag of tobacco and rolling a cigarette, without a hint of concern. I'd never laid eyes on her before, definitely not at mass.

We went inside to start setting up. 'Who is she?' Liz whispered to Mum.

Saving St Brigid's

'Teresa O'Brien, she's Gerry O'Brien's niece,' Mum said with that voice as if that should make perfect sense to us. She had a habit of introducing us to people expecting that we should know who they were and how they fit in, just because she has a mental map of the entire population of the south-west district.

Teresa flicked open a Mac laptop and showed us a slideshow of black-and-white photos. The first one was of two rows of men, sporting big black moustaches and dirty overalls. The men who built St Brigid's, Teresa explained. 'That's Dan Lane,' she pointed out for Dad. 'That's my grandfather,' said Dad proudly to us girls.

The next photo was of two rows, men again, this time suited up with neatly groomed hair. There was Dan Lane again, sitting next to Mannix.

'Who's Mannix?' asked Mary-Ellen.

'Archbishop Mannix. He opened St Brigid's in 1914. They say he wrote his famous anti-conscription speech walking along Killarney beach,' said Teresa matter-of-factly.

I wondered why this woman I'd never seen before knew so much about St Brigid's history.

'We believe,' she said gesturing to Shane Howard who'd just walked in the door, 'that St Brigid's is a site rich with cultural heritage and meaning and should be protected. That's why we called this meeting tonight.' I'd seen Shane Howard at the last mass the previous week; I knew he lived in Killarney these days, but still wondered what connection he had to this Teresa O'Brien.

Teresa asked for introductions, and we went around the room, asking for input as to why we'd turned up. I could hardly tell everyone that I was here because I wanted to get married at St Brigid's, and none of the words of my speech came to mind, so I mumbled something about 'not wanting to see it go', feeling the emotion well up in me again. Mary-Ellen, clearly inspired by the pictures she'd seen, told us, 'I guess we've always had a strong connection with the place, but seeing that photo, of our great grandfather, it really brings home how long that connection goes back, so yeah, I'd like to see if we can save it.'

Mum told us about her days at the old-time dances, with a smile that never failed when she relived those memories in her mind. 'There are so many memories in that place, and we've always tried to keep it going. I think it's still got some life left in it,' she said, both a wistfulness and an air of defiance about her.

Dad was more pointed, explaining that the parish was mad not to keep St Brigid's, with the huge influx of new residents the area had seen in the past few years. Dad informed everyone that St Brigid's hadn't been decommissioned and was still in fact a Catholic church. He laid out the challenge of needing to prove to the Bishop that an overwhelming majority of parishioners were in favour of keeping St Brigid's open. This stirred up lively conversation for the next half-hour, before Teresa went back to her powerpoint presentation.

Several leading historians, she explained, have identified our part of the world as significant to the story of Irish settlement in Australia.

'These buildings are at the centre of that story. We need to protect them, so that story can be recorded and preserved there', she said, and introduced the idea of creating an Australian-Irish Cultural and Heritage Centre at St Brigid's. I was impressed with the way she talked about its community benefits, culturally, socially, economically – she knew what she was talking about. I liked the way she talked about our history, as if it had value and should be protected. It made me feel less silly for bawling my eyes out in front of 300 people a few days earlier. Still, it felt like she was getting a bit ahead of herself. The Bishop has said to us that St Brigid's was still a Catholic church. I'd like to see how well her cultural centre idea would go down with the priest.

Teresa proposed that we form a community group to work together to protect St Brigid's and preserve our rich cultural history. A motion was forwarded, all hands were raised in agreement, and the motion was passed. It was all very unexpected and exciting. In order for us to become an incorporated association, we had to become members, and pay a fee to do so. She asked us what we thought was an appropriate fee, and we agreed upon ten dollars. Everybody opened their wallets and threw ten dollars on the table. A piece of paper went around and we all signed our names and details. And that was it: we had begun a community organisation.

Now we need a name, Teresa instructed. 'How about "The Friends of St Brigid's?"' Dad shot back straight away, as if it had been playing on his mind. It probably had – he'd been eating, breathing and sleeping Crossley since Christmas. A vote was taken, and we named ourselves The Friends of St Brigid's. It had a nice sound to it, in respect to the patron saint of our church. Yet we weren't a religious organisation, we were a group of people who believed that St Brigid's should be protected and preserved, kept as a Catholic church if possible, with the potential that the space could be used to create a cultural and heritage centre. And therein were the agreed objectives at the first meeting. We didn't consider that these things might sit at cross-purposes, or could become controversial in the community.

We left the meeting as high as kites. At home, Dad fished in the pantry for a bottle of wine to celebrate. With Dad's epilepsy and Mum's aversion to alcohol, neither Mum nor Dad drank, and the only wine we ever had in the house was left over from the previous Christmas. It tasted god-awful, but we optimistically toasted a glass of red to the formation of 'The Friends of St Brigid's' and the good fortune that there were people like Teresa O'Brien in this world (Shane Howard's partner, Mum explained).

Our first job was to get signatures on a page, to show the support in the parish for keeping St Brigid's open as a Catholic church. Dad drove house to house, asking for signatures. No one refused. He came home with 167 names on his petition to the Bishop. Our little community meeting had earned some interest further afield: in March, *The Standard* newspaper ran a story called 'Crossley residents search for a place to call their own', with a picture of Teresa and her little girl, Niamh.

I kept the Bishop informed of our progress, expressing my relief to have the status of St Brigid's confirmed, reiterated my previous requests for a public announcement of the status of St Brigid's, and for full and proper consultation for the community to participate in the future of their parish. I told him about the conversations we'd had locally of people leaving the parish, if not the Church altogether, because of the closure of St Brigid's.

'YOU HAVE MY WORD'

I seriously thought this would be of concern to him. Especially since he told us about Father Bryant's poor health – I thought that under the circumstances, including his own observation that consultation had been 'less than satisfactory', he would feel a certain sense of responsibility to resolve the situation.

A couple of weeks into February, I got the same response Dad received before Christmas: 'There are issues you raise that I should wish to discuss with Father Bryant.' Father Bryant was on holidays, so I would have to wait until sometime in March. Dad also received a phone call from the Bishop informing him that Father Bryant was sorry for the way he'd spoken to Dad before Christmas. The Bishop informed Dad that 'the Church will not be sold for an indefinite period of time'.

In that first month or two, as these letters went back and forth, we gave little thought to the future of the hall. It wasn't in question, and we weren't about to open another can of worms. Dad had informed the Bishop back in December about the most recent funding application he'd submitted to the Moyne Shire Council, for which he received a letter late in February granting the Crossley hall committee, of which Dad was Secretary, $2000 to repair some storm damage to the wall of the hall. Dad sent a copy of the letter direct to the Bishop and placed a notice in the church bulletin, as he'd always done, notifying the parish of the grant and the upcoming working bee to put the money to good use. He put his name and contact details down for further information. A month later, on the second of March, Dad received a call from the Moyne Shire Council stating that Father Bryant had contacted them, saying that he'd not given permission for Dad to make the application, and that Dad should get written consent before the grant could be processed. All this was new to Dad, but he went off to mass two days later, with Mum, my sister Mary-Ellen and brother Michael, to get the permission required.

Before the final blessing, Father Bryant asked the congregation to sit down as he had something important to say. He thanked those in the congregation who'd supported him, after the 'goings-on in the newspapers'. He publicly doubted that the new group that had been formed would ever be able to come up with the money to buy the church, and joked that 'maybe we should give them some Planned Giving envelopes as some of the people in that photo don't contribute to planned giving', a cheap shot that wasn't lost on my parents, whose regular faithful donations to the parish were given generously, even through great hardship. It was obvious to my family that Father Bryant was trying to undermine The Friends of St Brigid's, and one particular member within it. He then told the congregation that 'an individual from the Crossley Hall Committee had been undertaking parish business without my permission. No one can take it upon themselves to do business on behalf of the parish without the priest's permission. Not even the diocese can give permission,' he added. He need not have said my father's name; everybody in the church knew who he was talking about. They'd be few who wouldn't know Mick Lane and his role at Crossley. And if they didn't, they could read for themselves, as his name was on the church bulletin. Father Bryant was now taking issue with the Crossley Hall committee, an informal committee which Mum and Dad set up in 1990, to handle the maintenance of the hall. 'There is no such thing as a Crossley Hall committee. The only committee that makes decisions about St Brigid's is the one I formed (referring to the committee he'd formed to "consult" on the closure of St Brigid's).'

'Dad!' Mary-Ellen elbowed Dad in the ribs. 'You've gotta say something! You can't let him get away with this!'

But what was Dad going to do? There is no place for a parishioner to stand up against a priest on the altar and have their say. The priest has the power and no one has the right to challenge him, especially not during mass. The priest had spoken and his words were truth. He had implied that Mick Lane was breaking the law. The parishioners didn't know where to look. They hurried out afterwards, heads lowered, unsure what to make of what they'd heard.

Of course, Dad got straight on the computer and started a letter to the Bishop. The Bishop had indicated that he could move Father Bryant to another parish by the end of the year. Dad felt that he was helping the Bishop to build a case for when he approached Father Bryant, to have him transferred to another parish in the diocese. The more evidence that could be provided to show how he'd felt intimidated by Father Bryant's behaviour, the more chance there would be that the Bishop would take steps to address this. He laid out for the Bishop the comments that had been made, and the details of the offending $2000 grant which Father Bryant had objected to.

While Dad was busy letter writing, Mum was showing signs of the strain. As Father Bryant's weekly attacks intensified, so did the sciatica in her back, and for both reasons Mum began to find it difficult to walk down the main street of Koroit. All our upbringing church was a social outing as much as anything, and our orange Falcon station wagon was always the last car left in the car park – Mum and Dad chatted away to other parishioners long after mass was over. That all changed since the letter to the Bishop, and the 'goings-on in the paper'. Dad had simply stood up for what he believed in and on any other issue, it might ordinarily cause praise or support. But Father Bryant's words appeared to have sown seeds of doubt in people's minds, enough at least that people who used to stop to chat, hurried on by. Mum, a talkative, gregarious woman, for the first time felt alienated in her community and was constantly on edge whenever the phone rang, lest Father Bryant be at the end of it. St Brigid's was a constant topic of conversation in the household, and though Dad was busy letter writing, and we girls were organising ourselves in the newly formed association, without access to the church or hall Mum felt disabled and powerless to contribute, unable to roll up her sleeves and take a broom or mop to the floor of the hall she loved.

'People didn't stop talking to us so much as stop talking about church. That's what you talk about at church, you talk about what's going on in the parish. All of a sudden nobody wanted to talk about anything to do with the parish,' said Dad. It was the elephant in the room.

I rang home often to check on Mum. It was Mum I was worried about. 'She's alright,' Mary-Ellen said. 'Well, she's not actually. I'm really worried about her. She's crying a lot, she feels like people are looking the other way when she's down the main street. It's like she's lost her confidence in who she is.' In a small community, where everybody knows each other, people know their place. They know where they fit in, who they can trust and go to for support. For Mum, she was also the support of many who came to her, for strength and guidance. She wasn't dubbed the 'Lifeline' of Tower Hill for nothing. Mum and Dad had played such an integral part in the community for so long, but now felt that Father

Bryant's attitude towards them was rubbing off on other parishioners. Maybe people didn't think they had the right to object. Or probably, they just believed what Fr Bryant told them, when he said that St Brigid's was a financial drain on the parish and it couldn't survive. Perhaps they simply believed the priest when he told them that the maintenance bills were more than the parish could afford and the buildings were about to fall down. It was no use Mum and Dad explaining how far the Crossley hall had come since the state of disrepair they found it in back in 1990, when we walked into a hall that might as well have been a hay shed.

Plus, the parishioners at mass in Koroit weren't the same as those in Crossley. As Dad had predicted, closing St Brigid's didn't mean an automatic transfer of parishioners from Crossley to Koroit. When we knocked on doors, collecting signatures, we heard repeatedly that many of the regular parishioners at St Brigid's now preferred to make the fifteen-kilometre trip into Warrnambool to go to mass, rather than go to Koroit. That's if they went at all. One of the locals, unaware of the final Mass at Crossley, turned up one Sunday to find the doors locked, and decided there and then, 'If God wants to find me, he knows where I am'. Now that Mum and Dad were no longer necessarily sitting in mass alongside the Tich Kellys, Peter Maddens and Plunger Lenehans that Dad had known since he was a five-year-old, they began to feel, for the first time in their 66 years, on the outer in their community. They no longer felt in a position to speak up. It was simply too controversial, and better to keep quite lest people think they were stirring up more trouble. There was a great loneliness for my parents in this feeling.

One Saturday night, I took my turn to accompany Mum and Dad to mass in Koroit, my own little act of solidarity. Father Bryant didn't say anything about St Brigid's that night, but the vibes were just as bad as I'd been told. We always sat in the third row back on the left side of the church, almost directly underneath the priest when he stood in the pulpit. During his sermon, Father Bryant carefully avoided landing his gaze on our family, and although I was hardly paying attention to what he had to say, I could not help but notice his choice of theme for the night. He talked about the need to 'move on', and allow change to happen. Though he made the effort to come down from the altar to extend the gesture to the parishioners right in front of us, he quite deliberately avoided shaking hands with us at the ritual sign of peace, shaking hands with the family in front.

I was fuming.

'Why do you do it to yourselves?' I cried, flinging my criticism at Mum and Dad on the way home, driving around the darkening Tower Hill lake.

'Gina,' Mum said bitterly, on the verge of tears, 'I know Father Bryant would just as soon us not attend, but Mass means more to me than the priest who says it. It's not him I'm there for, I can look past him. He doesn't interfere when I receive the body of Christ.'

This talk frustrated me no end, but it was hardly fair of me to be having a go at her. Like the vast majority of my peers, I hadn't been to mass on a regular basis since before I left school; I wasn't a parishioner of any parish. I had faith in the power of humanity and believed in the good people doing extraordinary work in the spirit of Jesus' teachings, but was quickly losing all respect for the bookkeeping Catholic Church. It was the Church's call to action that inspired my faith, not a hierarchy obsessed with maintaining the letter of the law – a law, it seemed, that had been construed to preference those who held the power. That wasn't a Church I wanted to be part of.

Not that I had completely made up my mind on all this, but I was twenty-six, not sixty-six. Dad was born into this parish and Mum had been here since they were married at twenty-two. They're what you call 'rusted-on Catholics'. They went to mass every weekend of their lives here, and plenty of weekdays as well.

'We were here before he got here, and we'll be here after he's gone,' Dad said stubbornly.

I shut up and looked out the window.

It wasn't a choice for them, I realised. To question their faith would be to question who they were and the rock on which they had built their lives. For Mum and Dad, this battle was as essential as their very faith itself. This was what having faith *meant*, in fact. The words of a hymn came to mind, that we used to sing loudly and gaily as children: 'To live justly, to love tenderly, and to walk humbly with thy God.'

I had to hand it to them. I don't know how they did it.

Still, I felt a weird sense of déjà vu from my childhood, being lectured by my parents as we drove home from mass, looking out at the charcoal-coloured sky, the ancient volcano rising up from the shimmering water on the eastern side of Tower Hill Lake, under a brightly lit moon. No longer did water form a full ring around the volcano, like it had when we were kids. On the Killarney side, drought had turned the lake into savannah land. In this light, I could see the kangaroos hopping across the dry lake bed.

In some ways, it felt like everything, and nothing at all, had changed.

Bishop Peter Connors was clearly feeling the pressure of the barrage of letters. He rang Dad, and skipping the pastoral care bit that Dad might have once expected, instead begged Dad to allow him more time 'at least a week', to give him the chance to speak to Father Bryant. Though he didn't address Dad's personal suffering from the alienation he felt from Father Bryant, and the difficulty of being scapegoated as the troublemaker in a now divided parish, Bishop Connors promised what Dad had been waiting to hear: 'Michael, you have my word, the church will not be sold, it cannot be sold, while this controversy exists.' Dad was jubilant. This confirmed that the Bishop was on our side! It was just a matter of time before Father Bryant could be moved on, and this whole sorry sordid mess could be sorted out.

When Dad queried him, Bishop Connors repeated three times, 'St Brigid's will not be sold. It will not be sold. Michael, you have my word, it will not be sold!' A promise repeated three times, as hollow as the denial, three times repeated, of a well-known Peter that went before him. It would be a long time after the cock crowed that Bishop Peter would deny Dad his promise.

CHAPTER SEVEN

Locked out

Most of the window frames were rotting around the edges, the wood all chewed up and spilling out over the windowsill in a confetti of pink primer and white paint. We brought along the shifter to pry the window open, but we didn't even get it out of the car. The first window he tried was jammed shut, the lock firmly in place. The second had some give in it, as if it might stumble off its hinge with a bit of force. Thankfully none was needed, as the third window gave way with one touch, and slid upwards enough for a child to climb through.

Dad picked up his seven-year-old grandchild, Paddy O'Brien, under his underarms and hoisted him up. I interlocked my fingers and provide the foothold for him to get a hold on the windowsill, while he hoisted the other leg over. He reached out for the bar in the 'Men's Room' with his right leg, flattened his body, and slid through the window, like we sometimes did as kids, when we'd forgotten the key.

'Good boy,' we said proudly, as if Paddy had just told us he'd passed a maths test at school with flying colours. Instead, he'd just succeeded in his first, and hopefully last, break-and-enter attempt.

'Go through the hall to the supper room, and then out through the kitchen. You'll have to give the lock a good yank.'

Within a few seconds, Paddy swung open the kitchen door to our hall, with a big smile on his face. 'We're in!' he said gleefully, knowing as well as we did that this wasn't something to be proud of, but made necessary none the less.

The hall sits across the yard from the church. The key that had hung at our back door for the past two decades suddenly didn't fit the lock. Father Bryant had changed the locks without the courtesy of notifying his parish or the hall committee. And hence, we realised that the hall was headed for the same fate as the church. It seemed almost sinister to so rudely deny access to a community gathering space, especially when the committee had spent so many years diligently collecting donations and grants to build up the humble assets of the place. Forty office chairs, a BBQ, pie warmers and hot-water urns might not have much resale value, but are tools of the trade for a community just trying to survive. To be given no opportunity or forewarning to redistribute those items was simply unfair.

And since access had been denied, our community had to find another home. The Killarney Recreation Reserve sits five kilometres down the road from Crossley, near the beach. It sits on the cricket ground, not much more than a shed, used by the club for drinks after a match. It has a kitchen and a couple of toilets, so would do the job. It was a hard fact to swallow that we had to transport all our chairs and tables, pie warmers and urns down to Killarney, and then cram into that concrete pavilion with no atmosphere and bad lighting, when a perfectly well-equipped hall sat up the road, darkened and empty, all because one man deemed that it should, it seemed.

The salt in the wound was only more stinging because we had been told by the Bishop that 'St Brigid's would not be sold' and all we had to do was to prove that we had the parish on our side.

Dad had gone about seeking that support with the petition we'd taken door to door. But the Bishop needed to know that the sale of St Brigid's was not only of concern to those who lived in Crossley and Killarney. It was at our third meeting on 19 February, three weeks out from the Port Fairy Folk Festival, that I suggested we make the most of the crowds that descended on our district over that weekend and make the case that we had more far-reaching support.

I typed up a membership form, with a painting of St Brigid's red brick contrasted against the black-and-white cattle that dotted the fields below. The subtitle summed up our struggle, 'Preserve our past; Protect our future'. We were all a bit nervous about standing by a card stall plastered with pictures and articles about saving a church and asking people for their signature. The Port Fairy crowd is fairly typical of a folk festival, a moving mass of people whose politics can be defined by the slogans on their T-shirts and the loud applause they give to any musician who speaks or sings of justice and peace. We had thought it was a complicated message to sell – a church in limbo – given the confusion as to its status, even among ourselves, and our own ambitions for saving it, but we were pleasantly surprised to find that it wasn't so difficult after all. A community fighting for its gathering place is much the same story whether that place is a tennis court, a theatre or a pub. Communities the nation over, we heard, are struggling to hold their own against the tide of far more powerful forces. As we briefly gave our spiel, the sympathetic response told us that ours was a not an unfamiliar battle. It resonated enough that we received firm nods of support and a fistfull of coins.

That was before we told them about 'the Session'. The Session was Teresa's idea. It made sense to ride on the back of the crowds leaving Port Fairy and redirect them down the beach road to Killarney, if they had the luxury of not going back to work after the long weekend and were inclined to stay that bit longer for just a wee bit more music. Mum and Dad had catered for the Session before at Crossley, but it'd been years since the last one, now a distant memory. We were kids then, running around making cups of tea and sandwiches, like we always did. It was always a great fundraiser, but I don't remember much of the music, maybe because back then, the Irish cultural revival hadn't yet really kicked into gear. As an adult, the annual pilgrimage to the Port Fairy folkie had changed all that and given me, and thousands of others, a new appreciation of Celtic music. I love spending a weekend listening to the rhythmic inner worlds of creative brave souls and always leave the festival feeling half melancholy and half joyous at the beauty of the human spirit. The festival has also become such a tradition in our family calendar that not turning up to folkie would be like not turning up for Christmas. Fish and chips in the Guinness tent on Friday night, campsite cooking and watching my nieces and nephews try their hand at busking with a tin whistle they made in the children's tent, are as much a part of the folkie experience as the music itself.

The year we decided to save St Brigid's was different, though. We had work to do. There wasn't time for sitting round the campsite or whiling away the afternoon in a wine bar – we hardly got to see a single act that weekend. When we weren't busy at our card stall collecting signatures, we were debriefing and handing out flyers for the Session to those in the spirit of things at the Guinness tent.

'Who's the special friend?' people asked over and over. In a black marker scrawl across the page, the flyer simply said: 'St Brigid's Session. Local Irish music. Shane Howard and special friends. $10. Supper provided'. We knew as little as they did as to who else might turn up to play.

But on the main stage, when we watched the headline act for the festival, Irish singer, Mary Black, invite her special friend, Shane Howard to the stage to sing with her 'Flesh and Blood', one of Shane's best and a song she made famous in Ireland, to an adoring crowd, we realised who the 'friends' might be. So did the crowd, and we had no trouble getting rid of the rest of our scribbled flyers that afternoon.

After three days of music, camping, campaigning, and Guinness, we packed up our tents, rushed home to make sandwiches, and raced back to Killarney cricket ground to get ready. We'd hardly finished pitching our tents and tucking into fish and chips when the cars started arriving, a steady stream of folkie goers from Port Fairy. They were two hours early. I guess they'd come to get a good seat to see Mary Black.

'Where's the float?' said Liz, battling with the legs of a card table.

'Gerry's bringing it.'

'Jesus,' she said under her breath, looking up at the queue forming at the door.

I handed her an ice-cream container, and got busy with the raffle tickets. 'Which side do I write on?'

'God, I dunno, work it out,' she grunted at me. 'I'm sorry, do you have anything smaller?' she asked politely, turning to the couple waving a fifty in front of her.

Before long the ice-cream container was overflowing. We had more change than we could handle.

Gerry turned up, wearing his uniform akubra hat. 'What the frig is going on here?'

'Where have you been?' Liz snapped at him.

'I said I'd be here by 7 pm. You think you've got a system there, do you?'

'Well, you're late. They've been pouring in for an hour.'

The pavilion was packed to the rafters. You couldn't even cross the room without standing on people – bloody folkie chairs.

Some people turned up, but when they couldn't get in the door, they gave Dad $50 for the cause and went home again. 'I didn't expect to see so many here.' Nor did we.

'Where's Teresa? The musos?'

A week ago, she said we could do this. She said the musicians would come. Where the bloody hell were they? The crowd was getting restless.

Mum worked her magic in the kitchen, and the crowd was being treated to generous serves of homemade sandwiches, sausage rolls and slice. We had no idea of how many to cater for – thankfully Mary-Ellen had the good foresight to grab some bags of frozen dim sims from the supermarket just in case. It wasn't long before the hungry campers were passing steamed dim sims across beach chairs, couches and bar stools – no room for a waitress to pass through. It was comical to watch.

In amongst this chaos was an ABC television camera crew. Shane Howard had spent the week being filmed by *Australian Story*. They chose a good week and spent the night picking their way through the crowd to get the shots they needed. It all added to the 'anything might happen' atmosphere.

Teresa turned up and turfed some people out of the way to make room for the O'Shea Ryan dancers, girls in brightly coloured dress and jiffies to do the Irish jig. They were gorgeous and delighted the crowd.

Then Teresa climbed up on the middle of the table, laid out with instruments.

'I want to welcome you here to Killarney. We're sorry we can't be in our beautiful hall up the road, but the locks have been changed, and we can't access our buildings.

'Two months ago, St Brigid's church and hall were closed. We, the community, were not consulted. As you can see, we need those buildings. They are the centre of this community. They have been for 100 years …

'I'm doing this for my great grandparents. For my grandparents and for my parents.'

And with that she broke down.

I was standing beside my sisters, all decked out in our green St Brigid T-shirts. We cried with Teresa. She was telling our story, too.

The room was silent.

And then the music started. Around a large table, they sat cradling their favoured fiddle, drum, whistle, guitar or violin. They played, seamlessly and effortlessly, moving between harmonious ballads and fast and furious reels and jigs that had the crowd tapping their feet. In a Session, there doesn't seem to be a beginning or end to the music; it rises and falls from one tune to the next, the lay listener oblivious to the fact that protocol is very much at play here, each musician quietly awaiting their turn, joining in only when appropriate to do so.

As brilliant as the music was, there was no doubt it was Mary Black that many had come to see. This was a woman who could pack London's Royal Albert Hall and drew thousands to the best concert halls around the world.

Here in Killarney, there was no stage announcement when Mary came out. There was no stage. No microphone even. Just a bunch of people sitting around a table, playing the best Irish music you'll hear outside Ireland.

And then when the music stopped, you could hear the crystal-clear voice of a woman, singing in Gaelic, so beautiful the room was full of misty eyes.

She might have pulled thousands to her stage at Port Fairy. But this wasn't about her. When she finished her acapella moment, she joined in with the rest of them.

And this is how a Session goes, we learned, until 6 o'clock in the morning.

LOCKED OUT

Our first St Brigid's fundraiser was a raging success, beyond our wildest dreams.

As the numbers dwindled and the crowd shuffled forward, sitting lined up along tables and standing in doorways, we watched intently as the musicians, in almost trance-like movements, danced their fingers across their beloved instruments, paying homage to the homeland that their ancestors had left generations before. At first I wondered why tears ran down the face of the old man who sang in Gaelic as he bowed his violin, but when I looked around and saw he wasn't the only one with wet eyes, I felt a deep sense of yearning for a place I'd never been.

In recent months, I'd begun to consider making my own rite of passage across the world, to live and work in the UK and discover something of my own roots.

I leaned over to my friend, and said, 'See why I have to go? I need to find where I come from. I need to go and discover my roots,' I explained.

She leaned back, 'I don't know why you need to go across the world,' she said. 'I think you've just found them right here.'

My eyes were hot with tears as the thought weighed down on me. We'd only just started the fight to save St Brigid's, and already I was leaving.

SAVING ST BRIGID'S

Chapter Eight

Power and pride

Mary-Ellen is the nurse in the family. She's a gentle, nurturing type. She has that gift for deep listening, for being present and making you feel heard and cared for, whether you're a patient in bed in hospital or having a beer at the pub. I think that's why people often tell us what a great nurse she is – she has that capacity for deep empathy. It probably helps that she's highly organised and very thorough in whatever she puts her mind to. When we grew up, Mary was Mum's right-hand woman, always cooking and cleaning and keeping things in order. But Mary-Ellen was no homebody. She always had lots of friends. Even in my memory as a kid, I saw her as a leader and not just because she was a school prefect. I remember watching her and all her friends at sixteen dancing away in jeans and boots and linen shirts to eighties hits in the Crossley hall. Mary-Ellen organised it, of course, as a fundraiser for a school project. It was such a roaring success, she organised another one, just for fun. Unlike the school who eventually tried to ban them, and a lot of parents who feared 'what goes on' at those country hall parties, Mum and Dad encouraged them. Knowing the strong bonds they formed in their own youth at the dances, they gave each of us the opportunity to lead by example and prove that we could be trusted. Mary-Ellen and her mates earned it and share lots of fun memories of their nights in the Crossley hall.

The same circle of friends came back to Crossley for her wedding nearly ten years later. Still, another five or six years on, she didn't expect to feel quite the way she did at the possibility of losing St Brigid's. Like the rest of us siblings, her life had moved on, she didn't attend mass there and didn't feel that well placed to complain. But she also couldn't hide those red-rimmed eyes at the last mass and that uneasy feeling that it didn't have to be this way. That feeling was made worse by what she had witnessed that day in March, when Father Bryant accused Dad of acting without authority from the altar. His accusing words nagged at her in her sleep, with images of my parents' bowed heads, powerless to object.

She rang me in Melbourne.

'You've always had that fire in your belly, Gina. Now I know how you feel. I can't get it out of my head.' She told me how she'd bumped into two elderly women who'd also been at that mass. 'They told me to tell Dad to be careful of that man. It got me thinking. If I can advocate for students as a school nurse, perhaps I should be standing up for Dad.' It felt like she was asking me to empower her to do something she already knew she had to. Mary-Ellen is not a person I'd call docile, but she's also not the type to go out of her way to challenge authority. In fact it's fair to say that I don't think she ever has before. It was quite out of character to hear her sounding so compelled to act. She told me she could see the sympathetic looks towards Dad after mass, but she also thought she saw something else in their eyes: fear. To speak to Dad might put them in the line of fire. Best to keep quiet and stay out of it, their expressions said. She had seen it before, she said. Isolation and intimidation equals submission. It works.

For the past year, Mary-Ellen had been employed as a school nurse in two secondary colleges. Her job wasn't to hand out band aids so much as provide education and counselling in relation to the students' social, mental and physical health. Bullying was the number one issue. She attended conferences and seminars and was well-versed on the issue. She knew it when she saw it and was trained how to appropriately respond. Her message, for students and teachers alike, was that to be silenced on the issue was equal to condoning the behaviour. Her mantra kept her awake at night.

POWER AND PRIDE

Dear Father Bryant,

I attended mass at Infant Jesus Church Koroit, and I am writing to express my concerns about the manner in which you conducted yourself following Holy Communion and the period of reflection.

She talked about the public humiliation Dad had been subjected to, and how insulting it was to his contribution over decades to be told in such a manner that 'there is no such thing as a Crossley Hall committee'. She talked about the inspiration that The Friends of St Brigid's were, keeping the community spirit alive and fighting to prevent the breakdown of a rural community. She talked about the 'us and them' impression she felt he'd created when he talked about the 'goings-on in the newspapers', and how unhelpful that was to an already confused and disempowered community. She also reported the fear she'd witnessed in parishioners' eyes, and explained her professional background. She told him that on both a professional and personal level, she felt compelled to respond. She made enquiries in the Ballarat diocese, and because they didn't have one, was directed towards the Melbourne archdiocese workplace-bullying policy, which applies to parishes, priests and volunteers. In it is quoted a list of behaviours that constitute bullying: belittling remarks, isolation, putdowns, intimidation, manipulation and the imbalance and misuse of power. She listed these for Father Bryant, expressing her concern at having witnessed such blatant behaviour from the altar, to the undivided attention of the seated congregation who were not given any opportunity to respond. She called upon Father Bryant to retract his comments and apologise to Dad. She, like Dad, made it clear that it was the behaviour and not the perpetrator that she had issue with. She asked that he not take it personally, and take the steps that were needed to create a supportive and respectful environment for the parishioners to have their say.

A week later, Mary-Ellen joined Mum and Dad at mass to await a response. Perhaps naïvely, she thought Father Bryant would retract his comments, apologise for any hurt feelings, and she could go home and forget about it.

It didn't happen. So she did as instructed by the archdiocesan policy and contacted the Vicar General, Fr Barry Ryan, in Terang. Towards the end of March, Mary-Ellen and my other sisters Monica and Catherine drove to Terang to explain the situation. Father Ryan commented that hers was a thoughtful and well-written letter to Father Bryant, and took it upon himself to pursue the matter with the Bishop. Mary-Ellen felt great relief: her job was done, the hierarchy had been informed, action would be taken and things would have to improve. Her relief was reinforced the next day, when the Bishop phoned Dad yet again, to inform him that he'd instructed Father Bryant to make contact and resolve the issues with Dad. 'If he does not contact you within a week, let me know.' Dad was sure the Bishop was on his side.

A week later there had been no phone call from Father Bryant. Mum was beside herself with the stress. Mary-Ellen did her best to support her. Dad did as he was told and informed the Bishop. Ten days passed, then before Sunday mass, Father Bryant pulled Dad aside and told him that the 'powers that be' requested that he meet with Dad, and that Dad should ring him to make an appointment. He again reminded Dad that 'my lawyers are pushing for me to take legal action.'

Mary-Ellen was fed up. Common sense surely said that it was not good process to resolve this situation by leaving it for the two parties to meet in the absence of a mediator. Certainly, this is not what the Melbourne Archdiocesan Workplace Bullying Policy recommends, recognising that one-to-one contact can be inappropriate; especially in this case, when Father Bryant was continuing threats of legal action. It's this kind of outcome the policy appears to be designed to avoid. Disappointed, Mary-Ellen rang Father Barry Ryan and stated her complete dissatisfaction with the process.

And so a mediation session was arranged and a professional mediator from the Catholic social service organisation Centracare was appointed. Father Bryant insisted that the meeting be held at his presbytery in Koroit – hardly neutral territory, but Dad was given no choice. They would meet at the presbytery or not all.

Dad was well used to mediation. In his full-time job working in aged care, he often represented the elderly in family disputes. He knew that in order for this conflict to be overcome, everything must go on the table. He was well prepared, and had clear in his mind what he wanted. His requests were relatively simple: to drop all legal action and to commit to more appropriate issue resolution in the future. Essentially, he wanted to iron out whatever personal differences had come between them, so that the parish could get on with the central task at hand: addressing the future of St Brigid's in an open and honest way.

Father Bryant responded by sitting there with his hand on a large book – the *Code of Canon Law* - and declared that this book gave him, as parish priest, the authority required to make decisions in the parish.

On the question of the $2000 grant from the Shire, Dad explained what he thought were good reasons for accepting it – to maintain the hall in case it was not sold; to add value, if it was. 'It'd be a win-win situation for all,' said Dad. 'If we give the money back, the hall will deteriorate, it will lose value, and we all lose.' The mediator agreed it did make sense.

'But that would mean you'd win,' Father Bryant replied.

'No, we would all win. And if we don't, we all lose,' Dad said.

Eventually Father Bryant agreed to sign the paperwork. He also agreed to drop all threats of legal action and endeavour to discuss issues directly in the future. In regard to the way forward, he also agreed that Dad would, in his personal capacity, have 90 days to prepare a 'realistic proposal' for the future of St Brigid's.

This brokered agreement was something of a breakthrough. A resolution. A way forward. He even agreed to meet with Mary-Ellen, in lieu of not responding to her letter. But it was his final, departing comment that meant all was not well.

'We know about the issues with your daughter in the community.'

Taken aback, Dad questioned him on what issues he meant.

'There are some things a father doesn't need to know about his daughter,' said Father Bryant.

Afterwards, when Dad reported back to Mary-Ellen, she was ready to both laugh and scream. 'Who is this man? What is he on?' she said trying to make light of it, but it was beyond personal now. It felt like he was trying to drive a wedge between a father and his daughter. It was ridiculous, but it was too hurtful and too damaging to shrug off. Having a priest she'd never met make such abstruse remarks about her riled her completely, to the point where she felt she had to confront him. He was playing a game, it seemed, trying to plant seeds of doubt in Dad's mind, and Mary-Ellen wasn't going to put up with it. An appointment was made for the following week.

Koroit Presbytery is a big white, imposing building. Even as kids who were friends with the parish priest, a knock at the heavy wooden front door always made you feel nervy, watching the frame of the priest through the red leadlight that framed the door, descending the red carpeted stair well, as he made his way towards you. We looked upon them like they were kings. They might as well have been in our eyes, to have the privilege of living in such a big house all on their own, with a cook and a cleaner to wait on them. We were always half scared, half excited to make a visit to the presbytery, to sit in the puffy high-back chairs at the dining table, dragging our toes through the expensive carpets and running our fingers over the ornate fireplace, while the housekeeper brought Mum and Dad cups of tea in pretty little tea cups. We didn't really know anybody else that lived in such luxury. We always wondered what the priest did with so many rooms, but we never got past the front one.

I'm not sure which of these memories passed through Mary-Ellen and Dad's heads as they knocked on the door on that morning in May. When they got seated in the front room, Mary-Ellen, heavily pregnant with her second child, started out by explaining that she had a little 18-month-old boy at home. She told Father Bryant that she loved her child, but she didn't always love his behaviour. She said that today she wanted to be sure that Father Bryant knew that this wasn't about him as a person, but his actions of late. She then expressed disappointment that he had failed to respond to her letter, or action her requests. He responded by telling her that he hadn't read past the first paragraph anyway and after consulting his lawyers, was also considering suing her!

Mary-Ellen expressed her confusion and upset at the comments made to Dad about 'the issues concerning her in the community', and asked him to clarify what he meant by that. At this point, he asked Dad to leave the room. Mary put her hand firmly on Dad's arm. 'He can stay. I don't have any secrets. Anything you have to say to me, you can say in front of my father.'

Power and Pride

With nothing to say, no 'issues' to speak of, Father Bryant went red in the face and scratched his head with agitation. It looked like he was suffering with psoriasis, and clearly the stress was making it worse. The 'things a father didn't need to know about his daughter' suddenly receded into irrelevance.

Nothing needed to be said. The point had been made. Now they could move on and talk about the real issue at hand. But on broaching the topic of St Brigid's, the strong, confident persona Father Bryant presented crumbled away as he became increasingly agitated, unable to make eye contact. Mary-Ellen reassured Father Bryant that they were not there for confrontation, but for an open discussion, and to find a mutually agreed way out of this mess. Father Bryant put his head in his hands and turned away from them.

'I wish . . . I'd never heard . . . of Crossley,' he said, his voice cracking.

More words tumbled out, and they caused Dad and Mary-Ellen grave concern. The situation before them had suddenly reached a whole new level. This issue had been causing Father Bryant great distress, and Dad was the cause of it, he said. There was room for nothing but compassion in that moment. Dad and Mary-Ellen gently assured Father Bryant that a solution could be found – that he did not have to carry the burden of St Brigid's on his own.

'I don't want you here,' Father Bryant said through tears, hunched over the table.

Repeating reassuring words, Dad stood up, took a step towards the man and laid his hand gently on his shoulder.

'We're here to support you, Father Bryant. You're not on your own,' Dad said, softly, kindly.

'I don't want you here. I'm going to ask you to leave,' he said to them.

They offered to call a friend or support person, not wanting to leave him on his own.

'Get out,' came the response.

Mary-Ellen and Dad left silently.

Dad made a phone call to the Vicar General, who gave his word that he would act upon it and follow up with the Bishop. He agreed that he would make sure that Father Bryant was well and that he would be given support if he was under stress. This was some relief, but still neither Mary-Ellen nor Dad slept a wink that night.

The Vicar General agreed to meet Dad at a funeral he was attending in Koroit the following Monday. They met at the graveside, at Tower Hill cemetery. 'Leave it with me,' the Vicar General said. 'I'll handle it.'

Weeks turned into months as Mum and Dad continued the struggle of going to Mass, trying both to be careful to respect Father Bryant's space and not to inflame the situation, but also determined not to be alienated from their faith or their parish. Gone were the days of standing around in the churchyard chatting after mass. Now they slipped out quickly and quietly, doing their best not to arouse attention.

The silence from the Church hierarchy was deafening, with no reassurance or follow-up from the hierarchy, let alone the kind of counselling and support that the policy speaks of, and they once might have expected of their Church. There was no consideration for the fact that Mum and Dad were now even more isolated in the parish because of the sensitivity of the situation. There was really nobody who understood how serious things had become, outside our family. It was a very dark, disturbing time for Dad.

A month earlier, the Bishop had given Dad 'his word' that St Brigid's would not be sold amid this controversy and that he would see to it a resolution would be found. Now he knew full well that this controversy was causing the priest in charge, and a parishioner and his family, enormous distress.

The silence continued.

Though Mary-Ellen had just given birth to her second child, she could not forget the gravity of the situation concerning Father Bryant and St Brigid's. With some assurance that both the Vicar General and the Bishop were well informed, she was horrified to think that Father Bryant was being left to deal with the very issue that was causing his intense distress. He had made it clear he didn't want to be in this situation. Why on earth was he still being lumped with it? Where was the hierarchy's duty of care to their priest? She assumed that he was getting the professional support he needed, and that arrangements were being made for his relocation.

Apart from Sunday mass, Dad lay low, assuming that an internal church process was under way and respecting the Bishop's unmistakable instruction to 'back off'. As directed from the mediation session, Dad passed the weeks and months by researching and writing the detailed fundraising plan for the parish, including bequests, grants and a generous lease arrangement, whereby Crossley would take responsibility for St Brigid's upkeep and maintenance as it had done in the past. Despite it all, Dad was still convinced that the future of St Brigid's could be a 'win-win for everybody'. More than anything, he didn't want to lose St Brigid's because of some personal stoush that he never intended. When he eventually sensed that things had improved, and the time was right, Dad sent his plans to Father Bryant. His response confirmed that there was no getting away from it: the situation was still intensely personal. He didn't even acknowledge the fundraising plan.

'In future, I shall deal only with the secretary of The Friends of St Brigid's, and request that any correspondence or business be addressed through Teresa O'Brien.' The fact that Dad was a practising parishioner was irrelevant. The power play continued.

The future of St Brigid's remained sidelined.

In frustration, Mary-Ellen eventually rang the Vicar General. During the course of the conversation, it appeared to Mary-Ellen that he had failed to alert the Bishop to the matters earlier raised. Four months of sleepless nights and worry for Dad and Mum, and for four months Father Barry Ryan had done nothing, as far as we could tell. He obviously hadn't taken the situation as urgently or seriously as she had. Disgusted with his inaction, she made another visit to Terang to spell out her concerns.

She explained the situation with great concern and implored the Vicar General to do his job and take action.

Realising that he had apparently failed to report to the Bishop, her trust in his authority dashed, she rang the Bishop's office herself and without divulging the detail of her meeting with Father Bryant, she made an appointment to travel to Ballarat herself to visit the Bishop. During the course of the conversation, the Bishop made a comment that this appeared only to be a 'Lane problem' and that if it was in fact such a problem, 'shouldn't it be coming from all corners?' Exasperated, she hardly knew where to start to explain why it was that few other people in the parish had any idea, or were too afraid to stand up to a parish priest who continued to make divisive remarks from the altar in relation to St Brigid's.

During this time, a parishioner from Port Fairy unknown to Mum and Dad approached them to explain her own story. Dad asked her to join them in their visit, and before long seven people were sitting in a mini van on their way to Ballarat to visit the Bishop, an armful of handwritten letters from people who'd also experienced problems at the hands of Father Bryant. It wasn't just a 'Lane problem' after all. Up all night breastfeeding babies, they'd risen at dawn to organise nine children into childcare for the day, to make the important two hour journey to visit the man who had the power to put a stop to this stalemate. As they waited in the foyer, Mary-Ellen breastfeeding her ten-week-old baby, they had high expectations. Finally they had created the opportunity to have this whole sorry tale put to rest, and a solution found.

'Thank you for making the journey here today. I only have 45 minutes before my next meeting,' were the first words out of the Bishop's mouth.

Mary-Ellen slowly and carefully explained her concerns. His first response was that our family had been the only ones to complain. Clearly, he'd made up his mind that this was a 'Lane problem'. Smarting from the insult and the stress, her newborn babe in arms, tears pricked at Mary-Ellen's eyes. The Bishop told her not to 'get all emotional.'

'Well, Crossley doesn't mean a row of beans to me,' chimed in the woman from Port Fairy who'd been so far sitting quietly. She went on to explain her dealings with the priest several years earlier, when she was on a parish committee in Port Fairy, and the way he'd talked to her – words she would not repeat, but went along the lines that 'women who wanted power should find themselves another Church'. She explained that a group of parishioners had reported the problem in a letter to the Bishop, and how her mailing address had been on the letter. Just like Dad, she too had copped the brunt of Father Bryant's angry response when he got hold of the letter and read it aloud at a parish meeting. She explained that the comments were so threatening, demeaning and disgusting, she vowed never to step foot inside another church again, while ever he remained the parish priest. That was five years earlier. The Bishop fumbled through some filing cabinets, and after ten minutes he produced the letter and admitted that his usual practice of forwarding letters of complaint back to the priests concerned appeared to have inflamed the situation.

How on earth had he not woken up to this before? The little group had travelled up to Ballarat that day, aghast at the front page of the *Warrnambool Standard*, 'Paedophile capital of the South West', an article they left behind for the Bishop to read. The Ballarat diocese had long been under scrutiny for the abominable acts of abuse carried out by priests in their ranks, by those asking serious questions around the hierarchy's inability to respond, if not their possible acquiescence to the crime. Though our issue paled in comparison, it gave us more insight than we wanted to see about how the diocese, and the church in general, handles itself behind closed doors. On this day, the Bishop must have really been feeling the heat. No wonder he only had forty-five minutes to meet with them!

He excused himself with a well-worn mantra. 'What am I supposed to do? My biggest concern is that I simply don't have enough priests,' said the Bishop.

No, your biggest concern is the priest you've got, thought Mary-Ellen, with too much respect to voice her thinking.

They suggested that Father Bryant be given some time off, and proposed radically, that the parish might function without a priest as had become common practice in other parishes in the diocese. Dismissing the idea, the Bishop did acknowledge he might be able to suggest Father Bryant take a holiday, given the complexity in moving priests around. The Bishop explained that priests have rights, and he could not just move them around at will. Father Bryant had already refused a posting in Ballarat.

The question on the lips of those who'd travelled to Ballarat had been left to the last two minutes. They expressed their concern that they might soon drive past St Brigid's and find it sold and bulldozed.

'I assure you priests cannot just go around selling off property. I have to sign off on the sale of any item or property valued over $20,000, as does the Ballarat Finance committee,' he said. Again, he reiterated the words that kept us believing in him.

'You have my word; St Brigid's will not be sold.'

They went away with little idea of what would happen next at St Brigid's, but assured at least that they need not worry about finding a 'For Sale' sign plastered over the building.

Chapter Nine

Going home

'Thank you for making the choice between love and fear,' the tall, grey-haired man had said to me that day. He was a priest, I found out later, a Jesuit. 'You showed us that you were both strong and vulnerable up there,' he said. 'That's a lovely gift to share.'

Strong and vulnerable. That other one, the Marist brother, slapped me on the shoulder. 'Someone's got to keep the Irish rebel spirit alive.' That was very strong of you, they said. Strong and vulnerable. They saw my vulnerability. How could they not? It was pouring out of every pore of your skin, before you even opened your mouth.

It's OK to be vulnerable, they said.

I tossed the words around in my head as I drove home from Ballarat that hot January day in 2006, my eyes dry and salty from the tears, desperately wanting to be closed, as I drove into the blazing sun that bore down the Princes Highway, home to Tower Hill.

They were right. I did feel strong. When I was putting the words on paper, in the middle of the speech, when I was in action, I felt the full force of my strength. But these days, I was finding it harder and harder to choose the right words, to keep fighting back, to do it on my own. And I felt vulnerable.

Not surprising, really. I was working by myself. A young woman, in a little office on my own, a whole world of injustice out there. Getting nowhere. What was the point? The question rolled around in my head, day after day, as I trudged off to work. I needed to step back, to stand still; I needed time to think, to read and to meditate. To try and make sense of this messed-up world. To figure it out.

You can't leave, I told myself. You're committed to the cause. There's too much work to do. We need more young people like you, not less. You're lucky to even have a job that pays you to pursue these passions. You can't run away. You'll let too many people down. And plus, you can't quit your job with nothing to go to, I lectured myself. Where will you go?

It wasn't a question that needed to be answered. I already knew. Just struggled to bring myself to do it. I knew exactly where I wanted to go. I could see myself sitting in a sunny spot on my favourite log in the veggie patch, watching the sun rise up and over the tops of the messmates and the mountain ash. I wanted to sit on the deck as the night drew in and watch the changing shades of the silver wattles. They looked silver in the darkening light, holding the last fraction of light against the dark green foliage of the blackwood. Ah, the blackwood, the king of the forest! Deep within the forest, the blackwood was the master. On its own, standing tall, no tree grew up beneath it. Only ancient ferns, speckled by the sunshine, thriving in the dampness the broad black tree branches provided. It was a mystical place, so much that it forced me into silence whenever I parted the scrub to enter into that domain, as if I might disturb the fairies dancing on the fronds of the fern trees. To me, it was as sacred as if it was a house of God. It took me a while to realise that it *was*, in fact.

I had a partner, you see, and this paradise was what he called home. For at least a year now, I'd happily combined city life with my weekend retreat. But as 2006 marched on, I began to feel more vulnerable than strong. Unlike my partner, who was one of those rare souls at ease with himself in his corner of the world, I was the complete opposite, searching all over the place, for what I wasn't even quite sure. In the city I nervously ventured back into a church, many years though it had been. Compared to the clean energy of the bush, the smell of incense, the brass candles, heavy statues and starched cloths felt stuffy and overpowering. There wasn't any room for God there, it felt. And so I retreated back to the bush. On Fridays I escaped the Brigidine's office, with the likes of Thomas Berry's *The Dream of the Earth* and David Tacey's *A Contemporary Spirituality*, and wondered how we'd managed to place such a distance between ourselves, our Creator and the created. I did my best to bridge that gap: I enrolled in healing courses, learned to meditate and practised the art of being present. Sitting in the bush, I'd end up swatting away the flies and worrying about my future, my career, and how best to make a meaningful contribution to the world.

I battled away writing essays for my Masters of International Development and made long lists of possible places I might go to make a difference in this world: Cambodia, Uganda or East Timor? Who could I volunteer for? What would I do? Was I even qualified to achieve anything, I wondered? Not from what I'd learned. I felt destined to be just another well-meaning aid worker flown in to offer 'expert' views in communities where studies have long shown 'development' is generally better left up to the locals.

And so I'd go back out to the veggie patch, pull a few weeds, sit on the log, gaze out over the mountains at the clearing in the distance and wonder. Of course, I was plagued by guilt. As if being Catholic is not bad enough. At work, I'd read the science. I knew the world was warming, and it was lifestyles like mine that caused it. Living like mice on a treadmill, working to earn, earning to spend, spending to consume – what was the point? In the bush, I felt removed from all that, and wondered why our society had developed such an autistic attachment to stuff, living this misguided belief that we had to have more, to be more, to do more. In my lifetime our incomes had grown so much, our standard of living so high, that we could pretty much have whatever we wanted, go wherever we wanted, do whatever we wanted – and it had still left us wanting. All the while, the earth had quietly paid for it. And yet, in the city, it didn't feel like anyone else gave a toss. Everybody was so tuned-in to their iPods and Blackberrys, so caught up with themselves or where they had to be next, that the chances of the kind of universal awakening of consciousness that I read about seemed about as probable as finding a consensus on the future of St Brigid's.

So I made the conscious effort to switch off, unplug and let go. In retreating to the bush, I spent a lot of time on my own, weeded the garden, baked bread, wrote a bit here and there, meditated and relished the pleasure of being up to appreciate the sunrise, the dew on the grass and the crispness in the air. I was convinced that there had to be some kind of master plan for this perfection, that to deny the presence of a Creator spirit in our world was to deny the very essence of the planet we lived on.

Still, I was confused. I wanted answers. Answers to the ailments of the world, and of course, my place within that. There I was – the world at my feet and a strong sense of responsibility that I should do something with the skills I had to save it. And yet, another side of me quietly insisted that the best thing I could do for the world would be to stay put and live a simple life; grow my veggies and tend the chooks, reclaim the survival skills my generation had lost and celebrate my newfound interdependence with nature. And yet, either way I looked at it, it felt like an act of self-service. To stay would mean some sacrifice, but would essentially be to take care of my own lot in a place where I was comfortable. To go would also mean sacrifice, because it meant leaving this place; I knew I would never return. Travelling the world to find out what I could offer it also felt whimsical and indulgent. The journey I was about to embark on had no compass or defined route. It would start with an overseas flight, and where it might end I had no idea. I worried that I really didn't have the muscle for it, that my increased footprint would do nothing to serve the world and that it might all end up in vain. It was an equation that didn't add up, no matter which way I looked at it. Some part of me cursed the choices I had in life. There was a part of me that wished it could have been made for me. Our generation is so privileged, I know, with more opportunity than any that went before me. But it didn't necessarily make life easy.

Knowing I might leave soon, for how long who knew, I visited Nana every time I went back to Warrnambool. Nana had always been as strong as an ox. As a young woman, she'd be working on the farm at eight months pregnant, lifting twenty-five-kilo bags of spuds. I visited her at home one day, not long after she'd come home from hospital after her first stroke. She was digging spuds in her veggie garden in the backyard. 'Nana!' I panicked. 'You shouldn't be doing that!'

'They'll go rotten sittin' in the ground,' she said, waving her arm at me dismissively.

But I knew now, at ninety-four, though she very much had her wits about her – never short of a word to say about the debacle of St Brigid's closure – she was nearing the end, it was clear, and I felt the urge to make sure I learned what I could from her.

At the time, I read an article by a woman who found an old recipe book discarded in a garbage bin on the street. In it were dozens of recipes written in old cursive script, for making and preserving jam and chutney. It reminded me of the rows of jars of beetroot and relish that lined Nana's pantry, with chequered-cloth lids and labelled with her beautiful old handwriting. It was a superbly written article; an ode to the knowledge, skills and experiences of those gone before us, and a lament for what we are losing in our modern throwaway society. All of a sudden it became terribly important to me that I should know how to grow potatoes. Five generations of my family had grown spuds in south west Victoria, and who knows for how long before that in Ireland. Mine is the first generation not to make a living out of it. Perhaps I was just realising that farming was in my blood and I had an instinct to honour that.

I told Nana about the spuds that grew in my compost heap, and asked how to cut seed so that I could grow a small crop.

'You'd get four, maybe five eyes out of a spud this big,' she said moving her wrinkly wrists, her hands calloused and worn. 'You've got to slice it through like this,' with a gesture that showed she'd made that movement a thousand times before. It was an action I knew well and reminded me of Dad, sitting in a shaft of light in our darkened spud shed, cutting seed on a hessian bag on the floor.

As we talked, Nana told me stories of her past. She was born in Kirkstall in 1912 and had six sisters and a brother. She was sent to live with her cousins in Killarney when she was nine or ten because they needed help on their farm. Her older sister Alice had already done a stint, but didn't cope, so returned to the family home. 'Well, I'll go,' said Nana and, as a child, began her working life in Killarney. When she rode her bike back to Kirkstall to visit her family, her younger twin brother and sister would call out, 'Mum! That kid from Killarney is here.'

I loved the stories she told me about the Crossley dances, how people used to walk from 'miles around', how much they looked forward to the St Brigid's ball, and the year when Nana scrubbed the wooden floors of Mrs Sheehan's house in exchange for making Nana a dress out of purple crepe material she bought for sixpence a yard. With her dress fitted and her hair done in curlers Nana walked the mile up to Crossley. 'It rained like hell. I was wet through, and me dress shrunk up. I had to go home, before I even got there,' she said with a wry smile. I loved to imagine the waltz and the foxtrot, the women standing along the walls waiting to be asked for a dance, sure not to leave before the last dance at 2 am. 'We never danced with the same bloke all night,' she told me. 'They used to swing the old girls off their legs. Once they swung me so hard, I went flying out the door! I had cuts on me knees and everything,' she said with a cackle.

I watched her flick her wrinkly wrists as she told me stories of life on the farm, a life before tractors and harvesters, when she'd sow and pick the fields by hand.

'You kids don't know you're alive,' she'd say scornfully, never letting us forget how easy we had it in life. I could hardly argue, listening to her life story of survival and hardship, a life short on material wealth and long on hard work. But there was something in Nana's story that was missing in mine, something I was beginning to envy, something stable and grounded that was lacking not just in my life, but in the world around me.

Since Nana's day, we'd been sold the idea that 'you can make anything of yourself', an idea I was acutely aware of as I stood on the precipice of the next chapter in my life. Without the education, technology and standard of living our generation so took for granted, Nana had no such ideal of ambition to aspire to. And yet, there was something she took for granted perhaps, something that was a given in her world – but lacking in ours. Now that we lived in a world where one built their own identity from the ground up, we were losing that deep and comforting assurance that Nana took for granted – a sense of knowing who you are and where you fit in the world. Some of us might look back and dismiss the close-knit community as stifling and limiting and I myself, can attest to that feeling. And yet, in our liberation into a globalised, cosmopolitan world where anyone can be who they want to be, we had paid a price. The choice and convenience that defined our lives had a twin brother. It was called depression and disconnection. The choices that were so lavishly bestowed upon our generation were fun and exhilarating, but out there on our own they could involve an awfully daunting and lonely journey. There I was in 2006, Googling flights and jobs and far-flung holiday destinations, and dreaming of a simpler, no doubt tougher, life in a bygone era.

The months passed by. As summer turned into autumn, I made my own green-tomato chutney, proudly sharing it among friends and family. I fasted for two weeks, channelling my energies into whole grains and juicing fruits and veggies. I went tree planting up in the Murray Darling Basin and relished the hard work and the sun on my back. I kept up with what was happening in Crossley, attending the odd meeting or writing a letter when needed. As the winter rolled on, I hosted a French cuisine dinner party for my twenty-sixth birthday using home-grown produce. The physical work and my daily yoga routine left me feeling as fit and healthy as ever. Life was picture-perfect, though that was half the problem. I didn't fit the picture.

Travel had always been on my agenda. There was a world out there, and it nagged at me.

I was torn. I had learned a lot from my time in the bush, including how to live slowly and simply, grounding myself and getting out of my head. It wasn't easy. But I had come to realise that by being gentle on the environment around me, I could be more gentle on myself and others. I had come to realise my true interdependence with nature. I had understood these things on an intellectual level – I had to go and live in the bush to feel them at the core of my being.

But still, I had something more in me that had to be satisfied. Something that could only be discovered on my own, out there in the wilderness of the world. I knew it would cause me pain, and somehow I knew that to be good for me.

I cried all the way to Mumbai, India, the well-worn destination of those who go in search of themselves. I had three months in that country of contradiction to achieve my aim. A country of snow-capped mountains, and cities buckling under the weight of an incomprehensible population; of ancient worship and faith as deep as the skyscrapers of the software companies are high. Four days in, I escaped the oppressive summer heat in Delhi and sat cross-legged on the floor in a Buddhist temple in the Himalayas at four o'clock in the morning. I had embarked upon a Vipassana course (ten hours of silent meditation a day for ten days), and in the cold morning air I was questioning my sanity. It was the hardest thing I've ever done in my life. But I survived, and though no moments of pure enlightenment showed me the answers to my questions, on day ten when I was finally allowed to speak, I strangely didn't feel the need to. After our 4 am meditation session, I sat cross-legged on a stone fence, like I did every morning for ten days, watching farmers go to work in the foothills of the Himalayas, and had only one thought: 'I think I'm goin' to be alright.' Though I had no clue where my life would take me, how long I would be gone, or even what I wanted to do, I decided on that morning, that if nothing else, I would have faith in myself.

'I'm going to be alright,' I repeated out loud the thought to the farmers who were starting their work days in the fields below. I committed myself to that fact. It got me through, when I thought I might die from vomiting and diarrhoea. It got me through from Varanassi to Calcutta, on a night train, spent upright squished six or seven to a row intended for three, on a third-class carriage, choking from the hot dusty air blowing in the open windows, blinking from the fluorescent lights and swatting away insects that clung to my sweaty skin. I thanked God for my music player, plugged in Shane Howard and transported myself to a place where the grass is green and clean, and the south-west winds blow. 'I'll be alright,' I told myself.

When I first walked into Kalighat, Mother Teresa's House of the Sick and Dying, I reeled at the room of 55 women on MASH style bunks, all dressed in green with shaved heads, and one thought went through my mind: 'I can't do this!' But as I sat with these dying women, stick thin, or bloated with malnutrition or fluid, I wondered where they'd come from and how long they'd been there. They stared back with deep brown searching eyes; some, cloudy with blindness, simply squeezed my hand. I spent my days massaging their wafer-thin skin, chocolate brown and wrinkled like foil, to their disfigured and broken bones. It was raw and confronting but I took strength from the beautiful singing voices of the Sisters of Charity, in their blue rimmed saris and brown sandals, who sang in choir every morning from 5 am and prayed that we set aside our guile or worldliness and be guided by love and compassion. Once I overcame my reluctance and fear, I realised the power of those words and realised the true privilege it is to sit with somebody in their hour of need. And I was alright.

Before long I had to trade the fire twirling and flea markets of Goa for the cold winter days and grey skies of London. On my arrival, my brother Bernie picked me up, taking me on his customary tour to see the Christmas lights on Oxford Street, Buckingham Palace and Big Ben lit up at night. I couldn't get enough of London, its galleries and theatres and cosy old pubs. Not to mention its access to my weekend European getaways. I got myself a good job, one that easily occupied me for ten hours a day if I chose. I worked for CAFOD, the Catholic Agency for Overseas Development, employed to organise an anti-poverty rally on the River Thames, on the occasion of the G8, for the Make Poverty History coalition. I thrived on the challenge of an event that forced me to get up to speed with rock stars I'd never heard of, barges and river tides, British politics and climate change. It was exciting, and I loved it.

In July that year, my sister Catherine and her husband and four children arrived from home. We flew into Cork and an hour later were standing on the remains of St Erasmus church at Upper Aghada where Pop Maloney's grandparents, Edward Stafford and Mary Carey, were married in 1834. From there you could look out over Cobh harbour, sparkling in the summer sun, and try to picture the coffin ships that left these shores over 150 years ago, bound for Australia. In the museum, we learned just how many didn't make it, feeling a strange sense of privilege that our ancestors had. It was here in Ireland that I came to realise just why St Brigid's meant so much to me. No wonder our ancestors were so proud of their achievement in building such a grand monument as a symbol of their survival and their triumph in a new land. That pride was inbuilt in me. Somewhere in my genetic memory was a natural tendency to fight, a fear of dispossession, an attachment to land, an urge to stand up to the abuse of power. No wonder the closure of St Brigid's had struck such a chord deep within me, in all of us really. Perhaps it's true. If you're Irish Catholic there is no escaping that 'Irish rebel' blood.

I visited St Brigid's healing well in Kildare, set in a green field of wildflowers with the only sound the trickling of a tranquil stream.

Standing alone on this ancient and sacred ground, the energy of Brigid the goddess and the thousands who pilgrim here surrounding me, I got to thinking about this Celtic spirituality and how familiar it was to our Indigenous people in Australia. Both were born in readings of the land, an insight into the sacred in nature intimately bound up with personal identity. At each of the five prayer stones, I reflected on Brigid, the saint, the goddess, the woman of the land, the peacemaker, the friend of the poor, the hearthwoman, the woman of contemplation; and I prayed that the church in which she is named saint would not alienate itself from our ancestral traditions, but instead draw inspiration from a woman attuned to the cycles of nature, the fragility of the planet, who modelled equality and compassion.

With Catherine and her family, I travelled on to Shravokee, a few miles north of Limerick, overlooking the Shannon River in County Clare to the place where my great-great-grandfather, Thomas Lane, was born in 1833. Dad had told us about a graveyard where the Lanes were buried. We stopped at a corner shop in the middle of nowhere, it seemed, to ask for directions. 'The Lanes? Oh, if you just go just over the bad bridge and past the nice house, you'll find it,' we were told in the thickest of Irish accents. We laughed as we drove down the narrow country lanes, with boxthorn hedges and stone fences, which felt weirdly familiar. The economic impact of the Celtic Tiger meant there were far fewer bad bridges, and lots more nice houses, in Ireland now. Eventually we knocked on the door of a farmhouse, of a kindly farmer who loaded the kids in the car and drove ahead of us up the lane, where we climbed a fence and walked over the green lush fields, perhaps the same fields our ancestors farmed in the 1800s we wondered. The word etched in gold in the newly laid tombstone shone brightly in the distance: 'Lane'. Without a word between us, Catherine and I began running across the field. In the ramshackle old graveyard we tore back the overgrown vine to discover tombstone after tombstone of graves etched with our family name. 'In loving memory of Michael Lane b. 1788. His wife Catherine.' These were the graves of our great-great-great-great uncles and aunts. Being there made our story somehow feel complete. A story that began here in the green fields of Clonlara, and travelled across the seas and was made manifest in a church on a hill that overlooked the green fields of Killarney, at home in south-west Victoria.

A story that was still unfolding at home, and in Rome.

Nearing the end of my first year in London, after much deliberation, I made the difficult decision to forfeit my return flight home for Christmas. Approaching the shortest day of the year, it already felt like months since I'd seen daylight. The temperature in London was plummeting below zero, and with it my health. I was acutely aware that it had been more than a year since I'd left, and though my life had moved on, my heart was still stuck firmly in the middle of that bush. I was dying to go home, but equally couldn't bear the thought of it. By the weekend before Christmas, I was holed up in bed with a burning temperature, rattling lungs and a runny nose, while my flatmates cooked a special Christmas dinner. It was only three o'clock in the afternoon but it was almost dark outside, the windows fogging up from the hot stove. I promised I'd make the gravy.

Standing at the stove, stirring the pot, feeling rotten and homesick, I told everyone that 'Mum makes the best gravy.' As if she'd heard me, the phone rang.

'Love, I've got some sad news. Nana passed away today.'

I nodded, tears streaming silently down my face, as she told me how peacefully Nana had left this world, with Mum and Dad praying by her bedside.

I hung up the phone, kicking myself for the flight that left yesterday and regretting that I'd missed the opportunity for one last goodbye. We popped Christmas crackers and sipped mulled wine, and then I went to bed. Sleep didn't come, and so in the middle of the night I picked up the phone.

'Do you have any seats on a flight to Melbourne today?'

'Yes, we can get you on a flight at 12 noon lunch.'

'Can you hold that for a few minutes, please?'

I checked my bank balance. The cost was its entire contents. I rang my sister Angela. 'Is it silly if I spend everything I have to fly home for Nana's funeral?'

'It's only silly if you feel you have to. Not if you want to.'

'I want to.'

Six hours later, as I was quietly creeping out the front door of our terrace house, my flatmate came down the stairs. He took one look at me and smiled.

'You're going home, aren't you?'

'Yeah, I'm going home,' I grinned back.

The words had never sounded so good.

We couldn't grant Nana her wish, to farewell her from St Brigid's. The doors were still firmly locked, a grand old building stood idle, no chance in hell that the Church would allow us in. So, on the night before Nana's funeral, we had the ritual rosary at St Joseph's church in Warrnambool. Afterwards, Liz called us back to Crossley. There have been only a couple of occasions in my adult life where I've spent time with just my parents and siblings. They've all been married so long that I don't remember life without the in-laws around. This was one of those moments for just Mum and Dad and us kids. It was one of those hot summer nights, not a breath of wind in the air. We sat on picnic blankets and folding chairs in the dark churchyard and did what we hadn't done as a family in years. We prayed. We sang songs and told stories. It wasn't what Nana asked for, but I like to believe it helped her rest peacefully.

The next day we buried Nana at Tower Hill cemetery, summer rain gently falling over the fields of green. I sprinkled that rich volcanic soil on her coffin and said goodbye to a woman whose long life had fascinated me since I was young, thinking about the graves of her ancestors that I'd visited only a few months earlier in Ireland.

'You glad you came home?' Liz whispered to me, as I stepped back from the graveside.

'Yeah, it's good to be home,' I said, tears welling, both happy and sad, 'even if only for a bit.'

Chapter Ten

A ruling from Rome

For as long as I can remember, on our mantelpiece at home sits a big heavy yellow book called *The Catechism of the Catholic Church*. It's a hefty-sized tome which synthesises the doctrine of the Catholic faith – the 'rule book' in my child's world view, a seemingly inexhaustible list of all the things that were forbidden in the life of a Catholic, like blasphemy, adultery and other mortal sins about whose meaning we had no clue. And so, the big yellow book on the mantelpiece was quite an eye-opener for a twelve-year-old, sneakily scanning the list of 'good acts and evil acts' to decipher how much time I must spend in purgatory on my way to heaven.

In 2006, when I discovered the concept of canon law, I was relieved to know that there was also a rule book for the hierarchy to ensure good governance and decision making. In fact, I discovered canon law is a fully developed internal legal system, with all the trimmings, courts, lawyers, judges and a long legal code to abide by.

So, convinced that Father Bryant was playing outside the rules, and encouraged by the support of the Bishop, Dad did some research to see what canon law had to say. The book of *The Sanctifying Office of the Church* on 'Churches' was most applicable, carrying a very logical clause that seemed to fit our purpose: *If a church cannot in any way be used for divine worship and there is no possibility of its being restored, the diocesan Bishop may allow for it to be used for some secular but not unbecoming purpose.*

Saving St Brigid's

In our minds, the concept of an Australian Irish cultural centre fitted the bill perfectly. It was just the solution to a prematurely discarded church, one which not only provided some kind of sustainable way forward, but also celebrated the influence of St Brigid's on the Catholic Church in Victoria, if not Australia. Dad had argued quite persuasively that St Brigid's had been the 'cradle of Catholicism in south-west Victoria' and should be recognised as such. Dad was of the vehement opinion that one day in the future, people would return to church, albeit a necessarily evolved version. He laid out research and case studies. I didn't see the case studies but based on the numbers of young Catholics I saw when I attended youth conferences and festivals, I tended to agree with him really. They existed, and it felt like a pure omission or deliberate decision that in our corner of the world the Church was simply not bothered with engaging the next generation. So, we felt that a cultural centre incorporated into the existing church was a win-win solution that would recognise the contribution that the people of the district had made to the institutional Catholic Church in Victoria. We thought it was an idea that the Catholic Church would welcome and support. We felt that marrying together the cultural and religious aspects would add appeal and attract a new audience. We were on the side of the Church. At least some of us felt this was some kind of answer to a declining Church, some way these challenges could be addressed. We weren't radicals, but rather we saw ourselves as people willing to take practical action for the future.

At the very least, if the Catholic Church really was on the way out, a heritage centre which told the story of the Catholic Church in this part of the world would be an everlasting reminder, to the children of the future, of the central place it once held in our community.

And we thought, naïvely, that as direct descendents of those who built the church, and current day parishioners, we'd have a say in the decision making. We were wrong on both counts, despite clauses in canon law that appeared to indicate otherwise: *Before doing so [allowing secular use of the building], he must consult the council of priests; he must also have the consent of those who could lawfully claim rights over that church, and be sure that the good of souls would not be harmed by the transfer.*

There it was in black and white, it seemed to me. Our ancestors had built those buildings for the purposes of religious and educational usage, as stated in the trust, but it is also in writing and in our community's living memory that they intended for these buildings to be a community gathering place. We were convinced that for our ancestors, this wasn't just about ensuring the supremacy of the Roman Catholic Church. This was about a small farming community who were marking their triumph over a long history of oppression and asserting their unique religious and cultural identity in a new land.

We respectfully wanted to uphold this legacy, to carry on this story, this faith and cultural tradition and ensure it would be passed on to the next generation. We had shown our energy and commitment to reach a mutually beneficial solution, but our buildings were locked and the keys had been thrown away.

I consulted a canon lawyer, who let me down gently, doubtful we'd have much of a case. He was happy to assist us in an appeal to the Vatican, but at the time, such action seemed excessive and unnecessary. The Bishop had agreed with us that things had been handled badly and saw that there had been no dialogue, no facts or figures. He couldn't even confirm for us if it had actually been decommissioned, so talk of an appeal to the Vatican seemed way too premature.

It was clear to us that in his haste to close the Church, Father Bryant was not making a rational and sound judgement. He certainly hadn't employed proper process. We would sit tight and await the Bishop to fulfil his promise to move Father Bryant along. And so I had discussed with the canon lawyer what avenues existed in the institutional Catholic Church to address problems of bullying. Very few it seems. Though a professional standards board had been set up, there was really only provision to deal with those sexually abused. There was no protection or process to engage when a priest is bullying one of his parishioners.

It was a difficult time for Mum and Dad. As devout Catholics, going to mass to hear the word of God, delivered by a priest who was, they felt, actively ostracising them, was bewildering and deeply hurtful. All the way over the other side of the world from London, I could hear the strain down the phone in Mum's voice.

'We are the Church, they told us,' she said, with the sadness of someone who'd been reminiscing, thinking back to better days. 'Until you say something they don't like, and then you're not really the Church at all.' It was heartbreaking to hear.

Perhaps due to the lobbying efforts, Father Bryant did eventually seek the views of his parishioners on the topic of St Brigid's. He sent a letter to planned givers, advising them of the impending sale and giving them only three days in which to get back to him. A week later on the church bulletin he informed the parishioners the sale was a fait accompli, and he'd received 10 to 1 support. Mum and Dad said nothing, simply buying time, waiting for the Bishop to come good on his promise to move Father Bryant on. 'In our time, the priest was the only educated man in town. He could do whatever he wanted and he did. We didn't know any better, so I guess they put it over us. But they won't put it over you young ones. No wonder there's nobody going to church these days,' said Mum, half in lament, and half as a rallying call to my generation. She was beginning to see that the hierarchy she so revered her whole life was not only fallible but also seemingly incapable of the self-examination that they preached from the altar. And what is more, they seemed completely unable or unwilling to change, in response to the great exodus of people walking away from the pews.

This kind of conversation, liberating as it was to my childhood perspective, was strangely at the same time unsettling to hear from Mum. For the first time, she began to speak differently about concepts of faith, and parish and prayer. This period marked a definite shift in her, where she was taking as much heart from the wisdom in Shane Howard's music, as she was from going to mass on Sunday.

'I feel I can go to a St Brigid's meeting, and get that same feeling I have at Mass.' Having long tried to convince Mum that I felt greater communion with God sitting in the bush than I did sitting in the pews, this comment came as rather a revelation. Compared to the Mum of old, this kind of talk was truly revolutionary!

Still, I could hear the sadness in her voice, at a loss to comprehend what they had done so wrong to get into this mess. The parish priest, once their confidant and pillar of support, was now the thorn in their side. In the interests of their wellbeing, I questioned again from London whether church on Sunday was a good idea.

'We might have fallen out with the priest, Regina, but we haven't fallen out with God.' There was no doubt about them. Their faith was rock solid. I had to admire it, and trust it would carry them through. They took heart from an ex-priest, who told them, 'Remember, *you* have the faith. *They* haven't.'

In Europe, I wandered around the world's largest Catholic cathedrals, St Paul's Basilica in Rome and the Cathedral of Saint Mary of the Sea in Seville, Spain, thinking how far removed from its origins the Catholic Church had become. In the halls of the Vatican, I couldn't help but think if the Pope melted half of its gold, they could save all the struggling rural parishes of the world. Getting a hearing at the Vatican for our little church on a hill felt as likely as getting Father Bryant to say sorry of his own volition.

Overwhelmed by the opulence and grandeur of the buildings, it was hard to find any resemblance with the teachings it preached. We were taught that it was the poor, the meek and those who hunger for justice that would inherit the earth, and yet in Rome it was the Church hierarchy that inherited the wealth. It felt perverse and a complete discredit to the institution and what it had stood for, for 2000 years. Or perhaps I was just coming to realise that what I thought it stood for actually had little to do with how it operated.

But Europe firmed my resolve to fight for St Brigid's for another apparent reason. A hundred-year-old church is a modern building in the cities of Rome and Paris and Seville. We were so young in Australia, and it showed in the disregard we had for our heritage. Saving St Brigid's now became more than just my cultural heritage; it was part of the heritage of our nation. By allowing our buildings to be sold off, privatised and worse, demolished, we were paying no respect to our architectural, social and cultural history.

The Friends of St Brigid's continued to plug away, meeting every month in the cricket pavilion in Killarney, wearing beanies and blankets to keep warm and bringing a thermos for the cup of tea. There was no doubt they were committed to the cause, but I could hear their frustration over the phone in London. They had all the energy and commitment of a winning team, but the doors of the perfectly good and well-equipped hall that stood up the road were locked, and the keys had been thrown away. Soured relations with the Catholic Church prevented them from entry. That was the first hurdle. The second was that despite their impressive administration skills and an association with growing membership and increasing infrastructure, like the odd grant for equipment from local government, The Friends of St Brigid's was ineligible for serious funds to restore and upgrade the buildings and facilities, because they were coming to grips with their second hurdle: the buildings were owned by the Catholic Church. In order to attract large funding, we would have to become owners. It was a hopeless chicken-and-egg scenario, not helped by a Church hierarchy that couldn't give a straight answer about the status of the buildings. It was immensely frustrating.

It didn't stop the Friends. They carried on booking in meetings with local members, at local, state and federal level, even inviting the Irish ambassador down to Crossley for a cup of tea in the hall. It was of course our hope that our shire council might pitch in to buy our much needed community centre. Dad and Teresa took their concerns to a Moyne Shire Council meeting. Teresa presented the situation, spelling out the population shift, the changing demographics and the multiple needs of a community who now had no gathering place to bind it together. She suggested that the council consult with the local community as to their needs. Her request was met with a positive response from all but one councillor, the Mayor, Gerald Madden, who became flustered and agitated by the discussion, and hence the conversation stalled. He suggested that 'we take our time on this'. One of the councillors said she'd move a motion that the council meet with the Killarney/Crossley community.

Still flustered and agitated, the Mayor rose from the chair's seat, and announced in rushed tone, 'I have a conflict of interest here. I'm going to have to leave the room.'

In an air of confusion, all seven remaining councillors passed the motion. Dad and Teresa were not the least bit confused however; they knew full well the Mayor's position on the matter. Gerald Madden, a former St Brigid's student, was also on the Finance Committee of the Koroit Parish and was responsible for approving the decision to close St Brigid's.

The public meeting went ahead and the councillors acknowledged that the Crossley/Killarney/Tower Hill community indeed needed a meeting space, but were clear that the shire was not in a position to purchase the St Brigid's buildings on the group's behalf should they ever be sold. They did undertake to assist with any future grant applications members of the community wished to make to assist any community building activities.

From the other side of the world, it wasn't easy keeping up with progress. When I rang home for Mum and Dad's birthday in October, not much had changed in relation to the Father Bryant saga. He'd just returned from four months' sick leave, he'd had surgery, and everything to do with St Brigid's had been put on hold. On Dad's birthday, the whole family joined him at mass in Koroit, the 150th anniversary celebrations of the township of Koroit and 100 years of the Good Samaritan Sisters in Koroit. As the family lined up for Holy Communion, Father Bryant became extremely flustered and agitated at the sight of Mick Lane and his family waiting patiently in line. He called repeatedly to a parishioner sitting in the second row and beckoned him to take over the task of administrating the Body of Christ. He then stepped back and took his seat, mopping his brow, as the perplexed parishioner stepped into the fold for the next in line.

Via email, I caught up with the Friends of St Brigid's news. The report of their Annual General Meeting for 2007 went like this:

FOSB truly believe that every approach they have made to discuss the topic with the parish and Ballarat Diocese has been made politely, appropriately and in good faith that, as parishioners and supporters of St Brigid's Church, we would be given a fair hearing.

Communication between the group and the local parish is now virtually non-existent, with Father Bryant indicating he wishes to have nothing to do with the group or its members.

This means that, even 16 months down the track, we are still no closer to knowing what the future of St Brigid's Crossley will be: will this piece of local history, built by the strength and funds donated by the local farming community, be handed over to the community, or sold off to private developers? While this question remains unanswered, the future of the FOSB also remains something of an unknown.

Aside from Christmas, the most homesick I was overseas occurred during the weekend of the Port Fairy Folk Festival. I sat on the grass at Clapham Common in the chilly afternoon sunlight, staring at the planes flying overhead, wishing I was camping in Port Fairy with my family, drinking Guinness and enjoying the music I loved. I was fingers-crossed that somehow our community would gain entry into our hall for the second St Brigid's session.

A few weeks earlier, Teresa had written to the Bishop requesting use of the hall for our fundraiser. She had earlier requested use of the building from Fr Bryant, assuring him that although the Church had cut off power, water and insurance for the buildings, FOSB would happily arrange public liability for the evening and ensure adequate supplies of power and water to the building. Father Bryant refused, replying that he was not prepared to meet with The Friends of St Brigid's nor allow use of the hall while ever Mick Lane was a member of our organisation, 'even if he's sweeping the floor afterwards'.

The response from the Bishop was short and to the point. After speaking with Father Bryant, the Bishop discovered that Father Bryant 'had brought to the attention of the Congregation for the Clergy in Rome the manner in which I had interfered in his administration of the Parish of Koroit'.

Father Bryant had dobbed on the Bishop, to the Pope! Talk about 'going over his head'! To think that this whole debacle had been set off because Dad had complained to Father Bryant's superior. If Dad could do it, so too could Father Bryant, it seemed, complaining to the Bishop's superior – the head of the Roman Catholic Church, no less. We were the ones that thought we had a bone to pick with Church law, but just weren't bold enough to pursue it all the way to the Vatican.

We couldn't believe it! Not that he would go so far, though this in itself proved just how determined he was to win this battle, but the very fact that he had the power to 'go over the Bishop's head' was in itself rather a surprise. The Roman Catholic Church in theory is structured like a pyramid hierarchy. The Pope at the helm, with the fullness of power, delegates to around 4000 bishops across the world, who make up the 'College of Bishops'. Together, they exercise power over the universal Church and individually they have responsibility to administer governance for a diocese, which is 'a portion of the people of God, entrusted to a Bishop to be nurtured by him' (Canon 369). A diocese is made up of a collection of individual communities, called parishes, which in turn are entrusted to parish priests under the authority of the diocesan Bishop (Canon 515). The last in line are the people, without whom there would be no Church, we are told.

Clearly, this separation of powers is a vexed issue. Based on the above reading of canon law, one might have expected the Bishop of Ballarat to have the last word. In actual fact, his response to Teresa in that letter reflects that the exercise of powers in the Church is a far more mysterious business.

On account of the ruling from Rome, Bishop Peter therefore would not grant our request, contrary to the decision made by the parish priest, asking us to appreciate that 'Parish priests do have rights that a Bishop is duty bound to respect'. What those rights are in fact, we are still none the wiser.

The hierarchy, as we understood it, was suddenly a falsehood. The Bishop had given us his word that right up to the point of transaction it was his decision; and yet now he was mandated by the Vatican to sit silent on the issue.

The irony was now complete.

At first it had seemed like St Brigid's was a small local issue. But Father Bryant's appeal to Rome broadened the issue to one of much wider implications. It felt like we'd just become privy to information nobody else knew, and the behind-the-scenes vantage point was nothing like what was happening on the main stage at the altar. This kind of unfettered power not only goes against the grain of the life and teachings of Jesus Christ, but also has created the space for the harmful violation of the rights of individuals, by allowing unscrupulous, autocratic and now, we could see, even criminal priests to do what they like. If his power could be authorised so easily, what hope did laypeople have? It didn't make sense. Well, except perhaps to those poor souls and their families who were victims in the tragedy of the Catholic Church sex-abuse scandals, who had seen all this before. As Gerry O'Brien often said throughout these years, 'Thank God we're fighting for a building and not to repair the broken life of a sexually abused child.' One's heart breaks to think what those families have been through. I've read more stories than I wish to remember of families who with broken hearts went to the hierarchy to be given assurances of swift action, pastoral care and compensation, and instead were handed avoidance tactics, denial, and outright hostility at their claims. These were ghastly stories, not just of criminals and their despicable crimes, but of a hierarchy that behaved in an all too familiar way, silencing victims, hiding behind their own code of law, moving priests around, claiming priests were not under their control – seemingly more interested in protecting their own and the good name of the Church than the people whom they were apparently called to serve. Finally, the Australian Government has called a Royal Commission into institutional child sex abuse, undeniably instigated by the staggering extent of systematic child abuse in the Catholic church, and its irredeemable failure to appropriately respond.

Unfortunately for the Catholic Church, it is now the government, the police, the courts, the media and the weight of public opinion that will have the last word.

The tragedy for many Catholics still trying to 'keep the faith' is that it didn't have to be this way.

In 2007, after the ruling from Rome, Teresa gave the Bishop one more chance to intervene in the St Brigid's situation. She wrote to him to outline issues in relation to water, power and insurance, and to offer our support in relation to the difficult position the Bishop now found himself in since the Vatican ruling. Banging her head against a brick wall, she sent a plea for help: *We do not wish to inflame this situation any further but in light of the situation we ask your advice on whom we should speak to, as we are unclear as to our rights as parishioners and where we should go from here.*

She did not receive a response.

CHAPTER ELEVEN

On the market

In January 2009, I was backpacking through the Middle East as bombs were dropping in Gaza and hundreds of men, women and children were being killed. I was fascinated and surprisingly moved by all the religious and historical sites, and never so aware of their direct relevance to the present day – how faith, story and place combine to create a shared identity among people. In the West Bank and in Palestinian refugee camps in Jordan, I saw how under occupation this identity comes under attack and without a collective voice; the people are broken, diminished. Their pain and loss has translated into the one of the ugliest and most protracted wars of all time, the inability on both sides to walk in the shoes of the other, making a resolution appear unlikely. Leaving Israel, I entertained the idea of returning to the West Bank to volunteer with an international organisation that supports the Palestinian people in the simple but risky act of helping them harvest their olive fields. I'd just finished six months living and interning at the United Nations in New York and knew it was time I got my hands dirty, to start working 'on the ground' in a community and try to make something of a tangible difference. My key to get there was a work visa in London, the gateway to the world, it felt.

But it had been an eventful six months, two and a half years really, since I'd moved overseas, and for a few months at least, I was happy to go home. I had no intention of staying in Australia; I couldn't even imagine what I'd do if I did. So, with a return ticket to London and a highly skilled visa that didn't come cheap or easily, I planned my return home to finish the last semester of my Masters and get the first plane back to find work overseas. After a few days holed up in London, a city shut down from the worst ever snowstorms, I flew into Tullamarine airport at midnight on the sixth of February, the eve of Black Saturday, the day of the worst bushfires in Australia's history. My sister Angela picked me up and drove me home to her place in the bush at St Andrews. I woke up to the searing 46 degree heat, jet lagged and dehydrated, with no comprehension of what the scalding heat and hot north winds would bring. I spent the day in a daze watching smoke plumes rise on the horizon, while very alert to the threat, also very unaware as to the devastation that was wreaked just over the hill. While the family ran around dressing in jumpers and heavy boots, setting off sprinklers, and checking and re-checking hoses, generators and the like, I just sat there praying for a cool change – too late to go anywhere, too stunned to be of much help. When the cool change hit, with 130 kilometres per hour winds, it blew the fire away from us, up the hill, in the other direction. We celebrated by cheering and jumping in the pool, completely unaware that just one kilometre over the hill, people's lives were being blown apart – 22 people died in St Andrews itself, and more than 150 lives were lost in the Kinglake - Marysville region.

My first week back home in Australia was spent glued to ABC radio, on complete high alert, packing up our valuables and evacuating on a daily basis. I volunteered at the local community hall, overflowing with donated food, clothes and furniture, and helped them sort through stuff, feeling partly like I was intruding on a traumatised community and partly relieved that I could do something of use.

It wasn't a day, a week, or even a month for that matter, that I'll forget in a hurry.

The shock and continued bushfire threat meant that I had to readjust my plans to stay the few months with Angela and instead took my backpack and slept on the couch and floor of my inner-city friends, upgrading to their bed when they went away and left me to housesit. I picked up a waitressing job and went back to uni a couple of weeks later, stretching my scattered brain to try and take in the role of the UN in the Middle East and busily writing applications for campaigning jobs in London.

I was exhausted, but determined to make it all happen so I could get on with my life.

I was sitting at the kitchen table of my mate's place in Clifton Hill, ploughing through an essay on the partition of Palestine, when Liz rang.

'Have you heard the news?'

'What?' I said wearily, a million miles away from life at home.

'St Brigid's is on the market.'

'What??'

'Teresa just got a call from LJ Hooker. They advised her that St Brigid's is up for tender. We've got six weeks.'

'You're kidding? The real-estate agent advised her?'

'It's in the paper too. Listen to this: *"The finance committee advised me that we must sell. If we don't it will just sit there and rot," said Father Van de Camp.'*

Back in September 2008, Father Bryant had finally been moved on from our parish. We all breathed a sigh of relief and looked forward to an opportunity to have open and respectful conversations with the new parish priest, Father Van de Camp. The initial signs were good when he allowed The Friends of St Brigid's access to our hall to hold our meetings and community gatherings, as well as giving Shane and Teresa permission to be married, at long last, in St Brigid's church, by their friend, Jesuit priest Fr Frank Brennan.

But a month after Fr Van de Camp's arrival, my whole family were at mass again, for my nephew's christening, when they found out on the church bulletin that, after consultation with the finance committee, Father Van de Camp had come to the same conclusion as Father Bryant. 'St Briget's' would be sold. (Never mind the fact he spelt it incorrectly.) Mary-Ellen, Dad and Teresa went to see him on behalf of the Friends. It was here that Teresa originally mooted the idea of the Friends having first offer to buy the buildings.

Father Van de Camp's response was: 'The Friends of St Brigid's are more than welcome to turn up to an auction just like everybody else.' Based on this response, I guess it wasn't news to us that St Brigid's would be sold. But still, given the controversial history, and the group's attempts to build a more positive relationship with him, it would have been nice if he'd given the community the good grace to notify them before it went on the market.

'Sit there and rot?' I retorted. 'Are we invisible?'

He wasn't blind; he'd attended the Christmas carols at St Brigid's the previous year, and said he'd never seen so many children in one church at one time. 'Didn't change his mind, though,' said Liz flatly. 'There's a meeting on Monday night. You'll be there?' It wasn't a question that needed to be asked, and she wasn't expecting an answer – we both knew I'd be there.

On the chilly Monday night in May, walking into the brightly lit hall, the glow of the heater burning in the corner and the urn bubbling away on the bench, was as comforting and familiar as coming home to Mum and Dad's at Tower Hill. Except that Mum and Dad weren't there. They had decided to go to England to visit my brother and his growing family. They weren't going as tourists, it was important to Mum and Dad that their English granddaughters knew their grandparents. They were looking forward to sharing in the daily routine of life with the kids, like they did here. We were all so happy for them. Mum and Dad had been under undue strain over the past few years with the Church business. It's no exaggeration to say that it had taken its toll on Mum's bad back, ruined from a lifetime of hard work – too many hours scrubbing floors at St Brigid's hadn't helped, for sure. None of her children were surprised that when Mum was most feeling the strain of Father Bryant's bullying, her back pain was also at its worst. In the end, she had little choice but to undergo a last-resort back operation, which put her out of action for the best part of a year, and from which she'll never fully recover. Yes, it had been a rough few years. They definitely needed a break. They left the day before the sale was announced. My sisters and I made a pact that we wouldn't share the news with Mum and Dad, so we wouldn't ruin their holiday.

'Gina, you're back in town,' Teresa said as she gave me a hug.

'Not for long,' I grinned back.

I'd driven around Crossley with Liz the previous afternoon to hand out flyers. Putting in an appearance at the meeting and dropping off some flyers felt like the least I could do before I took off back overseas. It was a relief to see that unlike those long cold meetings in the Killarney cricket pavilion, where we were lucky to have half a dozen people around the table, the supper room was filling up. Thirty people were packing into the set-out chairs. Hopefully, they wouldn't notice me taking off again. The boost in numbers was good news, but not for Liz, who'd recently taken up the chairman's position (begrudgingly, it must be said). She looked as if she wanted to be sick, holding in her hand a book Mary-Ellen bought as a joke for $2 at an op shop: *How to chair a meeting*. Public speaking isn't her forte, and she wasn't pretending to be happy about it.

As people milled around, making cups of tea, I tried to step into my mum's shoes and struck up a conversation with a man standing on his own in the corner.

'Hi, I'm Regina,' I offered, sounding nothing like my mother, who by now would have already guessed from his 'look' if he were a Mugavin, or a Mahoney, or a Gleeson.

He stuck out his hand and offered me his name.

I tried, unsuccessfully, to place him in my limited mental map of the district, but he wasn't up for discussing his family tree, and so I introduced him to Monica, my elder sister, and escaped back to Mary and Liz on the other side of the room.

The meeting started with a sweep around the room for all present to share their reasons for coming. When the aloof man I'd just spoken to said he was here because he'd read the flyer in his letterbox and decided to come and find out more, Liz and I cheered, for our work had not been in vain.

An older lady with white hair who I didn't know, but had some vague idea she had a theatrical or poetic background, rattled on about the loss of heritage buildings in Koroit and the need to preserve them. She talked so long I lost track of what she was saying, distracted by the chunky brooch and brightly coloured scarf she wore. Some people talked about being new to the area and wanting to become part of a community. Some were married in the church and couldn't bear to see it go. Some were aware this was a massively booming population and wondered what community infrastructure we'd have left. A woman who sat knitting told us her daughters liked to use the tennis courts. Some were interested in putting Crossley on the south-west touring map. Next was a young hippy girl, younger than me who looked like more of a match to Brunswick Street or Byron Bay than the Crossley hall. When she opened her mouth and explained earnestly that she recently moved out to Tower Hill because she 'craved community', something inside me fluttered as it hit me that for me, so far this had really been about holding onto what we had, but for her, it was about creating something new for the future. In a community where people identify you by your surname, I guess I took it for granted that it would always remain that way; that those connections came ready-made. Her words reminded me of our changing times as I realised that community is not just a product of history and large families, but must be constantly re-created.

Next, an old man, perhaps in his eighties and wearing a tweed cap, waistcoat and green trousers, introduced himself by the name of Jim McCarthy and launched into a tirade about the Roman Catholic Church. 'Holding us to ransom, that's what they're doing. We can't let them get away with it. This place belongs to this community. They want every last cent they can get, they'll jack up the price just so they can pay some bills of the pedophiles. We can't let them get away with it. But they've been in this business a long time, 2000 years. They'll fight back. We'll have to take it all the way to Rome, I've done it before,' he steamed on, as people shifted in their seat and we looked at Shane to shut him up and move us on. I was part intrigued by what he had to say – he was evidently Catholic himself – but aware that many of the people in the room weren't, and this wasn't the most positive of introductions.

And in any case, we'd already written countless letters to the priest and Bishop and made numerous trips to Ballarat to state our case. His outburst evoked a general weariness amongst us on the committee, a feeling akin to when a child repeatedly states the bleeding obvious and refuses to be told that nothing can be done to change the situation.

'You're barking up the wrong tree there, Jim,' Teresa gently told him. 'Been there, done that.'

She explained the situation with the Catholic Church, how we'd pursued all avenues in Australia and that we didn't see much point in pursuing the case in Rome, since the Vatican had already ruled against us.

As infuriating as it was, it was almost a relief to feel that we didn't have to go down that path again. Banging your head against a brick wall takes a lot of energy. The room was filled with a mood of submissiveness as we realised we were now at the end game, and that we had to either choose our team and go out there and play, or give up and go home.

Teresa flipped open her laptop and got started. I was well and truly out of the loop, and wholly surprised to see how well-developed the Friends of St Brigid's Association was: an incorporated association, with auspiced deductible gift recipient status, 80 members and $25 000 money raised in the previous eighteen months. It clearly wasn't enough to buy the buildings, but for an organisation that until recently didn't have a home, or even a clear fundraising target, it wasn't a bad effort. Teresa read from letters of support from our local, state and federal members of parliament and explained our positive relationship with Moyne Shire. She even tabled a letter of support from the Irish Ambassador, Martian O'Fainain, who had joined the Friends for tea and scones one afternoon.

She explained the four core goals of The Friends of St Brigid's: to preserve and restore the buildings; to create an accessible community gathering-space for meetings and events; to provide a forum for discussion of local community needs; and to assist in the preservation and restoration of the unique cultural history of the Crossley, Killarney and Koroit regions. She spoke at length, and with great passion, about the need to preserve our history, to highlight the significant contribution the Irish had made to Australia, and with the highest concentration of them coming from our district, why St Brigid's was a prime location for a tribute to the Irish. But she wasn't talking about a static museum. She spoke about the 'living culture' that was thriving around us – the people who came from across Victoria and Australia to attend the Lakes School of Celtic Music, Song and Dance, to share and learn instruments, language and poetry. She spoke of the Ryan O'Shea Irish dance academy, teaching young local girls to dance. She talked about the huge success that our St Brigid's music session had been for musicians and patrons alike, who knew that they were enjoying a cultural experience, free of the manufacturing that so often taints our modern experience.

She talked about the need to preserve our family histories, our stories, photos and artifacts. She stressed that, stuffed in our sheds and piled under the beds, these pieces of history were useless, but if made accessible to the community, they formed a whole educational resource for the next generation to understand what had gone before. She talked about a meeting called by the Australian-Irish Association some years earlier, where a number of elder residents shared their desire to share their story. Teresa stressed the urgency of ensuring these stories are recorded, as a whole generation was passing on as we spoke, and with them a part of our history.

She explained that if this material was appropriately housed at St Brigid's, we could really put ourselves on the tourist map as part of an Australian-Irish trail that encompassed all the significant Irish immigration sites: Yambuk, Port Fairy, Killarney and Koroit. She raised the idea of developing a sister-city relationship in Ireland, as more and more Irish were travelling out to the new world to find where their ancestors went to, as opposed to us, who go to Ireland to find out where they came from.

It was exciting, visionary stuff. In her true style, Teresa delivered with passion and confidence.

She explained that the tender was split in two. We could purchase the hall and adjourning land or the church and adjourning land. The total land acreage was five acres. The buildings had heritage overlay placed on them restricting what can be done with them. It was difficult to do a valuation of the properties but they were worth something in the vicinity of $200 000 to $300 000, she said. We had $25 000 in the bank, enough for a deposit perhaps.

There was a long discussion about whether we should pay for buildings that rightfully belong to the community. The firecracker that Jim had thrown in the room had stirred up debate, and people expressed ideas and opinion from all viewpoints. Still, there was a general consensus that past issues should be left in the past, and that our job now was to acquire the buildings.

'This is crunch time for us,' Teresa explained. 'It might be daunting, but this is a good thing for us. It's what we've been working towards for three years. This will give us the focus we've needed for so long. It's the end game, and now is the time to bring others with us.'

It was a rallying call, strong and confident. People clapped, although there was an air of apprehension in the room. Teresa sat down, clearly pleased with the reception and the eclectic mix of locals, old and new, young and old, who'd turned up in support.

However it was the voice of the old that was the loudest that first night. 'But we can't let them get away with this,' came the shrill voice from the back row. 'I've written to Bishop Connors and Archbishop Pell. I'm awaiting a reply. We can do this,' he sounded indignant and not easily put off.

'So have we, Jim, so have we,' Teresa said with a weary smile. 'We got nowhere. Now we have to change tack.'

'But these buildings belong to this community. They were built with the sweat and tears of our ancestors. They've got a bloody cheek to think they can flog them off from under our feet.'

We looked to Shane to placate him, to quiet him down. 'They're fighting words, Jim. But I once had a guitar stolen. I had to pay money to get it back. That's life. It happens. We've got a job to do here.'

The heated exchange went on, and I felt my heart racing as I tried to resolve on which side I sat. Shane and Teresa had a vision, and it was a well-articulated one. It was massive, and daunting, but it was possible. And more importantly, it was worthwhile. I trusted their judgement that we had done what we could in trying to negotiate with the Catholic Church, and that there was no point in wasting further energy in continuing that fight. We had a plan. Now was the time to put it into place.

I understood, and supported that even, but something about it didn't sit right with me. Jim's voice rankled me, and I couldn't ignore my racing heart, as he stated in laymen's terms the injustice we faced. 'It's bloody wrong. These buildings belong in this community,' he repeated over and over, and I couldn't help but agree with him. Jim had raved on about a case in Port Fairy where the shire was trying to sell off a piece of land that had been donated for use as a playground. 'There's precedence for this. There has to be. There's a legal case in this.'

I couldn't decide if the bloke was a crack-pot, or a genius. Part of me wanted to give him the airtime, to see what else he had to say. But he was making a scene, and we had an audience that we needed to stay with us. Not everyone had an axe to grind with the Catholic Church. People just felt that we had to do whatever had to be done. If that required six weeks of fundraising, then so be it.

But there was a fighting spirit in Jim that made me want to punch my fists in the air in support. Perhaps it was the Irish rebel in him. Clearly, I shared it. And despite the measured voice of reason that Shane delivered, I sensed that he too was fighting the urge to punch his fists in the air.

But Teresa was focused on the task at hand. She spelt out the financials for us. Valuing the property had been difficult and neither the Church nor the real-estate agent would put a price on it; $300 000 was the figure that had been most bandied around. 'Jim, I'm right there with you. It's not right, but this is how it is. In six weeks we need to submit a tender if we want to save these buildings. If we don't, we lose them. Simple as that. We can give ourselves the best chance we have of saving these buildings, or we can fight on principle and risk losing everything,' she said with an air of finality that was hard to argue with.

This is serious, I thought. For so long, we'd been 'fighting' the Catholic Church, and we never really had any idea where the end point was. Now we did, and it wasn't comforting.

Teresa went on. 'In the next six weeks, we've got no idea who else might lay a million dollars on the table. LJ Hooker says they've had lots of interest. We're not the only ones in this game.'

Liz was looking uncomfortable, knowing that as chair it was her role to take stock of this situation.

Teresa did it for her. 'So, what do we want to do? We need to make a decision on this tonight, because whichever way we go, we've got a whole lot of work to do.'

Shane spelt out the choice more clearly: 'So the options before us are to either put in a tender to acquire the buildings, or disengage from the tender process and instead take up the issue with the Catholic Church.'

There was silence for a moment.

The man who runs the Lakes School of Celtic Music, Song and Dance, Felix Meagher, spoke up. 'I propose that The Friends of St Brigid's submit a tender to acquire the Crossley precinct.' A man I'd never laid eyes on before, who said his name was Chas, seconded the motion. It went to a vote. Everybody in the room raised their hand, craning their necks to see if the man in the back row would do the same. Somehow, Jim McCarthy reluctantly managed to raise his hand while retaining a look of defiance that said he wasn't going to be beaten on this one.

I raised my hand too. I didn't want to. But though I was idealistic, I wasn't stupid. We had a job to do, anyone could see that. And looking around the room at the steadfast expression on everybody's faces, now was not the time to split.

A motion was moved by Shane, for the community to place their faith in The Friends of St Brigid's to proceed with the tender process in the best interests of the community. The motion was supported by all present.

We had a lot of work ahead of us. We needed all the hands we could get.

Despite the unanimous agreement, I went home with Jim's voice ringing in my ears. 'We can take this thing all the way to Rome. We can't let them get away with it.'

Driving home, one of my favorite songs popped into my head, a song by Shane Howard, about a group of aggrieved Irishmen who decided to stand up for what they believed in. I looked up to Shane. I had always listened to and loved his songs. They were like the anthems to my life. When I looked around at the world I lived in, I saw injustice, and it either made me angry or made me cry. I guess Shane did too, and making music was his way of making sense of it. I drove home, wondering if his heart was telling him the same thing as his head.

Rise up, Rise up,
Eureka man,
Rise up, we need you here
For the principles you fought and died,
Are compromised in fear.

For freedom sing, a freedom song,
and sing it loud and clear,
That we never more surrender to

SAVING ST BRIGID'S

the politics of fear.

Take heart, take heart, men and women now,
Take heart from freedom's call,
When we stand together all as one,
Then greed and might shall fall.

^ 'Digging and Bagging Potatoes', near Koroit, 1881

^ Potato buyers and Sellers, 1865

Story Map

Shamrock House

Crossley

Hamilton >

St Brigid's Church & Hall

Princes Hwy

Killarney

< Port Fairy

Koroit

Port Fairy Rd

Lake View Rd

Tower Hill State Game Reserve

Tower Hill Cemetery

Princes Hwy

Home

Warrnambool>

Southern Ocean

Luke O'Brien
1799 - 1898 m Sarah West
1808 - 1883 Galway

Rebecca O'Brien
1848 - 1912
m
Bartholomew Lyons
1845 - 1942

Richard Lane
1811 - 1889
m
Anne Green
1813 - 1894

James Lane
1842 - 1934
m
Annie Paterman
1846 - 1932

Daniel O'Shannessy
1785 m
Judith Haydan
1785

Catherine O'Shannessy
1834 Co Clare
1904 Killarney
m
Thomas Lane
1833 Co Clare
1900 Killarney

Thomas Lane
m
Ellen Maloney

Sarah Lyons
1876-1937
m
Richard Lane
1879-1970

Constance Lane
1912-2007
m
John Jack lane
1908-1971

Michael Lane
1939
m
Loretta Maloney
1939

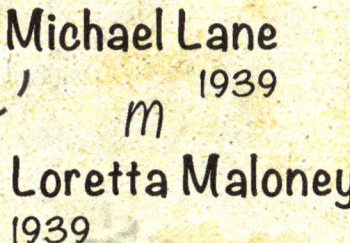

Dan Lane
1870-1948
m
Ellen Rock
1871-1964

^ Turning on the electricity at the Crossley Ball, 7 April 1938

^ The Crossley Church Committee at the opening mass of St Brigid's, 28 June 1914 with Archbishop Daniel Mannix and Bishop Higgins. My great-grandfather Dan Lane is third from the left in the back row.

^ The builders of St Brigid's, September 1913

^ St Brigid's church and hall

Four generations of the Lane family at St Brigid's last mass, January 2006

Chapter Twelve

Asking hard questions

The next morning I was on the 5:40 am train to Melbourne, a full day of class ahead of me. With a job interview coming up in London, I pulled out some reading and began jotting down a strategy for a child poverty campaign in London that I was expected to present over the phone. I was a few pages in when it hit me that if I had any kind of profession to speak of, campaigning was probably it and all of a sudden I realised I was smack bang in the middle of one. I switched from supporter engagement and recruitment of child sponsors and opened a blank page. If I could provide some kind of framework that was useful to the Friends, I'd know I had contributed something when it came time to get on the plane and leave.

Starting with our organisation's objectives, I wrote down our key demands, departing somewhat from last night's unanimous vote to purchase. Our first demand, I wrote, was that Crossley church and hall should not be put onto an open market and that the Catholic Church should return it to its rightful owners before a tender process is entered into. Only after that is lost should we resign ourselves to our second demand, that the Catholic Church should offer first bid to The Friends of St Brigid's before going to an open market. I suggested that in the first instance we wanted to get our concerns out there, without airing all the dirty laundry of the Catholic Church, to create the public mandate that the Church should act in the interests of the community. To that end, I wrote up a set of key public messages. 'Community buildings in community hands', 'Leave a legacy in honour of the faithful that made the Church strong', and 'Crossley should not be made to pay for the debts of Koroit', 'Let Crossley be an example to the area of a growing and vibrant community!', 'Keep St Brigid's in our community', 'People before profits', 'Community rots while Church profits!'

I reckoned that we needed an organised strategic approach. We needed to encourage people to write to the Church hierarchy to share this message and let them know our views. I suggested a viral email/letter campaign and a letter-to-the-editor campaign, for which I wrote a long list of possible topics. I set targets for how many letters we could possibly get published in the next six weeks, if we spread the word widely enough. I would need to write up a flyer with all of these contact details spelt out, to make it easy for people to take action.

I suggested that we host some public meetings outside of our area, in Port Fairy and Warrnambool, to take this discussion to a wider audience, those people who've used or had connection with the buildings but aren't residents. Lastly, I suggested we needed a massive public event, to harness all our energies, creating a buzz and life around St Brigid's and focus the region on our cause. In order to make all this happen, we'd need to divide ourselves into sub-committees, including a fundraising, events, campaigning, media and tender committee.

Three hours later, by the time I arrived in Melbourne for uni, I was pumped. 'I know we kind of agreed to get over the justice argument, put the past in the past and all that,' I wrote to Shane and Teresa in my lunch break, 'but I've been doing some thinking about the Jim McCarthy stuff. I think that principally, he's right. And rather than dismiss that, as "been there, done that", I think we should uphold that principle (Crossley is rightfully ours!) in everything we do and say in order to hold the Catholic Church accountable. It might be the best chance we have of getting a fair hearing.'

I didn't want to nag, but I also didn't want to give up, or give in that easily. Yes, we would submit a tender, I agreed with that. But it shouldn't mean we should do it quietly. The Catholic Church had behaved

ASKING HARD QUESTIONS

as if they could do whatever they wanted, as if people didn't matter. Still, I respected Teresa and Shane as much as I trusted my own judgement, which made me want to hold back and follow their lead. I fully expected a response much the same as Jim McCarthy received the night before.

By the time I was back on the 6:30 pm train on the way home again, my head was so full of war and conflict from around the world, I'd almost forgotten what I'd written and how fired up I'd been on the morning train. I was rather taken aback when an email arrived from Shane, with the subject line: 'Thieves in the Temple.'

Regina, I've been doing some soul searching myself since the meeting. I'm really angry. I think Jim McCarthy is right and I called him yesterday to say so. FOSB should not 'go gently into that good night.'

Whoever is behind the whole operation should be publicly accountable.

There is a gross injustice at work here that won't go away or let me rest. They should be drawn into the light and made to explain their actions. You're right when you say 'Crossley should not be made to pay for others' debts'.

What is happening is plain wrong . . . for all the reasons you've stated.

As a community we are left to sweat and worry about the outcome until July, that may well be unfavourable. Even if it is successful for FOSB, the burden is all laid at the feet of a small community and the worry of it all is grossly unjust.

Every guiding principle of the Gospels would affirm the wrongdoing that is happening here.

Well done Regina. I'm convinced they are wrong and a well-weighted campaign can put the pressure back where it belongs.

Shane

That was all I needed. I felt the strength surge through me. Perhaps there was still a fight to be had after all.

I stretched out over three seats and tried my best to sleep after the commuter crowd got off at Geelong. I couldn't. My head was racing with action points and campaign slogans and letters to write and meetings to schedule.

At Camperdown Liz texted me.

STAND UP PEOPLE OF CROSSLEY AND SURROUNDS. YOUR COMMUNITY NEEDS YOU. OUR ANCESTORS WOULD BE TURNING IN THEIR GRAVES

I dialled her straight away. 'What's that about?'

'LJ Hooker are advertising St Brigid's on their website!'

'What?!' 'The tender doesn't open for two weeks!' Can they do that?'

'It's on their website. "A PIECE OF HISTORY", it reads. "And it can be yours",' Liz said dryly. 'Bastards!'

'God, Gina, it made my blood boil. You know after the meeting the other night, I knew this was happening, but I guess I didn't really feel it. This is real, this is really real. They're really going to go ahead with this.'

I'd never heard Liz sound so passionate about anything before. I talked to her until I reached Warrnambool and she came to collect me. At her house we talked into the night, a ritual that saw us through the next eight weeks.

We received another call that night. Monica had just come home from dinner with friends where she'd connected some dots. 'You know who Matt was out with last night?' Matt is her husband, and while Monica was at Crossley Matt was at a school meeting, with a man who was a builder. That day he'd been out to Crossley 'to do a quote for a local man who is interested in buying St Brigid's . . . the one from the meeting!' she blurted out indignantly.

'You mean that bloke from last night? Got the flyer in his mailbox?'

'Yes, him', I could see her nodding down the phone. 'He wants to turn the church into a house, the loft into his bedroom, he wants to turn the altar into his bloody kitchen!'

I felt my anger rise, and realised immediately what we were up against. 'He *what?* The church our forefathers built as a legacy to their children, he wants to turn it into his house,' I said, spitting the words out.

'Can you imagine them up there cooking baked beans on the altar where I was married? It makes me sick.'

I laughed, darkly, thinking how stupid I was, we all were, to think that after all our fruitless meetings with the Church hierarchy, somehow they were going to do us a deal and hand it back. Of course, it suddenly clicked; they wanted all they could get for it. Now our biggest worry wasn't the Catholic Church but other buyers out there. Who knows how much other buyers were prepared to pay for it?

(When Gerry O'Brien got wind of this, he called up the bloke straight away. Turns out that he'd realised as soon as he'd got to our meeting the community need and passion for the buildings and he had already decided against tendering.)

Our first campaign meeting on a Sunday afternoon was three hours long and a shambles. Everyone spoke over the top of each other, so much to say, so much to do, so little time. It was hard to prioritise what should come first. There were conversations to be had with Father Van de Camp. 'Has anyone spoken to him?' Teresa called out over the din. Mary and Gerry O'Brien had gone to see Father Van de Camp, with a petition that we'd signed. It didn't make any difference.

'He treated us like lepers,' said Gerry. 'He put his clock on the table and said "you've got fifteen minutes to make your point."' They left him with our petition.

We, the undersigned, ask the Koroit Parish Finance Committee and Fr Van de Camp to sit down and negotiate with the communities of Crossley and Killarney regarding the sale of the St Brigid's precinct. The sale of the buildings on the public real estate market puts The Friends of the St Brigid's at a disadvantage, with no transparency in the process. We implore you to reconsider the public tender process being entered into.

Mary and Gerry had been lifelong friends of Mum and Dad, and as with most of their friends, I never really understood where the friendship started, except that they always had some connection to Crossley. It was only when the campaign got into full swing that I learned that Mary was in fact a Dwyer, related to Mr Bill Dwyer, who in 1913 donated the land on which St Brigid's stood. Mary and Gerry both went to school with Dad at St Brigid's, in the hall where we now sat, and the two went on to marry in the church across the yard. The O'Briens had a clan nearly as big as ours; in between having her own babies, Mary nursed Mum at St John of God, through the birth of all of us. Apart from Mum, Mary was the only person I knew who could whip up a batch of scones with her eyes closed; never was there a meeting at Crossley without a tray of scones, jam and cream or sandwiches, courtesy of Mary O'Brien or Loretta Lane.

Gerry is one of those salt-of-the-earth people; he never fails to give us a kiss on the cheek every time he sees us, and is always, *always* wearing his akubra hat. Perhaps it was that he too grew up as one of ten, sharing a double bed with two of his brothers as a kid, or maybe because he was a union man, but Gerry O'Brien would have to be one of the most straight-down-the-line people I've met. He never skirts around the issue, or is afraid to say whatever needs to be said to whoever needs to hear it. Whenever somebody offers an idea at a meeting, but then backpedals when its clear there's no one around to execute it, in the awkward silence that follows, Gerry has no hesitation in saying, 'Great idea. I reckon you're just the person to make that happen.' Gerry is an absolute godsend to St Brigid's.

Mary and Gerry were exactly the right people to approach Fr Van de Camp. Perhaps we were naïve to think their seniority should earn them favour, but Father Van de Camp was equally straight down the line with them.

'There'll be no goodwill treatment to FOSB. It's purely a financial decision, based on the needs of the Koroit parish,' Gerry reported dryly, but with not a touch of disappointment. Gerry never dwelled on the negative; he was a man that wanted to get on with it.

With Jim McCarthy in the room, there was no avoiding the legal questions. 'Can we put in an injunction? Can VCAT deal with this one?' A long discussion was had about the legal status of the church, and what jurisdiction it came under. It all seemed complicated and messy, and way above most of our heads. Fairly resigned to the fact we weren't going to get anywhere fast, most of us were prepared to let it slide.

But Jim wouldn't keep quiet.

'This is a case worthy of going all the way to the High Court,' he said, standing up with his arms spread as if he was preaching a sermon. 'It's Mabo!' he said indignantly, as if we wouldn't be told otherwise. We all cracked up laughing, for our story didn't feel so far removed from Dale Kerrigan's 'just cause' in *The Castle*. It felt surreal that we should even question engaging lawyers, but few of us were prepared to put the argument to rest, just yet. Teresa promised to seek legal advice in Warrnambool, and we moved on.

Teresa placed copies of my campaign plan in the middle of the table, and I worked through it. As I spoke, Teresa took out a black texta and wrote on a piece of brown paper; on the back was a poster advertising

ASKING HARD QUESTIONS

Shane's most recent tour. She called out the subject headings: ' "Legal", "Fundraising", "Media", "Heritage", "Church lobbying". Who wants to make another trip to Ballarat?' Teresa called out wryly. Mary-Ellen and I caught eyes across the table and simultaneously put up our hands. Nobody had been to see the Bishop in a year or more. Perhaps we could appeal to his sympathetic side. Plus, we'd never actually been advised, as he promised he would, of his decision to alienate the buildings. Sending an LJ Hooker agent to share the news was hardly good enough.

'Public action. What does that mean, Gina?'

'I think we need to get active. If the Church isn't listening to us, we need to create a critical mass, so they can't ignore us. We need to encourage people to write to the paper, ring local radio. We need to put ourselves out there.' I thought we could do up a flyer to distribute around the area. I was also thinking we could do up some placards to stick to our front fences.

'If the Church isn't going to favour our tender, then we need to win the favour of the wider community, so that the Church won't have anything to gain by dismissing our tender. The more active we are, the more publicity we get, the more we can turn the tide away from us,' I explained, feeling like the lecturer in the Social Action and Advocacy class I was taking at uni.

'So we need to get our messages straight. This is important. We're walking a fine line here. We want to win this thing, but we shouldn't have to play this game. We need to make sure people understand that. We have two weeks before this place goes on the market. We might have agreed that we'll tender for it. But we don't have to pretend we're happy about that. We need to stand strong in our message, that this is an injustice, that this place belongs to us.' I pointed to campaign messages on the flyers I'd copied for everybody and read slowly and deliberately.

St Brigid's should not be put on an open market. the Catholic Church should sit down with the community and negotiate. St Brigid's should be returned to its rightful owners.

'How we goin' do that?' Gerry looked skeptical.

'We need to spread this message as far as we can. We've got next Saturday to get this up in the paper, before the tender opens. We all need to go home and talk to our friends and families and get them writing letters that underline this argument.'

'I've never written a letter to the editor in my life. I wouldn't know what to write,' Liz said scornfully.

'Just tell your story, explain why you care about this, why this is important to you. I'll help you. I'll make a list of points to make. I'll email it around tomorrow,' I said gesturing to the table.

'I'll drop in a copy to you, Jim, and you, Mary and Gerry,' I said, acknowledging those in the room without email.

'But it's not going to change anything Gina. It's going on the market on the sixth of June. Father Van de Camp told us yesterday,' said Gerry, with an air of exasperation in his voice.

'I know. I don't expect a few letters will save the day. But look how many people are in this room. There's too few of us in this room to win. We need more people on our side. And we need them to know that this is urgent.'

'And then what? By the time the tender goes up, the Church will be well and truly pissed off with us.'

'I'm not suggesting we throw tomatoes at the presbytery. I'm not encouraging you to abuse anybody. I'm just saying that we need to stick to the principles. It's their bloody principles we're talking about!'

Why was this so hard? Why were they so reluctant to put themselves out there? Why did nobody see that we had a case to make publicly, and every right to make it?

I slumped down on my knees in the chair in front of me, remembering that writing a letter is a 'high barrier' action in campaigning speak, and when you're operating in a sensitive environment, like a conservative Catholic rural community, it becomes all the harder.

'Mary, you could write about your great-uncle, and what you believe was his intention for donating this land. Tell the world that you're his descendant, and that you're here to save this place for your grandkids. That's all you need to write. It doesn't need to be an essay'.

'As you say, Gerry, we may not be able to prevent the tender process. By the sixth of June, we're going to have to change our message", I returned to the paper.

Once the tender is open: The Catholic Church should show goodwill to the

ASKING HARD QUESTIONS

Friends of St Brigid's, the ancestors of those who built and maintained St Brigid's for nearly 100 years, and welcome their initiative to uphold and celebrate heritage and culture. The Catholic Church should prioritise the needs of the community, before profit.

'What do people think?'

I didn't get much response. I think they thought I was wasting valuable time we could have spent figuring out how to come up with $300 000.

Though my career had been reliant on it, and I worked alongside teams of people doing it, I hated fundraising. It just wasn't my thing. Money wasn't really my thing. I much preferred rallying people together, or organising events, or writing media releases. I knew the two went hand in hand, but now, more than ever, I was reluctant to set about asking for money for something I strongly believed we shouldn't have to pay for.

I'm not stupid, though. I knew we were going to need the money. I suggested we needed a public event, and everyone enthusiastically agreed. If there's one thing we know how to do, we know how to turn out a crowd. Shane said he'd talk to his mates and see if they would support our cause, in mutual recognition of dispossession of our respective ancestral lands.

'Who were the donors in 1914?' We needed to talk to their descendants, make sure they understood that this was their story too. There were names engraved in plaques underneath the stations of the cross that adorned the walls in the church. They were familiar names; those families all still lived in the area. It would be a powerful statement if a dozen families presented themselves to the Catholic Church to object.

And then, of course, there was the tender to consider. 'Tender', Teresa wrote in black letters on the brown paper on the wall.

Liz squirmed in her chair. She didn't want to have anything to do with it. Before last week, she hardly knew what one was. But as chair, there was no getting out of it.

'Members of the executive will form the tender committee, but anyone is welcome to join,' Teresa declared.

The tender committee, headed up by Shane, Liz, Gerry O'Brien as Treasurer and Milton Walters, agreed to meet on a weekly basis, and we all agreed their first task was to pursue negotiations with the finance committee in Koroit.

Saving St Brigid's

When it came to correspondence, Jim cleared his throat, shuffled his papers and shared a letter he'd written to Kerry O'Brien, presenter of ABC's *7:30 Report*. We giggled, imagining a producer's assistant trying to read Jim's scrawly cursive writing. But the letter was strong and well-written and from someone as captain Catholic as Jim, certainly was convincing. We had no idea, as we tried to hide our smiles at Jim's eccentricity, that his letter would end up on none other than Kerry O'Brien's desk and give our story the national profile that we secretly thought it was worth.

But another story about the Catholic Church was making headlines. The following night (Monday, 26 May), *Australian Story* ran a feature called 'Holier than Thou' about a priest in South Brisbane, Father Peter Kennedy, who was accused of not wearing vestments at mass, of allowing lay women to preach and of using alternative Eucharistic prayers. Always a promoter of the down and out, Father Kennedy had a strong orientation towards social justice. As a result, St Mary's parish in South Brisbane was perhaps one of the most socially active parishes in the country. The Micah Project, the social welfare arm of Saint Mary's, received some seven million dollars in state and federal funding for its extraordinary work.

People were drawn to St Mary's because of the strong participation in the liturgy, the effective voice the women held and the acceptance of all comers. While other parish numbers were declining, St Mary's was expanding. But it all began to come apart because of a small group within the Catholic community, caricatured as the 'temple police' (a term that comes from the Gospel of John 7:32), who are said to go around parishes, taking notes on sermons and reporting priests and bishops for any 'deviations' from what they believe to be Church orthodoxy. This material was sent on to Rome. Church historian and commentator Paul Collins says essentially this group 'try to take 'the "catholic" out of Catholicism and try to reduce the church to what is essentially a sect'. Collins says 'Catholic faith is about freeing people and deepening their ability to love and serve others'. It was Kennedy's ambition to truly make his a people's church, but it was his willingness to include rather than exclude that led to the undermining of his ministry. In the end, he was sacked.

Father Kennedy became the priest without a church. At Crossley

ASKING HARD QUESTIONS

we had a church without a priest, at least one who was willing to welcome and to include and to allow the hard questions to be asked. 'Perhaps we should give them some planned giving envelopes,' Father Bryant had remarked at that mass in 2006, letting it be known that many in our group weren't churchgoers and therefore didn't count. And of course there were plenty who agreed with him. When you are brought up to see the sinfulness in the smallest of things – missing Church on Sundays and eating meat on Fridays – your brain becomes hardwired to view the world in black and white terms. Either it's right or it's wrong. There is no grey area. Having spent ten years studying, travelling and working among people thinking, questioning and challenging the structures of power, it was something of a rude shock to come home to my home town and find I could be labelled a 'radical' or a 'rebel' for asking questions that seemed so obvious they shouldn't even have to be asked.

Peter Kennedy's story gave voice to our struggle. 'To doubt, to question and explore is what he's attempting to do,' said Paul Collins. 'And that is why people respect him, because they are involved in the same quest. This doesn't mean that their faith is weak; it is simply that they have the strength to ask hard questions.' We cheered at the television and spent the night on the phone pondering what would become of the Catholic Church when it became so obsessed with its own doctrine that it felt compelled to silence and exclude those who questioned it.

The next day, I drove into the familiar car-park of my old workplace, the archdiocese of Melbourne. The car park attendant remembered me after all these years and kindly waved me through. I had an appointment with a Father Kerin, a canon lawyer, because I had questions that I needed answered.

As I sat in the foyer, waiting patiently for my meeting, I thought what a different person I was from that girl who sat here, seven years earlier, dressed in my neatly pressed shirt and pants, my carefully typed resume tucked in a plastic folder, brimming with outrage at what I'd recently witnessed from Woomera to South-East Asia and back. At that time, there seemed no institution better placed from which to speak on these issues, and I couldn't wait to get started. I was proud of the principles that I held dear, had been proud to credit them to my Catholic upbringing. Now, I wasn't so sure.

When I walked into Father Kerin's office, looking out to the edifice of St Patrick's cathedral, I felt like I no longer belonged in this place. I still struggled to believe that the values which had drawn me here, which had given me the means to make sense of the injustice I saw in the world, were in the end meaningless when it came to its own. I felt a prickly sensation run through me, that uncomfortable feeling when you're the only one left in the room who doesn't get the joke. I felt stupid for falling for it.

I launched into the story. Father Kerin held up his hand. 'I'm familiar with the story. I've read about it.'

The Age had recently run a story 'Community fights to keep its Church' (Saturday, May 23) and not surprisingly, the online Catholic news had picked it up. We were well and truly in the news. When I asked what he thought about our story, he commented that Melbourne had well over 250 church parishes, and said he expected the numbers of parishes would fall dramatically in the next twenty years.

'That's really sad. What will happen to all those communities, do you think?' I wondered out loud. 'Where will those people go?'

'Parishes will amalgamate. Services will be more centralised. People will have to travel further.'

There wasn't a hint of regret or lament in his voice. He sounded like a business consultant called in to restructure a company, as if the outcome had no effect on him.

But I didn't think of the church as a service provider. I wasn't just talking about what would happen without a local mass on Sunday. What I meant was, what would happen to the community that had built itself up around the local church, for whom the building was much more than just a weekly ritual, but a place where they connected with others, made friendships, shared stories and forged a common identity in a place you call your own. The intangible stuff that a car and a ten-minute drive can't fix. Again, I wondered out loud to Father Kerin, what the Church would look like when all those churches were closed and services had been centralised.

He didn't really respond. It was like he hadn't thought of it. Or perhaps he didn't like my asking. Or perhaps there was no answer. I found

ASKING HARD QUESTIONS

it confusing and somewhat irritating how little thought the Church leaders we'd spoken to appeared to give these massive and pressing questions. People were walking away from the Church in droves, and its leaders seemed to be shrugging their shoulders with a 'such is life' attitude. It was as if they were only concerned with having enough priests, filling their own ranks, when I would have thought they'd be focused on new ways to function without priests.

I reminded myself that I hadn't come here to discuss the future of the Catholic Church with him. I came here to discuss the future of our church. 'I'm here to talk to you about where the parishioners stand in these circumstances. Do they have any rights under canon law?' I asked bravely.

He paused. Again, no real answer was forthcoming. I rephrased my question. 'So are there any principles which uphold any kind of model of democratic decision-making?' I could still feel the sting of Father Bryant's, 'the Church is no democracy, I am the power' comment.

'We don't call for a vote, if that's what you're asking,' Father Kerin said rather curtly.

I was a bit taken aback. In this very same building, I'd written articles, speeches, flyers, that outlined the Catholic Social Teaching which upheld that very principle, like the preference toward decision-making at the lowest possible level – I didn't expect it was such a stretch to expect some translation in canon law.

He explained that priests appoint finance committees to advise them on these matters. 'Yes, but committee members aren't necessarily representative of the parish.' Gerald Madden, the former Moyne Shire Mayor, who'd been so opposed to community consultation, doesn't even live in our parish, and yet is charged with making a decision on behalf of those that do.

He told me that what was most important was that those people could read the balance sheets. You need somebody who can do more than read a balance sheet when you're looking at a wholesale restructure, I thought to myself in frustration. Why didn't they seem to recognise the magnitude of the decisions they were making, or not making?

It annoyed me that I cared so much, when clearly they didn't.

When it came to ownership in the eyes of the law, the response was equally confusing. Under canon law, ownership rests with the parish, and therefore the person responsible is the parish priest.

'So what does that mean when it comes to civil law?' I asked casually.

He explained that parishes don't have standing under civil law. They are covered by the trust corporation, which comes under the diocese. The diocese does not 'own' the buildings, but holds the titles under state and federal law.

Had I missed something? Did that just sound like a bit of double-dutch?

I asked what would happen if a church building came under question in civil law, 'Who is responsible?'

The answer wasn't clear, or at least not to my untrained brain. I wondered if he was being deliberately obtuse, or if that was the nature of their set-up – intended to be difficult. I felt another prickly sensation run through me, a familiar feeling that I couldn't put my finger on. Later, I recognised it as the same feeling I had when I visited Woomera Detention Centre in 2002. A sense of knowing that I wasn't meant to be seeing what I was seeing, or hearing what I was hearing. That was how the authorities wanted it. After Woomera I wished I could just go home and pretend it hadn't happened. It would be much easier not to worry myself over something so huge, so wrong and so carefully designed – to fight it one would need the resilience of a pit bull. There would be no guarantee of victory, but it was better to fight than to sit on my hands and lose sleep at night. I wondered for a moment, sitting in the office of the Archdiocese, whether the fight was in me.

I moved on.

'The parish priest has told our community group recently that there will be no favourable treatment to the community, and that the decision would be based purely on the financial needs of Koroit.'

I asked if he could explain what legal code that was based on, because to me it seemed purely illogical to drive one parish community into financial ruin, just to prop up another. Robbing Peter to pay Paul, as Jim McCarthy would say.

ASKING HARD QUESTIONS

He sat forward in his chair, with an expression that said, 'That one's easy.' 'The parish priest *must*,' he said, emphasising the word, 'sell parish buildings at market value, in the best interests of the parish, so that he does not compromise the patrimony of the Catholic Church.'

'Patrimony?'

'The material wealth of the Church.'

Of course. How could I be so naïve?

'It's a very good system,' he said proudly. 'It's there to protect all concerned, the priest, the Bishop. It prevents the occurrence of a rogue parish priest who decided to go and sell off a church to his mates.'

I nodded my head, in pretend agreement. Protecting all concerned? Where were the people in that equation? He didn't even pay them lip service.

A piece of scripture rose to mind: 'For what will it profit a man, if he gains the whole world, and loses his own soul?' (Mark 8: 36). If it sells to the highest bidder, what will it profit the Church, in the long term, if it loses its own soul?

I wasn't there for a philosophical discussion of the future of the Church, but I couldn't help myself.

'But to me, making a decision against the needs and wishes of the community surely will only end up compromising the wealth of the Catholic Church.' I explained to him that the story didn't augur well for a Church with dwindling parishioner numbers and it didn't have to be that way.

Either the Church didn't care about PR, or they fundamentally didn't care about spreading the word of God. They were only interested in the bums on seats of paying parishioners, but didn't appear to be making much effort to keep them, or welcome new ones.

These priests reminded me of an old cranky caretaker who refused to use a rider mower on a huge unkempt and overgrown property, but determinedly persevered in a corner here or there, with the old push mower, that clearly could not keep pace with the size of the work that needed to be done. Rethinking the strategy of caretaking strangely seemed more than the priests could handle.

In my mind, I saw 'for sale' signs dotted around the country.

Selling off property to pay the costs of the property it had left to cling to the few remaining parishioners and priests, the Catholic Church looked like a business about to go into liquidation.

'Small but pure': the words of Pope Benedict from the previous night's airing of *Australian Story* played on my mind. The idea disturbed me.

For the third time that day, a fundamental question rose to my lips – 'What future is there for the Catholic Church?' – but I'm smart enough to know there's a time and a place for such questions. Sitting in the headquarters of the biggest Archdiocese in the country, I knew the question wasn't welcome. And I knew I wouldn't get an answer. I wondered where and when such an opportunity might arise for the million people who call themselves Catholic in this city.

CHAPTER THIRTEEN

The legal challenge

The sun was setting over Melbourne's skyline as I stood in the driveway of my mate's place in Northcote, trying to jam my bike into the back seat of my little brother's Commodore. I didn't have the time, or the patience, to figure out how to take it apart. I was too frustrated by the Church's legal code that protected 'everyone' except the people for whom it was built.

I was running late for a meeting, tired and flustered, when my phone rang.

'Hello, Regina?' said a sweet English voice, foreign, but familiar – the human resources officer from ActionAid.

Work. London. Life. I'd almost forgotten I'd come home to 'sort out my life'. I had about as much luck making that happen, as I did getting the damn bike in the car.

'We've made a decision about the position.'

'Yes?' I sighed, plonking myself down on the concrete driveway.

After two interviews over a period of a month, and a series of writing tests and presentations, I was down to the last two applicants. I knew from the last interview that I had a good chance. Two years earlier, I spent a month temping at ActionAid, and then worked closely with them organising the rally on the River Thames. I felt like I knew them. Easier to go back to start again working somewhere I know, I'd convinced myself.

I took a deep breath.

'I'm really sorry to inform you, Regina, but on this occasion, we've decided not to offer you the job.'

Relief. Thank God, was my first thought.

'Oh. Ok, thanks.'

'I'm really sorry. We would love to have you on board. We can tell you're a very passionate person. I can see you driving around town with your car loaded up with campaign materials. I expect we'll see you on TV one day.'

I smiled. It was unnecessary, but generous encouragement. She liked me, I could tell. I looked at my watch and the darkening skyline.

'We'd very much encourage you to apply for future positions with us. You're a very good fit here.'

'Thank you, that's lovely to hear,' I said, ready to close up the conversation, eyeing off the size of my bike, and the back seat of Michael's car. I had to get going, I had a meeting at Crossley in less than three hours.

'What do you think you'll do now? Are you in for other positions here?' she asked with genuine concern. I was a little taken aback; it's not her job to care.

'Um, yeah,' I lied. It wasn't like I was putting all my eggs in one basket; I just didn't have time for more job applications. 'I've actually, kind of got my hands full here, I'm in the middle of a campaign in my home town to save a church.' I briefly explained the campaign, feeling exhausted at the reminder that I also needed a job and an income.

'I'll find something,' I said reassuringly, more for her sake than mine I thought.

I jammed the bike in the car and drove down the Princes highway, waves of relief rolling over me as the clouds darkened overhead. 'I don't have to go back to London,' I smiled to myself, then laughed out loud when I realised that the only person that had said I *had* to go back to London, was me.

'Don't make decisions based on "shoulds". Listen to your heart, before you listen to your head,' a professional counsellor had told me way back in 2006. It wasn't that I'd forgotten what she'd said, but I was still young and felt like I was still reaching for that career defining moment that would validate all the knowledge and the experiences and the work that I'd gathered so far in life. London and New York are places where you either sink or swim. I guess I kept my head far enough above water, but I'm not fast enough to be called a swimmer. 'It's a jungle out there,' said a young actor to me at a darkened bar in New York one night, and I agreed. In a place like that you have to be your best – whether you're an actor or a diplomat or a merchant banker – it's cut throat, and there's something addictive about that. At my going away party in Warrnambool, my family surprised me with a rendition of Frank Sinatra's 'New York, New York'. As I flew into Manhattan, the lyrics rolled around my head: 'If you can make it there, you can make it anywhere.'

Something in me felt like I hadn't made it yet. I knew part of the reason was because I hadn't stayed put anywhere long enough. I'd learned a lot, but not in the one place, and it was hard to fit all the pieces together to make it mean anything. I'd never really committed to the long term success of a project, or an organisation, or even myself really.

But as I drove the back roads to Warrnambool, I allowed myself to acknowledge that running away to London was as much about escaping the unknown that I faced here. If I was honest with myself, I also knew that I was avoiding going back to Melbourne, because life as I knew it wasn't there anymore. My job, my comfy little apartment and my partner were long gone. While I'd been gone, my friends were getting married, having babies and buying houses, behaving like grown ups, while I was still living out of a backpack and budgeting the little money I owned as if I was still twenty. It was as if after dipping my toe in the water of a stable, committed rural life in the bush, I was rejecting stability wholesale, and any fragment of the familiar life I used to live, in favour of a disordered, floating, non-committed life. Now that I no longer had all that to come home to, I feared my overseas experiences would be reduced to nothing, would be rendered meaningless. That it had all been in vain. And so I must go overseas again to make the most of it, I told myself.

I had always been an all-or-nothing kind of girl. Every so often I wean myself off my caffeine addiction, only when I am also denying myself alcohol, wheat, dairy, sugar and salt in a two week detox. In lots of ways, it felt much the same choice when I thought about which country to live in – it would be easier to face square one in London, where things were meant to be difficult and challenging, then to start over in Melbourne, where everything had changed.

It's a strong pull that will put you on a plane to the other side of the world, away from everything you know and love in order to make it in life. I'd convinced myself in 2006, sitting in the veggie garden, looking out over the Mountain Ash trees, that 'I wanted to do something good for the world.' I felt like I still had my work cut out for me.

In the dark, the illuminated clock on the dashboard told me I was running late for the St Brigid's public action meeting and jolted my roaming mind back to the present challenge.

'Perhaps I should stay,' I said aloud, sounding out the words to myself. Perhaps you should do as they say, and listen to your heart for once. You need to be here for this one. There's more to life than a career, I reminded myself as I began thinking about the strength of the bonds I was rebuilding in my hometown. I know how Teresa drinks her tea, the secret ingredient in Liz's meatballs (anchovies) and which CD will quickest get her little girl, Stella, off to sleep (Colin Hay). These are the things you miss when you're on the other side of the world. Facebook and Skype might have made communication easier, but with the pace of our lives, you don't share these seemingly meaningless, but telling, details. And in the process something is lost. When you live the restless life, moving from one place to another, you learn to detach yourself from these things – from the details of the everyday lives of those you love. While I was living in London, I was relieved to hear that Mum's back operation had gone well and that the operation on my baby nephew's skull was a success, but by not being here, I'd missed out on what were massive moments in their lives, and everyone else around them. I picked up the gist of it, but it's the gristle in the stories – the fear of the unknown as Angela waited for her baby to be delivered from the operating theatre, the pained look in my Mum's eyes as she battled to open the back door – that can't be passed down the phone line across hemispheres. When those stories come up, I feel compelled to say that 'I missed all that', as way of explanation for not really 'being there', for understanding the major moments in the lives

THE LEGAL CHALLENGE

of those I loved. I guess I was just coming to realise that the only way to really be there, is to actually *be there*.

As I headed out to Crossley, I picked up a six pack. Chas and Elise, who'd I'd only met weeks before at that first community meeting, had signed up to help with the media work and were standing in the car park waiting for me to open the hall. In the clear blackened sky, a full moon formed a bright halo around the Celtic crosses that adorned the church steeple.

'I'm not going back to London,' I said cheerfully, as if they were old friends and knew what that meant to me. In the crisp night air, we toasted my good news.

My career defining moment would just have to wait.

Though it was nearly midnight when I got home, I couldn't help but ring Teresa to update her on my meeting with the Canon lawyer. It says something about what had become of our lives that it became acceptable to ring each other after midnight. We talked philosophically about what all this meant for the future of the Church, especially in light of last nights' airing of Australian Story. 'It's just like our story,' we exclaimed as we wondered where all this might end. Clearly, we had no rights within the Church code of law, and Peter Kennedy's story taught us that it was hardly worth appealing to Rome. While I'd spent my day investigating Canon law, Teresa had been to see a community lawyer in Warrnambool to check out our options.

'She said our story has a "Maboesque" feel to it, and we should apply to the Public Interest Law Clearing House in Melbourne to see if we can find a pro-bono barrister to investigate it.'

I laughed out loud. 'Was she swearing her head off and kicking the photocopier at the same time?' recalling the scene from *The Castle*. It seemed laughable, and like an impossibility, but it gave us a lift to think that there might be some clause, somewhere in some book of law, that would protect the intent of our forefathers and our right to uphold it.

At our next Sunday meeting, more unfamiliar faces sat around the table. There were Peter Keogh and Sue Elms, who lived in Crossley and turned up to a meeting after Mary and Gerry had knocked on their door inviting them. They weren't from the area originally, and though they had good relationship with the neighbours in their lane, they saw this as a good opportunity to really get involved in a community. They were sold on St Brigid's at that first meeting, by the energy in the room. There was Kate Sloan from Survey Lane in Killarney, who spent the meetings knitting brightly coloured scarves and beanies. Kate is nurse unit manager of the emergency ward in Warrnambool. She's lived in a few places around Victoria, and though some places, like Castlemaine, had a vibrant community, it was an expatriate one, and not too many people carried the stories from five generations prior. She said she liked how the farming community at Crossley and Killarney mixed with the newcomers, who came from all sorts of backgrounds. 'It's hard to get to know people in a new place,' she'd told us, but from the first session she attended back in 2006, she felt at home, welcome, like she was meant to live in this corner of the world. 'Everybody is welcome here,' she said proudly. 'St Brigid's is a true community group.' Plus, her teenage daughters love hanging around St Brigid's, always helping out in the kitchen or carting around the babies and the little ones.

'This place has given them community values, they've developed their awareness of how important this stuff is, right here at Crossley.' The girls wanted to play tennis on the courts, and they dreamed of having their 21sts in the hall. Like a lot of people around that table, Kate had never really been involved in a community group or a campaign. She wasn't Irish or Catholic either – hardly stepped foot inside a church before. There was a lot about the spiritual connection with St Brigid's that she didn't really share, but she respected it most definitely and couldn't deny that losing St Brigid's evoked a certain sense of loss of something greater. By working together, by fighting for something, we were creating a new meaning in our lives and a new sense of purpose. You didn't need to be Irish or Catholic to share that.

There were Milton and Bernadette Walters, the couple that lived in the old Bushell's house, and divided their time, like me, between Melbourne and Killarney. They told us they loved that farmers still tipped their hats in greeting when you drove down the back lane. Beside his grandparents' old Edwardian home, Dennis Bushell grew up in a modest

THE LEGAL CHALLENGE

little conite house with his five brothers and five sisters. He followed our story in the paper closely, until he couldn't ignore that pull from inside any longer. His respect for his parents, grandparents and great-grandparents' sacrifices saw Dennis become a pillar of our group, from that day forward. There was Ondrea Howie, from the new housing estate that used to be the Madden's farm. She was a family lawyer, who'd given birth to twins with great support from Mary O'Brien and had been along to a St Brigid's session before and had a great night. For some of us, it was holding onto our cultural heritage, for others it was about handing something onto our children, but mostly, people came because they simply wanted to protect the little things that communities are made of – a wave as you pass by, a hot casserole when you've just had a baby, someone around to feed the chooks while you're away. Life in Killarney and Crossley was a reminder of how life used to be, before our pace of life became so frantic we began to outsource these things and our culture became so individualistic, that we forgot that we used to ask our neighbour for a cup of sugar when we needed it.

It is through these most insignificant of daily interactions, across the fence or down at the corner store, that the strength of a community rests. It's knowing your neighbour's dog's name and taking it home when it's lost its way. It's when kids feel safe to knock on doors to sell raffle tickets. It's hitching a ride with the neighbours when you missed the bus or handing out sandwiches after a funeral. These were the routines and rituals of my childhood that gave me a sense of my place in the world. When I'm asked *Where do you come from?* it evokes a memory for me, of more than the potato fields and the ocean, the volcano and the Celtic crosses – it evokes images of people; people who know each other, and had time to stop and talk. People who were settled and happy with who and where they are. When I lived overseas, asked the same question, I always answered 'Melbourne', for ease of reference. Then, my mind is filled with far different characteristics – speed, restlessness and a sense of anonymity. Saving St Brigid's, for me and others like me, was more than just fighting for a building, it was fighting for the survival of something, something hard to put our finger on, but something we could feel slipping away in our world.

Crossley and Killarney and Tower Hill aren't the places they used to be. No longer is three-quarters of the population Catholic; the other quarter Protestant. No longer does everyone grow potatoes and have eight or nine children. Nowadays more people live in huge houses with glass frontages facing the ocean, and less of us live in weatherboard houses with faded tin roofs that face the highway. Our community these days is changing. There are people of different backgrounds, different religions and very different life experience and living standards. We need more opportunities to gather and meet, not less. With the corner store and the local pub gone, and while St Brigid's doors were locked, our community had less opportunity to gather than it had in 150 years of its white history. Saving St Brigid's wasn't driven by nostalgia, but by practical reality.

Communities aren't just a given, they have to be created. Our great grandparents understood this; we would be fooling ourselves if we thought we could survive otherwise.

I once heard it said that the sign of a good campaign is when you don't know everything that is going on all the time, even when you're right in the thick of it. If that was the case, the 'Saving St Brigid's' campaign was on fire. After that first meeting I had gone home and busied myself writing media releases and fact sheets and helping people fire off letters to the editor.

Liz was listing off options to the tender subcommittee, suggesting they approach Fr Van de Camp to agree on a 'win-win' situation. Liz suggested Milton, the businessman from Melbourne, and Shane, attend. Gerry had already had his turn, with no joy.

'We need to act very fast,' she wrote in an email, in a way that told me she was typing just as fast, 'because if this strategy is to work we need to have met with the finance committee before this goes to tender so they can cancel it. Or am I just wishful thinking?'

'I don't think it would be useful for me to attend as I am purely emotionally involved,' Liz said in her email to the men on our committee, 'and I have absolutely no business sense and anyway, it's all a bit of a boys club in that place.' Didn't we know it?

Shane wrote back to her trying to quell her anxiety and steady the

THE LEGAL CHALLENGE

horses. 'We need to hold fire at the moment, Liz. Are we agreed on a figure we're prepared to offer at tender? The big question is "What level of debt can we realistically service as a community?"'

Gerry, not one for email, simply shared this simple message with the subcommittee, 'Bloody oath, you should go meet him. May the force be with you!'

Mary-Ellen, on the other hand, went home the night of that first meeting and transcribed from *The Warrnambool Standard* the article from June 1914, to highlight the intention of our forebears to leave a legacy for their children. She also emailed the historian, Dr Helen Doyle, who had recommended to the Moyne Shire Council back in 2006, as part of the Moyne Shire Heritage Study, that St Brigid's be recognised as a place of State heritage significance and be included in the local heritage overlay. The Council had accepted this report back in 2006. At the meeting, there had been lots of discussion about what level of protection the overlay provided.

'I'll be buggered if we'll stand by and let the buggers knock it down,' Gerry had assured us. Still, we needed some clarification on the matter. If we couldn't buy it as a community, the least we could do was protect it from demolition.

'I would be grateful for your support, given your expertise in the area (I have little expertise but a whole lot of passion),' Mary-Ellen wrote in her email to Helen.

Helen wrote back noting that the former local Mayor Gerald Madden might be related to JJ Madden from the 1880's. 'Surely, he is supportive of your cause?' she asked innocently. She couldn't have been further from the truth – Gerald Madden had been one of the key people driving the sale. Helen promised to investigate the heritage overlay and get back to Mary-Ellen.

The next day Mary-Ellen received a phone call from Helen. Her enquiry had turned up an answer we hadn't expected. The buildings, in fact, didn't as yet have a heritage overlay. The Shire had not yet implemented the recommendations in the Moyne Shire Heritage Study of 2006 and so St Brigid's sat exposed and unprotected from being knocked down by the first developer to get their hands on it. It seemed with every little glimmer of hope, there was always a knock back following close behind.

Helen emailed the councillors to request their support for the imposition of an interim heritage overlay. For good measure, she also wrote to Fr Van de Camp, Bishop Connors, *The Age* and the *The Warrnambool Standard* newspapers and was published in both. It constantly surprised me how many new arguments and angles there were to save St Brigid's. Helen then went about submitting a very detailed report to Heritage Victoria (which formed the basis for her published history book, *The Church on the Hill* – see afterword for more information) in an effort to fast-track St Brigid's onto the Victorian Heritage Register. It was reassuring to have people like Helen with specialist skills and expertise to aid our cause.

It was also heartening to hear the emails that were flowing thick and fast through Teresa's inbox. People from everywhere were regaling their stories of people against power – saving golf courses and churches and children's playgrounds. There was the story of St Michael's, in the Hunter Region of NSW, a Catholic Church bought at auction by a community in 1991. After many years as a community centre, it is once again dedicated as a Catholic chapel.

'We did it, and have now completely paid off our loans. Good luck,' said an unknown voice of hope at the end of the email.

But for all the joy we took from their victories, there were plenty of people that wrote to us sharing their hard loss after a battle came undone - especially those in the Catholic community. We weren't the first to take up the battle; aside from the one or two good stories, it appeared that few had got the better of the Catholic Church and so we relied upon the well wishes and leg ups from people around the country who emailed to say 'Keep up the good work', 'More strength to your hands. Adh mor', 'Don't give up,' 'Yours is a real test case and the rest of us might benefit from your efforts.' We received all sorts of advice, from people with varying experience and relation to our cause, and varying degrees of usefulness. People suggested mass demonstrations and sit ins; real estate advertisements of recent church sales, government grants and lobby trips to Ireland. Some people simply sent an email with one line: '$500 cheque in the mail. Good luck with it all.' People's generosity never ceased to amaze us.

An email from East Trentham explained that the Sacred Heart

THE LEGAL CHALLENGE

Chuch was sold against the wider community's wishes and is now owned privately and run as an accommodation venue.

We had no avenue of communication, we also were not as well organised as yourselves. Much frustration and letter writing went to no avail. I think what you are doing, planning a cultural centre sounds like a fantastic idea, however raising enough funds is possible but will not be a walk in the park and if you don't get the money someone else will have it and the buildings will be sold. Getting a loan is not easy in the current climate.

So everybody kept reminding us. This was May 2009. Less than twelve months after the day Lehman Brothers bank fell in New York, (living with a Wall Street banker at the time, it was a day I remember well), and the global financial crisis had hit. Now, the nightly news was full of dire predictions of interest rate rises and growing unemployment. If the decade prior was remembered for being 'relaxed and comfortable,' then this was the dawn of a new era that was anything but. Were we crazy to expect that a bank would hand out a loan to a group of young and old, who were big on ideas and high on passion, but less endowed when it came to business management and financial know how? It's the way it goes, reckoned Gerry.

'The people with the ideas never have any money and the people with money, too often have no idea.'

The banks surprised us.

The tender committee approached the community banks, and the response was more positive than we'd expected. So while we might have had a bank willing to give us a loan, we still needed a hefty deposit, to secure heritage protection on the buildings, and mobilise the wider community. It was exciting but daunting to say the least. Teresa's inbox was overflowing. How she managed to keep up with the deluge is beyond me. In the space of literally a few days, hundreds of emails and dozens of pressing issues, few that were inconsequential, passed through her inbox, vying for her opinion or action. I was talking media releases and Canon law and billboards and can you please send the St Brigid's jpeg? Liz was talking about interest rates and council tax and the possible reallocation of boundaries and do we need a generator to power the sound system for the concert? Elise was talking about hosting a children's fun day and drumming up raffle prizes and can you please design something for the flyer? Mary-Ellen was trying to dig up information on insurance costs via Ballarat diocese, and sending around 'Food Event Forms' for catering purposes and how can we lobby the Shire to impose a heritage overlay? Chas was organising a forum with local businesses and trying to tee up an open day with LJ Hooker and attempting to implement better online communication and documentation of our media clippings. Teresa was asking Ondrea, the family lawyer, if we were barking up the wrong tree on conveyancing issues and Ondrea emailed back the conveyance and title deed documents she'd painstaking transcribed from the old English version. She was now faithfully researching the trust laws of 1887. All this and the week wasn't even through.

Attached to every email was the latest letter to the editor or tidbit of support on the street and a pat on the back to keep it up, and generally a reminder that it was time to go to bed, since a good lot of our emails were sent in the darkest hours. 'My God Teresa, did you go to sleep last night?' Liz exclaimed after receiving an email from Teresa at 3:46 am. Day by day, there was a growing sense of camaraderie between us, getting to know each other and the details of our daily routines in a way we never would have otherwise. When I since asked Teresa her memory of those chaotic, frenzied days and weeks, she searched for some kind of explanation, and then offered me this:

'After one of our meetings, four hours long and still so much to do when I got home, I opened the boot of the car, and I could smell something. Someone, I still don't know who, knew there was no time for cooking dinner for the kids and had made me a casserole and quietly slipped it into the back of our car. I guess that's how we did it. Each of us did what we could.'

Our community was alive and thriving, and what had seemed impossible only a few weeks ago was beginning to look within our grasp. Although not all of us were so sure. Not all of us even agreed that we should have to buy back our buildings anyway. And so when Teresa told us one Sunday

THE LEGAL CHALLENGE

late in May that local lawyers were questioning whether there had been a breach of trust, we were all ears.

Our questions were simple, but potentially groundbreaking. The land on which the hall stands was conveyed in 1878, in a transaction that took place between a John Dwyer and his mortgagee, Margaret Birmingham, for which the Bishop of Ballarat gave a peppercorn payment of £50. The indenture reads that the Bishop holds the property on trust for the 'purpose of a site for a Roman Catholic Chapel and school house and for general education purposes'. Our question was, given the Catholic Church no longer saw fit to maintain these buildings for said purpose, did the conveyance create a trust in favour of the local community, to maintain the purpose of 'general education'. If this was the intention of those who donated the land, then clearly an Australian-Irish cultural centre, where Irish language, music and dance lessons were held, would fit this purpose, would it not?

Given that no answer existed within the Church Canon law, our second and related question was what obligations were incumbent on the Parish of Koroit, to consult the community (who were direct descendents of those who made the transaction in 1878) prior to the tender process or to give the community a first option to purchase the property?

'She suggests that we have grounds to make an application to PILCH for legal advice'.

'What's PILCH?' asked Gerry.

'Public Interest Law Clearing House, they match up community organisations with pro-bono lawyers if they deem your case to be in the public interest,' I explained.

'What's pro-bono mean?' Monica whispered across the table.

'They'll do it for free,' I whispered back, loud enough to respond to the confused look on a couple of other faces.

The looks of confusion were quickly swapped with shining eyes of excitement. 'They reckon we've got a case?' asked Gerry, trying to get to the guts of the matter.

'No, they can't say that. They think they shouldn't have any trouble finding us a lawyer, to look into the grounds of our case'.

'On what basis?'

'Look, I'm no lawyer, but it looks like they're could have been a breach of trust. The conveyance documents show that that this building was built with the intention for "general education purposes". We need to find out if we, the descendents of the people who donated the land and money for the buildings, should have been consulted with regards to the disposal of assets and given the opportunity to negotiate.'

'Plus, there's also the question around the break in the chain,' chipped in Ondrea. More confused looks.

'There seems to have been a lack of continuous title transfers on the hall,' explained Teresa, 'which raises the question 'is it legal to sell the church and hall without the title appearing in the Section 32? Plus, there's also some funny wording in there about ownership of buildings in the name of the 'Catholics'. There may be nothing in it, but strictly speaking, the legal transfer of title should be in the name of the Roman Catholic Trusts Corporation. The use of the word 'Catholics' leaves a fair bit of room for interpretation.'

Murmurs of excitement rippled around the room. I had very little idea what Teresa was talking about, as did most of us, but the idea that there might be some legal record that the 'Catholics' were, as we were always told they were, the people in the pews, not the Corporation, was pretty exciting stuff.

'How long will this take?'

'Given the timeframe we're on, they think they can process our application quite quickly. Then if they get a lawyer to look at it, they can assess whether there is a case and then put in an injunction while the case can be further investigated.

'So whatever the legal result, it might buy us some more time to get our hands on some more money to buy the thing.'

It'd had been three years since we'd first taken up the fight to save these buildings. Now that crunch time had come, it all seemed to come at once. It was crazy that we had given ourselves six weeks to investigate if we were sitting on a 'Maboesque' legal challenge at the same time as we were meant to fundraise for $300 000 and bring a whole community along behind us. It felt like insanity.

Then I reminded myself how much hope we'd pinned on our

THE LEGAL CHALLENGE

letter writing and visits to the Church hierarchy – how some of us were still waiting for the Bishop to come down to St Brigid's and call a community meeting. We'd been fooling ourselves, at least my own sisters and parents had been, and we were only just beginning to realise it.

'So we need to agree that this is the way we want to go,' Teresa said looking around the table in each of our eyes.

'If we get assigned a lawyer, that means they'll assess the case. They may find nothing in it. But if they feel we have a case, then we'll be down a path, and we might find ourselves in the position to take legal action against the Catholic Church.'

Legal action against the Catholic Church. A surge of adrenalin ran through me, as the magnitude of the words set in.

'Is that what we want, do we *really* want to take on the Catholic Church?' Teresa asked slowly and deliberately, as if she was a school teacher explaining to her students that they might get in trouble if they did the wrong thing.

Like school children, we didn't really have the capacity to conceive of what she meant. We couldn't comprehend that we were talking about taking on one of the oldest, richest and most powerful institutions in the world. We couldn't fathom the consequences of our actions, and where all this might end, but the energy in the room was expectant, eager, looking for a way we could turn wrong into right.

Taking on the Catholic Church was a crazy prospect, but there was a feeling in my gut, a belief that cut right to the core of my being, that we were fighting for what was right, and when you believe in something that strongly, that's all you need.

Maybe there was one other thing. That is, belief in each other. When everybody around the table nodded firmly at each other, I could tell they felt it in their gut too. Yes, we'd take on the Catholic Church, if that's what it came to.

I wondered what Mum and Dad would have said. Liz, Mary, Monica and I exchanged a look that only we understood. 'We won't tell Mum,' it said. Writing our objections to the Bishop had been stressful enough for her. I hated to think what might happen if she found out we were pursuing legal action against her Church. But we could see a slight crack in this massive edifice of power. For so long, we'd been made to feel like little people leaning ever so gently on that wall. Now, we felt the full weight of the responsibility to choose a bigger tool and give it a good whack, just in case a whole chunk might fall away and reveal the answers to our questions.

CHAPTER FOURTEEN

'Old and empty'

Not everyone around town was in favour of Saving St Brigid's. Not even everyone in my family. At 21, my little brother, Michael, was less than interested in the whole affair, and as one of the last remaining 'young people' attending Mass in Koroit, he found the focus on Mum and Dad all a bit embarrassing. It didn't help that Michael's bosses, dairy farmers in Toolong, were great friends of Father Bryant, leaving Michael feeling like the meat in the sandwich. He just didn't want to know about St Brigid's.

Michael was a dairy farmer, up at 5 am and gone all day. Having now stationed myself comfortably in my old bedroom while Mum and Dad were overseas, I made an agreement with him that if I did the cooking and cleaning, he could pay for the groceries, since I didn't have two bob to rub together. Thankfully, he was agreeable. But it had been more than ten years since we'd lived under the same roof. Add the fact that I was running on the high of adrenalin, suffering chronic insomnia and incapable of talking about anything but St Brigid's, and I think Michael got more than he bargained for.

I organised billboards with 'Keep St Brigid's in our Community' and 'Save St Brigid's', emblazoned in giant red letters, to stand on our front fence, so that the thousands of cars that drove each day down the Princes Highway past Tower Hill could not ignore what we were about to lose.

We had only a matter of weeks to display them before the tender closed. I lost one of those weeks fighting with Michael, who flatly refused to have it in our paddock, let alone help me erect it. In the end, Liz and I drove down the paddock, baby in the back, and hammered and heaved until the five foot bloody thing was on show for all to see.

For someone who couldn't care less about St Brigid's, Michael had a funny habit of delivering the newspaper to me every morning before he left for work and reporting precisely how many letters to the editor covered our story, whether they were for or against us and what page they were on.

'You didn't tell me you'd have your head in it,' he said scornfully, my pitch-black bedroom suddenly flooded in bright light, the morning of the sixth of June – the day St Brigid's officially went to tender.

'Michael! Can you stop doing that?!' I screamed, as he pitched a rolled up newspaper at my head.

When we were kids, Mum was always up at four or five o'clock in the morning. She said it was the only time she ever got any work done. Pop Maloney used to go to work at that hour, and Mum and her brothers grew into the same routine. If we ever heard the phone ring before six o'clock in the morning, we weren't worried – just Mum on the phone to one of her brothers. Dad, on the other hand, took after Nana Lane and was a complete night owl. During my childhood, when Dad was studying for his Bachelor's, he only ever got started after 10 pm and it was nothing to go to the toilet in the night and find Dad furiously handwriting his essays. I figure because Mum is an early bird and Dad is a night owl, is how I ended up an insomniac.

During the campaign I didn't even try to rein it in. I just gave into it. I forgot how to sleep. It was nothing to be sitting in someone's kitchen organising until midnight, after which I'd be on my computer for a couple of hours before lying in bed trying to switch off my brain, gagging at the smell of lavender oil and writing more letters in my head. I always felt like I was just dropping off to sleep when Michael threw the paper at me at 5:30 am. Still, I wanted to read what they'd written and would drag myself out of bed, sitting in the kitchen with a cup of tea and relish the break of dawn as the crater wall of Tower Hill emerged from the darkness.

'OLD AND EMPTY'

Saturday the sixth of June was the day people began to dub *The Warrnambool Standard*, 'St Brigid's newsletter'. On page 9 there was a full-page feature, 'A passionate community is refusing to let its church go' with Mary O'Brien and I sharing our stories, our family histories and our fears for the future of St Brigid's. I punched the air in jubilation to find the letters-to-the-editor page entirely dedicated to our cause.

The featured letter of the week came from Jim McCarthy, of course. It was a brilliantly written letter, arguing that it was 'a moral outrage to sell St Brigid's, aware and informed, in detail, of the community's needs and plans for its future'. But it also placed St Brigid's within our contemporary regional challenges and opportunities. 'There is a profound total lack of vision by the hierarchy,' he wrote, given 'the projected population explosion' and the prospect that the South West might become 'the energy capital of Victoria'. There was a bigger picture here, and Jim was well aware of it.

Impressed, I rang to congratulate him. 'We'll get the buggers Regina, we've just got to keep up the good fight,' he said with a cackle. So buoyed by the coverage, I almost forgot the reason for it. It was still something of a shock to turn to the Real Estate section of the paper and see St Brigid's photographed from every angle, with 'Rare opportunity for a divine investment' emblazoned across it and LJ Hooker's name all over it.

'St Brigid's Church has been part of the Crossley community for almost a century and the hall for even longer. Now they can be yours.'

It made me feel sick to see something so sacred so crassly commodified. To see our sacred church, everything from the confessionals to the altar, splashed across two pages, felt as intrusive as one might feel seeing their childhood home, with all their secret hide-outs and favourite spots, on a billboard above a freeway. LJ Hooker's name had no business plastered across our place, but now that it was, it felt cheapened somehow. St Brigid's was a place where we found our spirit connection, where we believed, and doubted and questioned, and dreamed of how the world might be. When we went out into the world, some of us continued to believe and some of us gave it away; knowing and hurting more than they should have to, some of us paused and looked back, confused. Some of us kept coming back for Christmas mass, or even just to sit on the steps on a quiet day and look up at those Celtic crosses and be glad that it was there. Even for a lapsed Catholic, it's not so easy to disregard that St Brigid's meant something to you once, and because of that, in some small corner of yourself, still does. And that something was meant to be beyond what can be bought and sold in a marketplace.

Sitting at Dad's desk, the double-page spread open in front of me, the rain falling on the bright green fields outside, St Brigid's standing tall on the hill, I felt something tearing at my soul. By handing our church over to the cut and thrust of the market, the Church was doing more than offending the intentions of our ancestors and ignoring the needs in our community, it was actually failing to see the reason for its own existence.

It reminded me of one of my favourite songs, 'Cannot Buy my Soul', written by Kev Carmody and sung by Archie Roach. It's a deep spirit song, a song that sums up in a line, something as a society we too often forget: 'Humanity's more important than a constant quest for gold.' When Kev Carmody talks about the spirit of this ancient land, the spirit in the trees and the rocks and the rivers, he says we need to show the kind of reverence one would in a temple or cathedral. I wished our church leaders could sit down with our Aboriginal spirit leaders, because they know all too well what it means to have your sacred space destroyed and desecrated. And yet, here were our church leaders with their eyes on the money, perfectly happy for our church to be sold off to a developer, to do with what they will, for a price. It was perverse, and conflicted with everything we'd learned sitting in those pews on Sundays and with everything that 200 years contemporary Australian history had also taught us. Archie's voice rose up to meet my thoughts:

> *For two hundred years, we've been beaten down, too long on the dole,*
> *My dignity I'm losing here, admittedly, I'm old.*
> *There's a system here that nails us, and we're left out in the cold,*
> *Ah, they took our life and liberty friends, but they could not buy our soul.*
>
> *Jesus woke one morning, rode a donkey up through that gate.*
> *He could see quite clearly, he was going to meet his fate,*
> *And the powers-that-be could see that he could not be bought or sold;*
> *They took his life and liberty, friends, but they could not buy his soul.*

'OLD AND EMPTY'

There was a reason the real-estate and insurance agents could not put a price on St Brigid's, and it wasn't because they lack experience or there's not a market for churches. Fundamentally perhaps, even they knew that there are some things that money can't buy. That there is more to a church building than the bricks and mortar, and it's the stuff that you can't touch or feel that has the most value. It's the shared story and song, the belief in something or someone greater than ourselves – these are the experiences that warm and sweeten our lives and bond us together as human beings.

That's not to say that I believed churches should stand just so we can all feel warm and fuzzy about ourselves, but because I truly believed that Church still had a role to play in our society. Not so much these days to provide answers, but to help people explore the questions. Just like being deep within a forest, to me, a Church is a place where we can find the silence within ourselves, and be nourished by sharing it with others. Just as in the destruction of our old growth forests, it worried me that we were blithely throwing it away, believing we no longer had need for them, with little thought to how our children would one day encounter the mystery of life.

It was an emotional argument, they told us. It was. It was the stuff of the heart, which had always been the point, I thought.

That first Saturday in June was a busy one. Liz and I spent the day sitting on a stall at the Port Fairy market, fielding questions from people who recognised us from the newspaper, signing up new members and taking money. Our story had long been in the local paper, but today was the first time we'd told it from our family historical perspectives; what it meant to us. And not just us whose families go right back, but people like Elise and Chas and Kate who wrote to the paper to say what it meant to them.

Afterwards I took Stella home so Liz could go in peace to see Teresa. As secretary and chair, they had serious business to dicuss. There was talk among the committee that we should put in a bid early, that perhaps we could save everyone, not least the Church, a lot of pain by avoiding a campaign that was already taking its toll.

When she returned, Liz looked completely wrung out, like she was carrying the weight of the world on her shoulders. Or at least the weight of the community – I guess in a way, she was. It was Liz that would have to sign off on the bank loan.

She hadn't signed up for that when she took on the role of chairperson. She hardly knew how to chair a meeting, let alone the right thing to do when it came to keeping a building in public hands. Like all us Lane girls really, she'd got involved, at least at first, to show support to Mum and Dad. But the train had left the station now, and there was no getting off along the way, even if you wanted to. It was full steam ahead, sometimes downright scary, but there was something exciting, thrilling that kept you buckled in your seat.

'I can't walk away now,' she told me wearily. 'I'm addicted to it.'

St Brigid's was taking over our lives. It was like something we couldn't do without, but didn't always feel like it was necessarily doing us good. Not for Liz at least, trying to get to work on time, have dinner on the table and deal with a two-year-old who threw mum's files on the floor every time Liz sat down at the computer or picked up the phone. Stella could definitely have done without Saving St Brigid's.

'Do you think we can do this, Gina?' Liz asked me, searching for the right thing to do. The executive had discussed a figure that they would offer the Church. The thinking was that the figure should remain strictly with the executive, so as to be sure the media didn't get hold of it and we weren't one-upped by another bidder. Standing at the back door at Tower Hill, absent-mindedly feeding Stella one chocolate after another, Liz would have preferred to be anywhere else, than in that position.

'It's a big thing, taking out a loan on behalf of a community. We don't really know how we're going to pay it back.'

She was right to be cautious, anxious even. Liz had attended every meeting since the place closed in 2006. Only now that it was on the market were we getting such widespread community support, and were new people turning up to our meetings every week. Liz had sat through plenty before, when it was just the four of them. It was fair enough that she questioned the ability of our small rural community to pull it off.

'I'd better go,' she said wearily, thinking about dinner and how to tell her husband that she might be signing her name to a bank loan. It

'OLD AND EMPTY'

would be on behalf of The Friends of St Brigid's Association, but still, it's not something you do lightly.

I went back to writing an essay, wishing Dad was here. They were due back in a week, and we'd kept our promise to each other and not told them about St Brigid's for sale.

At 10 pm, Liz rang me. She sounded much better. 'I rang Dad. I couldn't help it. I had to know that I was doing the right thing, that he supported us.'

Dad had always believed that St Brigid's didn't have to close. He believed it still had a future as a Catholic Church. Perhaps it was the influx of residents in Crossley and Killarney, but Dad seemed convinced that there would come a time when people would turn back to the Church. Even though the behaviour of the Church hierarchy had Mum and Dad questioning the institution like they never had before, their faith never wavered. For the first time in my life, Mum and Dad respected my decision not to go to church on a regular basis, but they didn't see this as a sign of the future for *the* Church. Among us, there was lots of talk about the future of the Church, whether it was doomed for ruin. Mum and Dad never entertained such thoughts. As such, as far as our family went, we always wanted St Brigid's to remain a church. As far as I was concerned, I was determined I would get married in my church and until now, hadn't really considered that I might not be able to. (No matter that marriage was the last thing on my horizon, I didn't have time to go to the pub, let alone have a boyfriend!)

However unrealistic keeping a Catholic church open with fewer priests and dwindling numbers, we believed we had good reason to think otherwise. It was in phone call after phone call, that the Bishop of Ballarat had told Dad that 'You have my word. St Brigid's will not be sold'. It's a hard nut to swallow when you realise that you've been made to feel a fool by a Bishop whose role it is, among other duties, to confirm the faith of young Catholics in the ritual of confirmation. There was a childlike part of us girls that believed that Dad might win the day, and the Bishop might come good on his word. But Dad was on the other side of the world, and had no idea that St Brigid's was even on the market.

Until now.

'What did he say?' I asked Liz.

'He was so excited about his travels in Ireland. I couldn't really take it in. I kind of cut him off, had to get to St Brigid's. He was great, Gina. He couldn't really take it all in either, but he said he trusted we would do whatever we needed to do to save St Brigid's. He said that was the most important thing. He would support us all the way.'

She was in tears. Sitting on the kitchen table, stars shining bright in the sky outside, I shed a tear with her.

'Alright. I guess that's your answer then. I guess we have to do whatever we have to do.'

While Liz had to get on with meetings with solicitors and bank managers and insurance agents, I had something I had to do too. The line 'You have my word' played on high rotation in my head at night when I was trying to get to sleep. Same goes for Mary-Ellen. We'd both sat face to face with the man who'd promised us that 'St Brigid's would not be sold'. Only a few weeks ago, the first we heard that it would indeed be sold was a phone call from LJ Hooker. Not a word from the Bishop. Though our expectations were low, we still felt we had one last chance to state our case. We booked an appointment and off we went.

Mary-Ellen got straight to the point. She reminded him, that on that day in Ballarat in 2006, that he had clearly stated that, 'St Brigid's would not be sold'.

'Why are we in this position today?' she asked in a tone that highlighted how ridiculous this whole thing had been.

'Look, I know that Father Bryant didn't go about things the right way,' he said exasperated, seeming to wish he could just sweep the whole thing under the carpet. 'But since Father Van de Camp has been there, he's done the right thing, he's consulted his finance committee, and the parishioners.'

'How do you think he's consulted parishioners?' Mary-Ellen challenged, bravely.

'I'm not sure of the measures he's taken,' he said. 'But I'm assured that he's done his job. The Church doesn't work like a democracy.'

As if we hadn't figured that out by now.

'OLD AND EMPTY'

I asked if he might come and meet with the parish community now. He laughed and flatly rejected my invitation.

'So when exactly did you give the permission for St Brigid's to be sold?' Mary-Ellen enquired. I wondered where she was going with it.

He was vague in his response. Mary-Ellen referred to a statement Father Bryant made during his final mass in April 2008, the previous year, stating that the Finance Committee had made a decision and Father Van de Camp would inform the parishioners when he arrives shortly at the parish, making it sound like the decision had well and truly been made under Father Bryant's tenure.

'Father Bryant told my father and me in a meeting we had in his presbytery in 2006, that "he wished he'd never heard of St Brigid's". He said he should never have done what the Bishop had told him to do.'

Mary-Ellen paused. Bishop Connors looked uncomfortable. He could see where this was heading. So could I. If it wasn't so awkward, it might almost have been funny.

'So, it begs the question, *was* it Father Bryant's decision, or was it yours?' she asked politely, but firmly.

'The parish priest has his reasons for wanting to close the church. If I was to go into every parish and make decisions, then the priests would tell me to run the parish. I'd have forty parishes to run.'

'But Bishop Connors, you gave us your word, that our buildings would not be sold. We *trusted* you. We were guided by your *word*, we did everything you asked us to do. You told my father to back off and he did. What else were we to do?'

She didn't wait for a response. She was on a roll.

'Was it *your* decision to close Crossley? Is that the reason why priests scaled back activities at St Brigid's?'

'Oh no,' he said, 'That was only while Father Bryant was in charge. I couldn't put a stop to it forever.'

'But you're the Bishop of this diocese. Surely you can exercise your judgement, and intervene where you think it is necessary.'

When he didn't respond, Mary-Ellen changed tack.

'Bishop Connors, in my work as a nurse, I often have to put myself in someone else's shoes to understand their pain or their suffering. Can I ask that you do that today, so that you might begin to understand where we are coming from?'

She was brilliant. I sat back and let her go for it. When I opened my mouth, I felt like I sounded accusing and angry, and I knew that wasn't helping anyone. Mary-Ellen's voice was firm, but gentle and smooth. She was in control. I was happy to hand it to her.

'In November last year, Father Van de Camp told us "we are not simply selling for the sake of selling, this is not purely a financial decision". I asked him if it wasn't a financial decision, then why sell now, and like this? He replied that "they're old and empty and will be left to rot". We've come today to set the record straight on that.' She shifted in her chair as she prepared to list her reasons why.

'St Brigid's is most definitely old. That's why they are such treasured buildings. People all over this country come to St Brigid's because it has a history that makes it unique. It might be old, but it's not falling down; in fact it only needs very superficial work done to it. Everybody who visits St Brigid's is amazed when they see what a magnificent building it is. Have you been to St Brigid's?'

No, he hadn't, he'd only seen it from the outside.

'St Brigid's was not empty when it was closed.' Mary-Ellen explained again that at the last census more people were attending Mass at St Brigid's than they were at Koroit. 'If St Brigid's was "empty" it was because people were actively discouraged from using the buildings. First the playgroup was shut down, the tennis club not consulted, people were refused permission to have weddings and funerals at St Brigid's. St Brigid's draws crowds of up to 500 to 600 people every Christmas Eve. Everything about St Brigid's has been done wrongly,' she said with genuine sadness in her voice.

'I can't comment on such factors. Father Van de Camp would know about those things', said Bishop Peter dismissively. 'Look, the church in Koroit is only five kilometres up the road. The distance is not enough to warrant two churches,' he said impatiently.

'But they *don't* go five kilometres up the road, Bishop Connors,' I said. 'They drive to Warrnambool instead, or they've stopped going altogether. We went door to door and asked people. That's what they

'OLD AND EMPTY'

said.' I picked up the argument my sister Angela used when her letter was published in *The Age*. 'No one in their right mind would tell the people of St Andrews or Kinglake or Marysville that the next town is only five kilometres away; they don't really need their community hall or church.'

The point appeared lost on him.

Mary-Ellen threw in the population figures, to show how much our district is growing.

'They're not bums on seats,' he replied flatly.

'But closing down churches like this isn't the way to get people to renew their faith,' I said, exasperated for feeling the need to explain to him something I thought he should know better than I. A car won't keep you going to mass, but a community of people who share your faith might. Why did he not seem to understand that?

So that he didn't just take us for a pair of emotional women, we moved to the financials. Mary-Ellen produced a recent letter about a block of Church land in Koroit. 'If the parish needs money so badly, why not sell the block of land next to the presbytery in Koroit,' she asked seriously, 'rather than take away the meeting place of a community?'

'It's too late now,' he said.

We explained how in the past three years, The Friends of St Brigid's have repeatedly asked to see the financials and offered to cover the insurance and renovation costs. We even offered a significant amount as a yearly 'donation' to the parish, to keep it afloat. We had plenty of experience in our group in fundraising and seeking grants, and were happy to support the parish in getting back on its feet. If only we could see some figures.

'This could be a win-win situation,' I said.

Our offers were rejected, snidely. The Bishop laughed at the fact that so far we'd only come up with $30 000. 'You'd better get organised,' he said, informing us that they were expecting the building to sell for some $300 000. He told us, as if we didn't know, how much work a church like that requires to maintain.

Mary wasn't going to let that one slide. 'Since we were kids,' she said assertively, 'right back to our ancestors who built the place, *we* have maintained those buildings. We've spent half our life keeping that place going,' she said in frustration. Dad could tell the Bishop for a fact that since 1960 he knew of not one dollar that had been spent from the parish on Crossley. Instead, all the money from the plate at Crossley went to Koroit. Robbing Peter to pay Paul, as Jim McCarthy would say.

Mary-Ellen told the Bishop about the man who wanted to turn the altar into his kitchen. She asked what he thought about it. No reaction. Not a frown or a sigh or any sign of discomfort with the image.

Mary pushed him. 'But as a bishop, as a Catholic, doesn't that bother you? How do you feel about that? It bothers me.'

'I'm not here to share my personal opinions,' he said.

We asked if we'd be given a favourable tender over, say, the man who wanted to turn the altar into a kitchen. The Bishop simply said he'd support the decision of the parish priest.

We clarified, again, what role the Bishop had in the decision making. It was a rubber-stamp role, it seemed. The Bishop would not tell the priest what to do. It seemed a very different story three years ago. We wondered what had changed. Had the ruling from Rome really made that difference?

For years we placed our faith in this hierarchy, and for the first time I saw, with absolute clarity, that their agenda was about as far away from Christianity as it was possible to be.

'Bishop Connors, our great-grandparents built that church. Our great-grandfather told that congregation, in front of Archbishop Mannix, that they wanted to hand down that place as a legacy to their children. I reckon my great-grandfather would be turning in his grave to know what's happening to their legacy.'

'I reckon he'd be turning in his grave to see how few people are going to Church.'

Please don't insult us, I wanted to say. These people are our grandparents. I didn't. It was like talking to a brick wall. He hadn't heard a word we'd said. Or if he did, he simply didn't care. I couldn't understand how somebody in his position could be so heartless.

There was a long silence. I was done, ready to leave, when Mary-Ellen threw in something from left field.

'Bishop Connors, can I ask you something?' she said softly. If

'OLD AND EMPTY'

Jesus was here today, what do you think he'd say about this?'

I nearly cracked up laughing. In every campaign meeting Jim McCarthy banged his fist on the table and said that.

The Bishop grimaced. There was a long, awkward silence.

'I think that's actually a sick question. What would Jesus say about St Peter's Basilica?' He paused again, as if in deep reflection.

'I doubt Jesus could ever have imagined what the Church would become. Perhaps we're at a turning point, perhaps we might go back to the small communities as they did in Jesus' time,' he said, almost wistfully.

'Bishop Connors, that's what this is all about. That's the reason we're here,' Mary-Ellen said, with a deep sadness in her voice.

We got up to leave. We knew we'd lost. He didn't care for our arguments, but in that last comment, we knew he heard our message loud and clear. It only made us more determined. We would save St Brigid's if it was the last thing we did.

Saving St Brigid's

CHAPTER FIFTEEN

Saving St Brigid's

It was a wet winter. The wettest we'd seen in ten years, the locals said. I loved it. It gave me permission to sit at my desk all day long, often just gazing out the window, watching the paddocks grow greener by the hour. It reminded me so much of Ireland. I kept having déjà vu type feelings that I was back there. It was kind of the flip side of how I felt when I was in Ireland – like I was at home in Killarney. I wondered if a day would come when 'home' would mean something different to me, when I laid down my hat permanently and bought a house perhaps. But ever since I'd moved away ten years ago, everyone in my life knew when I talked about 'home' I wasn't referring to the place I laid my head at night. Now, it was a bizarre feeling to be at 'home' and sense that same connection to a place far across the seas, a place I only spent a few weeks, off and on. I remember my uncle once told us how he'd felt himself welling up with tears the first time he took that ferry across the Irish Sea. It's like something deep in your psyche remembers where you come from, all those generations ago, and why your people had to leave.

Shane Howard has a beautiful song called 'Silvermines'. It's about his great-grandmother, Mary Cleary, who left Ireland an orphan girl at the age of ten or eleven. She sailed out of Cobh harbour in Cork, knowing there was no home to go back to. It's not just a sad song about a little girl; to me, it's an ode to a whole generation of people, who came to this country in desperation, as a beaten people, with little but the will to survive. When I hear it, it tears at something fibrous in my soul, and I can't ignore the rising lump in the back of my throat.

Every day during the campaign, I walked around the back lane where we live, 'Lane's Lane' they used to call it. For years I've been coming home and appreciating my country in new ways. Now it took my breath away. It was wet, so wet, but the sun would always seem to find its way through the clouds and cast a soft milky glow over the fields, down through the cluster of houses in Killarney and across to the pine trees of Port Fairy. Aside from the bark of a dog, or a cow mooing, everything felt still and quiet, as I tried to cast my mind back to a time when hundreds of men and women worked those fields by hand, stopping only to eat and to say the Angelus prayer, as they did in Ireland every lunch and dinner time. The prayer, about the Angel of the Lord, sits on a little card on Mum's altar at home.

Just as soon as I'd made the decision not to go back to London, I saw a job advertisement with a well-known organisation that campaigns on social-justice issues – refugees, climate change and Indigenous issues, among others. GetUp! are based in Sydney, but maybe I could work from Melbourne, and anyway I didn't have time to think about it, so I just threw together an application and sent it in before I questioned my sanity. A few days later, I was rushing from an interview with our local paper to a job interview in Melbourne, hoping to God they didn't ask me tough questions about what was going on in the world. I had no idea. On the train, a pile of newspaper clippings sat on my lap – my attempt at pretending to be across current affairs. I spent the first hour or so on the phone back and forward to Teresa, who was locked in serious negotiations with Moyne Shire about St Brigid's. Around Colac, I thought I'd close my eyes for a minute before I got up to speed with the news. I woke up as the train pulled into Spencer Street station, drool running down my chin and my face creased from the seat. I don't have much memory of the interview, I was completely exhausted. They asked questions. I talked about St Brigid's. I was incapable of talking about anything else. The day after that, I had a job in Sydney. I convinced myself that it would satisfy those itchy feet, of needing to 'go away' to make it in life, while keeping me at least in the country. I didn't contemplate whether it would be good for me. All I knew was that Mum and Dad were due home soon, I needed an income and GetUp! were happy to wait four or five weeks until I'd done my job at St Brigid's.

I rang a friend I made in New York who lived in Sydney, to tell her the news. Literally five minutes later, she sent me an email of her friend, a girl we'd interned with at the UN, who had a spare room in the inner west of Sydney. It was fifteen minutes from Surry Hills, where my work was. I could ride my bike, she told me. Perfect. I rang her straight away. She described the house and the room.

'I'll take it.'

'Don't you want to come up here and see it first? It's painted aqua.'

'Sounds great. I'll take it.' It had been so long since I'd had a bedroom of my own, that I didn't care if it was painted pink with purple polka dots. I had a job and I had a house. Life was sorted. Now I could get back to St Brigid's.

But I still had essays to write. I was doing a subject at uni called Advocacy and Social Action. I was writing a 5000-word essay on Bill Moyer, who came up with 'Eight Stages of a Social Movement'. I decided to write about the refugee movement. The next Sunday, there I was powering through a thousand words before the St Brigid's meeting started. I was writing about refugees, but I was living and breathing a social movement in my own backyard. According to Moyer, I reckoned, we were in Stage 4, called 'Take off'. We'd passed through 'Normal Times' – the stage of widespread ignorance of the problem, when only a small group of people are aware and actively trying to address the problem through official institutional process. We'd just spent three years in the 'Ripening Conditions' phase I reckoned, where 'recognition of the problem slowly grows, as tensions build and conditions worsen'.

Now we'd hit 'Take off', the phase where 'an event occurs that starkly and clearly conveys the problem to the public, the problem is put on society's agenda, and a new movement rapidly takes off'. That would be when the Catholic Church put our buildings on the market and let LJ

Hooker deliver the news, giving us six weeks to come up with $300 000 to stay in the game. The closure and potential sale of St Brigid's had violated the values that we, who'd grown up in the Church, held dear. Now, it was clearly cutting close to the bone of plenty of people who didn't grow up Catholic. The local newspaper was full of letters to the editor; 'Sale a Travesty', 'Join the Fight', 'Not Impressed', 'Legacy Lost', 'Judgement Day', were the headlines. Our individual words of protest were even making it to *The Age* newspaper. Something more was going on here. Day by day, we were realising that this wasn't just a local issue, about our church and our priest. The sale of St Brigid's was offending something much larger about what we hold dear as a society – about justice and fairness and openness. People were stopping us on the street to offer support; emails flowed in from around the country. People offering their own hard-fought battles, mostly fought in vain, but it was their unwavering conviction that told us that we were standing on the right side of history. We too felt the threat of failure, that feeling you have before an exam, when you realise that no matter how hard you studied, if you lost your nerve it could all go horribly wrong.

But our little eclectic group of Catholics and lapsed Catholics, Protestants, atheists and everything in between, was still a mystery to most. Who were these people who spoke so passionately about protecting culture and the need to revere sacred space? When the rest of the baby boomer generation, and those who came after them, had long realised their powerlessness and turned away from the Church, why did this group think they had the power to fight it? 'That's the way it is,' they said, or rather didn't say; it was the look of apathy and resignation on their face that told us that they thought our fight was futile.

From other quarters, there was suggestion that we were rebels, radicals. Father Bryant called our group 'Fenians' from the altar, for standing up for what we believed in. We walked a fine line in espousing our belief in protecting the sacredness of the buildings and all the chattels that sat inside it, without insinuating that we were about to form some kind of breakaway church. There were, no doubt, people who suspected this.

And then of course there were the people who bought hook, line and sinker the Church line that St Brigid's was 'old and empty'. Just about everyone I spoke to in the supermarket would finish with 'Ah well, I guess it does cost them a lot to maintain'. People couldn't comprehend that bar insurance costs, the Catholic Church spent not a cent on St Brigid's in at least 40 years (as long as my father's guaranteed memory can stretch). People didn't believe us when we told them that it was our families, my Dad mostly, who'd kept the money pouring in, at least since 'The Back to Crossley' in 1989. I wanted to show them the list of community grants Dad had obtained, where the money was spent and how many volunteer hours had gone in. People don't want to hear this level of detail though. It's boring and complicated. We only see the world through sound bites these days, so when the priest says in the news that St Brigid's is 'old and empty', then that's what they become. In media terms, it's called 'cut through'. Tony Abbot is also very good at it.

Lastly, people questioned our naïvety direct to our faces, about how on earth a small rural community would manage to finance payment of such a building. We only had a few weeks left, they'd tell us helpfully.

All of this doubting and opposition only served to make us stronger. We convinced ourselves that we would do it, whatever it took. There were enough people from far different walks of life joining our cause to affirm that this was about more than us. It was fighting for the survival of something greater. Believing that we were on the right side of history only steeled our resolve, although, it wasn't like we agreed upon everything.

After packing up my books, another essay almost done, I rushed off to a meeting at St Brigid's. I loved those meetings. At 3 pm on a Sunday, the light shone through the white lace curtains that ran along the Western supper room wall and cast their pretty patterns on the wooden floorboards. For mid-winter, the sun had surprising kick in it, hot on the back of half the room and blinding in the eyes of the other. Our meetings never started on time; the first half-hour or so was spent talking ten to the dozen about meetings with real-estate agents, conversations in the supermarket or about the letter that was most recently published. Kids ran in and out of the supper room, grabbing glasses of green cordial and slamming the door behind them. Shane and Jim were invariably caught up in debate about the kings and queens of medieval Ireland, while Mary

O'Brien was faithfully buttering scones in the kitchen. At every meeting, people asked how my job hunting was going and when Mum and Dad were coming home. It was hard to believe that only a few weeks earlier, I didn't know half of these people. Now they were friends, in the truest sense of the word.

On this day, things got particularly heated. Teresa had proposed that we should put in a bid early, so as to avoid the stressful weeks ahead. Create a win-win for everybody, she reckoned. I didn't. Going on Bill Moyer's take of a campaign, we had only just reached stage four, I explained to the group, feeling like I was boring them with my theorising. We still had a long way to go. Victory is not just about winning the war, I told them. 'People are just waking up to our cause right now,' I implored. 'We have to bring them along with us for the journey. Pull out of the game, and we risk losing them,' I explained.

'Miss the opportunity to make a bid now, and we risk losing St Brigid's,' Teresa responded. We were on two different trains of thought.

Normally, I tried not to get a seat next to Jim, lest I not get a word in. Today, I was grateful he was beside me.

'I think she's right,' he said in a tone that sounded like I'd just struck gold. 'We can't give into them. We can take this further. I've written to Cardinal Pell. I'll send a letter to Rome.' Jim faithfully believed you could change the world with a well-written letter.

'We need to throw a few well-aimed spears in at the right places. That'll get 'em. They won't get away with it.'

On the one hand he sounded like an old crackpot. On the other, I completely agreed with him. I found my voice, but it shook as I spoke. My eyes were locked firmly on Shane and Teresa.

'People responded to our story last week, because they saw for themselves the injustice. People with histories and memories and a will to protect them, and a Church out to make whatever they can get. That's the story they took away. It's still only half the story,' I said, exasperated, thinking of the layers and layers of arguments that we've laid out for the Church for so long.

'If we quietly submit a bid now and they accept it, we haven't won. We're playing their game, underhand and secretive. That's the way they want us to play. Hand over the money and it will all be over.'

Monica was nodding furiously at me from across the table. 'I agree,' she said solemnly.

'We know now this is much bigger than us, and if we're going to win, we'll need the long-term support of far more than just those around this table,' I said, gesturing to the twenty or so whose eyes were firmly locked on mine.

'We're not just fighting corporate development. We're fighting an institution who bloody well taught us about justice and fairness.' My words were tumbling out, angry and indignant.

'I'm not saying we should spill all the beans. I'm not saying we need to slam the Catholic Church,' I said, careful not to forget the promise we made to ourselves that we would, at all times, not get into a slanging match with the Church.

'But there's so much more people need to know before this thing is through. People need to know that we've tried everything we can. That we've taken the softly softly approach. That they promised us and they lied. If the public are demanding answers, then shouldn't that make them think twice before they give it to the highest bidder?' My voice was getting stronger, defiant and angry.

Shane and Teresa were staring straight back at me from across the table. I didn't really know what they were thinking. Looking back, I can't believe how naïve I was to think that the Church would bend to the interests of the community and that a mandate from the wider public would hold any sway in the Church hierarchy.

'I hear you, Gina,' Shane said softly. 'But getting angry now, won't help anyone. I'm angry too. But you know you catch more flies with honey.'

Jim was huffing beside me. Clearly, he didn't like that approach. Neither did I. I was more inclined to throw spears myself.

'We've fought the good fight,' said Teresa. 'We're so close to owning these buildings. Can we really afford to take that risk now?' Teresa was always the pragmatist. I was the idealist.

'Powerholders are more effective when they operate out of public scrutiny. Putting an issue in society's public spotlight takes the movement towards 75 per cent of its success,' I said quoting from my study notes, aware that I was probably irritating everybody. 'Teresa, there's no guarantee they'll take our offer. I mean we don't even know how much the place is worth. We're just playing into their hands. It's how they operate. All the secrecy, behind closed doors, I don't like it.'

I was getting upset now. But I couldn't help it. Everything about this whole situation was wrong. And it felt more wrong, the more we went along with it.

I was thinking what Dad had said on the phone to Liz the other night, 'Do whatever it takes'. For three years, Mum and Dad had sat quietly on their story, on their pain, lest they cause more division in the community. Was now the time to tell the whole story?

In the end, we agreed to place our trust in the tender committee to make the decision they felt was in our best interests, given everything that had been said. And I went along with it, because to do otherwise was suicidal. We could stand together and lose, but I couldn't stand on my own and win.

It was the most impassioned meeting we'd ever had. I was the most vocal I'd ever been. The challenge before us was as stark as ever. This wasn't just about buying a building. It was about re-creating a community, possibly even a new kind of Catholic Church.

We broke for a cup of tea. I was so confused, I wanted to get in the car and have a good cry. Shane held his arms out to me, ruffling my hair. 'What are we going to do with you, Regina Coeli?' he said playfully in a mock-Irish accent, using the old Latin term for Mother Mary. I tried to hold back my tears. Shane was a bit like Dad, calm and gentle, but strong and principled and with me every step of the way. Poor Dad, I thought. I wished he was here.

Mum and Dad flew in a week later. Angela picked them up, and I met her halfway to the airport, careful to pack the newspapers in the car.

They looked fantastic. They'd had the time of their lives and talked non-stop all the way home about their adventures, mostly in Ireland. As only ever happens to Mum and Dad, they stopped at the church I've visited, where Mum's great-grandparents were married, and after asking the gardener, were sitting in a beautiful house overlooking Cobh harbour with the Stafford family. They'd pulled out an Australian family history book, opened on a random page, and asked Mum if she knew anyone in the book. In one of those moments that gives you goosebumps, the man had opened up a page, with a photo of our family. 'That's our family!' said Mum incredulously. Mum and Dad spent the afternoon having tea and scones, and looking to the place where our ancestors set sail for Australia. As the Staffords explained to Mum and Dad how our ancestors would have left that shore, their eyes brimmed in tears. The famine might have been a hundred and fifty years ago, but it's still recent history in Ireland. Shane often told us that in Ireland it's still too sensitive to talk about. When he questioned this, they told him, 'We're walking on their graves.'

In County Clare they met the Madden family, who lived close by the Lane family. Of course, they discovered that we are related somehow. Perhaps it's no surprise that the next farm alongside ours in Tower Hill is owned by the Maddens. Mr Madden told them they should stay the night so they could attend the church where Dad's great-grandfather, Thomas, used to go. He showed them the way to a hotel, and after checking for a vacancy, he bade them farewell. When Dad went to hand over his credit card, the woman at the counter said it had already been paid.

'But we just arrived,' Dad said confused.

'The gentleman paid for it. He said you were family.'

'We only met this morning,' Dad said shaking his head, feeling like he was at home away from home.

We didn't have time to sit around and listen to their stories. Liz and I had been working on an 'action' flyer, encouraging people to write letters and ring local radio. We also had a concert to advertise. Only at the last meeting a week earlier did we agree we should have one, and Liz left the meeting charged with coordinating the thing. She sat down with a local musician, Lyn Eales, and put together a line-up of local talent. We're pretty lucky in this part of the world, that we have that kind of talent to call upon. Shane asked his great friends, Indigenous singer-songwriters, Archie Roach and the late Ruby Hunter, who lived in Killarney if they would headline, and before we knew it we had an all-star line-up.

Saving St Brigid's

Liz, Monica and I spent the afternoon driving around Crossley, Killarney, Koroit and Tower Hill, putting flyers in gerry cans and plastic drums that served as letterboxes and getting very good at explaining why we wanted to 'Save St Brigid's'. Up a back lane in Crossley, I leant over a stone fence to hand a flyer to a farmer who was driving down the paddock on his tractor.

'I'm Regina. Lane. One of Mick and Loretta's,' I said, by way of explanation.

'I know who you are.'

It's a funny thing to have spent the past ten years living away, the best part of the past three overseas, and even though my feet felt like they'd hardly touched the ground, at home I was once again simply 'a Lane girl'. It's the reason I would both love to live in the country, and hate it at the same time. It can be comforting to be told 'I know who you are', when you hardly know yourself. But it can also be suffocating. The beauty about travel is not so much where you go and what you do, but it's the different way you learn to see the world and perhaps more importantly your place within it. It's also about the dreaming it allows you to do. In my years away, some of the dreams were fulfilled, and others not. The beauty is that when you can live vicariously through your dreams, you get to experiment in being whoever you want to be, just for a little while – an aid worker in Africa, a foreign student in Barcelona, a diplomat in New York. It's easier to dream those dreams when you're a long way from home – anything seems possible. And yet, you can't live like that forever. Spend too much time on the road, and in your head, and you start to become restless, never satisfied, adrift in the world. In this globalised world, we're meant to value adaptability and risk-taking as if they are skills to enrich your life, so that when you come home, you'll be better for it; but the more you travel, the more places you live, the less you feel you really belong anywhere. Living overseas, you begin to feel detached – from your nation, from your home town, from your family even, or perhaps these are the methods of self-preservation, keeping yourself afloat in the drifting seas you sail. In the state of disorientation and impermanence that characterised the life I was living, there was something grounding about being told by a man on a tractor – though you don't know his name, you know his mob too – that in this part of the world, no matter where you've been and what you've done, you'll always be a 'Lane girl from Tower Hill'.

'Should we drop in on Teresa and Shane?' Liz asked as we drove the back lanes of Killarney. A bit like dropping in at Tower Hill, you can't drop in on Teresa and Shane with only five minutes to spare. Mum and Dad had barely touched home soil, and we just dumped four kids on them while we did our letterboxing. We probably shouldn't. But every day of the campaign something else was happening and we all felt the need to spend our days in endless round robins of phone calls and cups of tea at the kitchen table, catching up on the latest, from meeting with the lawyers, a last-ditch lobby effort, a spirited email of support from Ireland. As each day went by, the pendulum swung from good to news to bad, raising and dashing our hopes like we were a boat bobbing around in the high seas. It was exhilarating and addictive and the only way to handle it was to simply hold on tight for the ride.

We stopped in for a cuppa.

It was one of those bright winter days, nearing four o'clock, the paddocks and sand dunes drenched in golden light, before the sun slipped over them and set across the ocean. Smoke was wafting from the chimney of the 'Shed' – Shane's recording studio – and inside the two of them were sitting by the fire drinking tea and talking about what 'Saving St Brigid's' meant for the world. Conversations with Shane and Teresa these days always meandered through the vagaries of the future of the Church, the Irish struggle for independence, the impact of Archbishop Mannix on secular education in this country and how it enabled the en masse education of Catholics everywhere. Sit with Shane and Teresa for a while, and you'll get a seamless education in history and philosophy and religion and politics with quotes and scriptural passages and lines of poetry thrown in to illustrate the point. Somehow in the past few weeks, we'd all established roles for ourselves – event coordinators, bean counters, sandwich makers, media advisors, advertising agents – and we all crossed from one to another on a daily basis. But there was no doubt that one role was played uniquely. Teresa and Shane were our visionaries whose role it was to continually remind us what this was all about, taken from the long view. We would never have got this far without them.

Liz and I sat nursing our steaming tea and lingering over our history for longer than we should, until we finally got up to leave. In the car, the conversation didn't stop, as Teresa and Shane stood at the window, still so much to discuss. The motor running, Liz and I laughed at how much like Mum we were becoming, mimicking the hour-long conversations she used to have in the car park at Crossley, while we kids wondered how on earth she always had so much to talk about. The longer I spent at home, the more I realised I was becoming her.

'Liz, Gina, come back inside. I've got something I want you to hear,' Shane said excitedly.

Looking at our watches, we went back into the shed and Shane sat down at his weathered old blue and yellow piano. 'Tell me what you think,' he said as he launched into a new song.

There's a Church up on the hill.
Some days it's peaceful and still
and the world seems a million miles away.

There was something perfect about that moment, the sun streaming in the window, watching an artist at work, finding the words to share a piece of history that stands in full view in the distance – from Shane and Teresa's house, you can just see St Brigid's steeple rising above the gums trees.

He continued his ode to our ancestors, while Liz and I stood there, choking up.

'It's beautiful, Shane,' was all we could manage, before we said our goodbyes.

On our drive home, Liz said to me, 'You know, Gina, growing up here, I never really thought about us having a culture. The Greek kids at school seemed to do things differently; we were taught about Aboriginal culture, but nothing in our life really stood us apart. All of a sudden, it's like I've just realised who we are. Shane and Teresa are so proud to call themselves Australian-Irish. It's kind of cool, isn't it?'

I laughed. It *was* kind of cool to figure out who you are. Driving down the back lane of Killarney, it was for me a rare moment of pure presence, grounded in the secure embrace of what it feels like to belong, a homecoming to the hearth of the soul.

Tickets went on sale eight days before the concert. People bought eight and ten a piece. Liz's phone was running hot. Everybody wanted to see Archie and Ruby. On Friday night the committee brought our dinner to the hall and rushed around setting up dozens of raffle prizes, pasting 'Save St Brigid's' to green cloth on the stage; Shane was putting up lights and sound checking. And then he called us all up to the stage.

'I want you to sing with me.'

We all cracked up laughing.

'Shane, have you ever heard Regina sing?' my sisters jibed. Ever since I was a kid, I was always known for my loud screech. As the ninth child, it was the only way to be heard.

Shane was adamant that The Friends of St Brigid's would sing with him. We trooped up onto the stage, helplessly laughing at the idea that among all of our newly learned skills, we were now becoming backing vocalists for Shane Howard. It was good fun.

However much our voices were left wanting, the song wasn't. It told a moving story of our ancestors who'd left Ireland with children starving at their feet and started afresh in a new land, with little but the faith they carried inside. After the frantic pace of our days and the way we'd come to talk in hurried shorthand to each other, there was a moment of release when as a group we stood in choir, sharing a prayer to the faith of our ancestors and the hopes of our community.

On Saturday, we requested that LJ Hooker come out to Crossley to open what they called a 'divine piece of real estate'. It felt like a risk; no doubt it could inspire a potential buyer, but we felt St Brigid's should be open for all to share, for, who knows, what could be the last time.

At 1:30 pm on the dot, as the newspaper had advertised, the cars streamed in. Dozens of them, filling the Crossley yard like it used to at Christmas mass. Everybody wanted to see this much-talked-about church. Was it really falling down, like the priest had repeatedly said? People were visibly moved when they walked inside the church, their heads instinctively swivelling upwards to the domed ceiling. 'It's beautiful,' we heard them say over and over. The mood was one of voyeuristic curiosity, but people spoke in hushed tones, reverent to the sacred spirit in the air. Money was freely thrown in our buckets, raffle tickets bought and real disappointment expressed when we told them our concert tickets had sold out.

While we had laughed at Jim McCarthy's staunch belief that the world would hear our story, it was him having the last laugh when Kerry O'Brien read his hard-to-decipher handwritten letter and sent a camera crew and journalist to record our story. Having a *7:30 Report* camera crew moving among the crowd, asking locals for their opinions on 'Saving St Brigid's', only served to add to an already surreal atmosphere. In this church we used to bow quietly in prayer. It was now becoming the scene of a national news story.

Meanwhile, in the hall there was work to do. A stockpile of food and flowers was overflowing the supper room, as men dragged hay bales and arranged fire pits outside. Mary O'Brien's daughter, Donna Dixon, laid out her screen-print T-shirts and session CDs were put out for sale, along with signs and bumper stickers bearing the slogans 'Keep St Brigid's in our Community' and 'I had a ball in the Crossley hall'. The room was buzzing, as people pitched in any way they could. I smiled quietly to myself when my couldn't-care-less-about-St-Brigid's little brother Michael turned up and spent the day on a ladder hanging green cloth and signage around the hall. Something happens when a community comes to life – the energy becomes infectious and you start doing what you didn't think you would, or cared about.

Like Liz. As chair, she had the responsibility of making a speech to thank everybody involved. Liz doesn't do public speaking. She looked like she was about to throw up. Her phone was running hot, as people rang; some rudely and abusively to complain about the fact our tickets were sold out. Trying to coordinate who'd made it on the list, and who hadn't, turned into a nightmare, and all of a sudden there were far too many cooks in the kitchen and a heated debate erupted. Stress levels were running high. The advert had said tickets available at the door – what do we do when a whole lot of people make the drive out to Crossley and they can't get in the door? We hated the idea of turning people away. If this was our last stand, we should jam them in any way we could, some suggested. Others highlighted health and safety concerns. Others said we needed to consider the musical talent and the quality of the sound. Three hundred and thirty tickets had been sold. How many people, exactly, can we fit in the hall? We had planned on a fairly casual affair where people could bring a hamper and a bottle of wine and sit around a table. A quick count of our chairs showed we were going to be well short; the tables were hauled out, a rushed trip was made to the party hire place in town, and we were set for the night.

Like everything to do with St Brigid's, we had to think on our feet and hope for the best. It was the way things often went that we didn't really make a decision but came up with a backup plan: open the church (LJ Hooker didn't have to know) and ask the musicians, after playing in the hall, to play a second time in the church. St Brigid must have been looking down on us, because somehow we figured it all out and became friends again.

Still suffering from jetlag, her back playing up and completely overwhelmed by the chaos in our community since their absence, Mum stayed close to home that day, making sandwiches and fielding phone calls from old timers who were on their way to Crossley from afar, some with tickets, some without. When I rushed home to pick up something, she kept asking me, 'Do you all know what you're doing?' For so long, it was Mum and Dad that made things happen at Crossley; but in the six weeks they'd been gone, a changing of the guard had occurred. They were now turning up to meetings, wondering who these people were, twenty-odd gathered around the table, non-Catholics and all, who were spending day and night fighting to save St Brigid's.

And compared with Mum's long to-do lists of my childhood, our tools of the trade were far different. These days, we were more likely to post our news to our hundreds of unknown 'friends' on Facebook than the church bulletin; when we needed a piece of information in a meeting, we Googled it on our iPhones; in the course of a day, I'd have multiple conversations via email to solve multiple challenges without so much as picking up the phone. In Mum's time, everybody brought a plate and shared it around. These days we did the same, but each of us had to have food-handling certificates and we had to fill out a form itemising every last ingredient of our donation for Moyne Shire health and safety concerns, in case someone was allergic to something and sued us for it. The world had gone mad and there was no better example of this than how things had changed at the Crossley hall. We had witnessed a seismic shift from a time when people freely donated time, food and labour to an over-regulated society, hamstrung by the threat of litigation and bogged down in bureaucratic process.

'No wonder people won't put their hands up to help anymore,' Mum would say in bewilderment. It was all rather perplexing to a couple in their seventies. Having said that, Mum has adapted very well to changing times, and stationed in her usual spot at Crossley, at the by-donation tea and coffee station, she does everything she can to accommodate the various requests for soy milk, chai tea and vegan butter that flow thick and fast these days. It's been quite an education for all of us! When somebody asks at Crossley 'Do you have espresso?' even I, an unashamed coffee snob, wish I could tell them to get over themselves and have a Nescafe. In my mind, it's refreshing to know there's some place left in the world that doesn't feel the need to be gourmet, to be trendy. A point well taken at Crossley – people lick their lips at the hearty soups, chunky steak-paste sandwiches and tasty biscuits and slices doled out in ridiculous quantities (always by donation – none of us except Gerry have the time or inclination to count dollars and cents) and once they realise this isn't an espresso kind of place, it ends up somehow adding to the appeal. The philosophy at St Brigid's is we'll serve you well, and hope that in return you'll help us along the way. And hopefully Saint Brigid is up there, warding off the litigation.

This afternoon, as the phone rang off the hook and Mum made sandwiches with a worried look on her face, I could only assure her that everything would be alright, and it wasn't her job to carry the burden anymore.

Back at the hall, Liz was doing enough of that for all of us. She was wandering around, doing everything and nothing at the same time, muttering about insurance and things catching fire, like there was an imminent threat, when her husband rang. At home chopping down a tree, he'd fallen and then afterwards, backing out of the driveway, he knocked over the front fence.

'Are you alright?' I heard Liz ask impatiently.

She didn't wait for the reply, before she barked back, 'Can you not come here tonight? I need you to keep Stella at home with you. I can't handle anything else right now.'

She hung up. 'Sam just fell out of a tree and crashed into the front fence.'

I cracked up laughing. It sounded like a funniest home video. Liz burst into tears. 'I don't think I can do it tonight, Gina.'

Shane took her outside and lit a cigarette for her. He told her that even he gets nervous on stage. 'You'll be alright,' he said. She dragged heavily on the cigarette, pulled herself together, and came back inside.

At 6 pm, the fire pits were alight, children in scarves and beanies played on the hay bales, a billboard painted with 'Our community for Sale' rested against the front entrance, women cut sandwiches in the kitchen, musicians did sound-checks in the hall – the electric buzz in the air told us that something memorable would happen here tonight. By 6:30 pm the crowds were arriving. Liz stood at the door, still looking faint, negotiating politely with people who hadn't pre-booked a ticket. The queue snaked out the door and across the car park. The south-westerly wind blew up from the ocean; people pulled in their scarves tighter and inched towards the warmth of hundreds of other people packed inside.

Brett Clarke welcomed us to country and wished us well in keeping our beautiful church in our hands, before a spirited rendition of 'Keep the Dream Alive'. Then Andy Alberts took to the stage and belted out a song that had me tapping my feet and clapping away: 'How many times did I try to leave this town, / But this town will always bring me back'. I cheered louder than anyone else in the hall and in my mind's eye I saw on my calendar my first day at work in Sydney, two days after we were due for a decision on St Brigid's. Why do I do it to myself, I wondered.

Shane's daughter Myra sang 'Silvermines', the one about her famine-orphan, great-great-grandmother, in her stunning, sweet voice, punctuated by the sorrowful sounds of the harmonica.

Then it was Lizzie's turn. For someone who said she would faint, she did brilliantly. She looked out at the crowd, and when she told them that 'we are completely overwhelmed by your support' she, more than anyone, meant it. It's one thing to sit around a committee table and convince each other we could make it happen, but it's another when you're sitting in a bank manager's office, trying to prove your community is worth the twenty-five-year loan. She reeled off a list of thank-yous, and then finished by simply saying, 'to anyone who has helped us, in any way, we love you. Please stay with us on our journey.'

Then it was Teresa's turn. 'This hall is all the warmer for your being here tonight,' she said. She talked about what it meant to belong in a community, a universal feeling we all knew. We all have that feeling about a place that means something to us – the house we grew up in, the park where we used to play. Hers was an open invitation to make St Brigid's a place for all to share, to gather and reconnect.

She spelt out, for those who didn't yet know, the challenge we faced: 'These buildings are currently up for tender. On July 17, we run the risk of losing them. If we lose this hall, and we lose that church, all of a sudden we don't have anywhere to meet anymore, nowhere for the girls to practise their dancing; for the musicians to play. We won't have these gatherings anymore. We believe we have a responsibility to this community to save them.'

Standing on the stage beside her, Liz bowed her head. Those words cut deep. It was funny to think that only four weeks ago, we said to each other we would attend the first meeting 'for Mum and Dad'. Four weeks had felt like a lifetime. The responsibility we now felt had far less to do with our parents than a realisation that we, too, felt a responsibility to leave a legacy in this place.

Teresa spelt out our dream of turning St Brigid's into a cultural and heritage centre. She talked about demographic change in our area, the booming population, how many more young families and children now lived in the district. 'We believe this is a vibrant and thriving community. We have what it takes to keep this place alive.'

Listening to Teresa, anything felt possible. She made a lot of sense; it was hard to imagine anybody could object to her. Anybody except the hierarchy of the Catholic Church.

And then came the plea. 'Your generosity will not go unnoticed.

We will not let you down. We're serious, we're determined and we have great faith in each other to make this happen.'

Shane sat beside me, urging Teresa on.

'This may be the last time we're all here at St Brigid's. Or it might be the night we say "Do you remember that night when we saved St Brigid's".'

The crowd erupted in rapturous applause.

Next was the new Mayor of the Moyne Shire, Ken Gale. His message was short and to the point: 'We've been told over and over again that the Catholic Church owns these buildings. But we all know deep down that historically and morally, they belong to the people of Crossley.' His voice strong and sure.

The crowd whistled and cheered.

Next, it was time for The Friends of St Brigid's to take to the stage. Or the 'choir of hard doers', as Gerry dryly told the crowd. To the searching sounds of the violin, Shane and Myra launched into the first verse of 'The Church up on the Hill'. We joined in on the chorus – for a choir full of people who last night couldn't hold a note, tonight we felt like we could raise the roof. On a roll, the choir of hard doers joined Marcia Howard in a spirited rendition of 'When Irish Eyes are Smiling', for old times' sake. No one could help but smile, watching the grin on the faces of Mum, Dad, Shane, Gerry and Teresa arm-in-arm on stage.

Afterwards, the Friends of St Brigid's choir followed the cue of the musicians and went across to the church, and climbed the sagging stairs to the choir loft. We've often been told by visiting musicians that the acoustics in the church are amazing. The church was softly lit, candles and lamps dotted around, collected from our bedrooms and desks at home. We were standing high above the overflow crowd who couldn't squeeze into the hall, their eyes glued to ours, the sound of our voices reverberating across the domed ceiling down to the altar, off the stain glass windows and back again; as we sang in full voice, hairs on the back of my neck stood on end, etching the memory in my brain. We sang the chorus over twice, three times, stronger and louder each time, almost as if we were willing ourselves to victory. It was a moment I'll never forget. The look on the faces of the crowd below told me they felt the same. The applause was long and loud. It was a song written for that precise moment, and everybody in the room knew it would never be sung in quite the same way again.

There's a church up on the hill
Some days it's peaceful and still
And the world seems a million miles away
This church that's made of stone
Was built with love and love alone
A light still shines from that church up on the hill

Our people died on Ireland's streets
Their children starving at their feet
Or out into the great wild world young lives were sent
With little but the will to live
The old ones cried first day they went
Into that church up on the hill

Well they laboured down below
In the fields their crops they'd grow
And then walk the well-worn way to Sunday church
Daniel Mannix rose to talk
St Brigid's blessing be on you all
And your children's children in that church up on the hill

And the Angelus rings
The working day to close it brings
Through the struggle and the laughter
Every day
So devoted so devout
They had so little but went without
To build that church up on the hill
Fade away, not fade away
Survive and live another day
The light's still shining from that church up on the hill

Saving St Brigid's

And the Angelus rings
The working day to close it brings
Through the struggle and the laughter
Every day
So devoted so devout
They had so little but went without
To build that church up on the hill
Fade away, not fade away
Survive and live another day
A light still shines from that church
Up on the hill

To welcome all to that church up on the hill

We were then treated to the wisdom and the experience of someone who knows a thing or two about community and the pain of having it taken away.

'When Shane told me what was going on here, it offended me. When you take something from a peoples, something precious, they are diminished. They are lesser for it,' said Archie Roach softly, wearing his signature red beanie, lingering over each word.

'We talk about not a place so much belonging to us, but we belonging to a place. This is the sense that I get here. You can feel the belonging. The people, they belong here.'

He had so much to teach us, I thought. There was so much we had yet to really learn from our history.

'Once they keep chipping away, chipping away,' he said slicing the air with his hand, 'at that old community spirit, it's just goin' up and go and walk away and leave us.'

'That old spirit had a name before it was called community. It was called place,' and then in tribute to what St Brigid's meant to all of us who belonged here, he played 'A Child was Born Here'.

Archie talked about not knowing his mum and dad, taken away in the stolen generation, but said he remembers them through the stories and memories of others. 'They told me, your folks were good folks, they were good people,' he said. 'It's some consolation. It makes me feel good.'

I am always amazed at how gentle he is, in the face of what he has been through in life. His words rang like warning bells to me, that if we weren't careful, we might end up repeating the same mistakes of the past by devaluing our heritage and the sacred space and communities our Irish forebears built for us.

In the same way I've asked my parents the question 'Why didn't anyone do anything?' to prevent the stolen generation, I imagined my children one day peering across the fence of a privatised St Brigid's church, transformed into a block of apartments perhaps or a bed and breakfast, and asking me the same, 'Why didn't anyone do anything?' Whatever happened from here, at least I could say we tried.

Ruby Hunter talked about how their people are always fighting to find a place to meet, that in a world where there is so little space left for community to gather, we should protect the communal places we have left.

'To be invited here, it makes us feel that we're all together, at least we understand that meeting is a great thing, and we can share our strength.'

More applause.

In today's *Warrnambool Standard* newspaper, Shane wrote a beautiful feature article on 'why St Brigid's matters', summing up why we needed to preserve memory and history. On the opposite page, the paper's editorial entitled 'An Act of Betrayal', sat alongside a cartoon of Shane Howard, guitar in hand, outside St Brigid's, with his hit album title, *Spirit of Place*. Father Frank Brennan once credited Shane Howard for sowing the seed of Reconciliation in this country, with his hit song 'Solid Rock'. I grew up on Shane's music, but it wasn't until I was 20 year old, driving the back roads to Melbourne, 'Solid Rock' blaring from my stereo, when the power of it fully hit home. For some reason, on this particular day, that one little word, 'genocide', cut through me in a way it hadn't before, and I pulled to the side of the road, sitting under the gum trees out the back of Camperdown, crying my eyes out for this land, carved up and spoiled and sold. I cried for the children, their sense of self and identity forever damaged, crying for their broken mothers, their lost language and ruined communities. And then I cried at the sense of responsibility that this knowledge entailed. Now, thirty years after his song hit No. 1 and bravely challenged white Australia to face its black history, Shane had brought together two ancient cultures in our little country hall in south-west Victoria and by doing so, was gently asking us to think about what we'd learned.

Listening to Archie and Ruby, and the powerful messages of the amazing singer-songwriters that shared their stories, I was again reminded that Saving St Brigid's was about much more than just us.

We would save this place if it was the last thing we did. We'd pulled together an absolute treat of a concert in only ten days. In the music and the food and the warm words said around the fire, we knew people's hearts had been touched. When we danced to Andy Alberts' song at the end, 'Gunditjmara Land. This is my land, this is my home, it's in my veins, it's in my soul', it felt like an open door, an invitation that we could join together and share this land, if we respected its sacredness and upheld the spirits of our elders, black and white, Irish and Indigenous. Tonight, it felt like more than an important step in Saving St Brigid's. It felt like what reconciliation might look and sound and feel like: people coming together to celebrate their song and their story and their strength. Tonight, we were no longer a community divided by religious or racial difference or intolerance. We were writing a new chapter, one characterised by respect, tolerance and compassion, as a legacy to our children.

SAVING ST BRIGID'S

^ Stained glass window in the church loft

^ View to the altar

^ Billboards that line the highway tell the story.

^ The community rally around to save St Brigid's, with Liz and baby Stella in the foreground: *The Age*, August 2007.

^ Mary O'Brien (left) and Regina Lane (right) pose for *The Warrnambool Standard* to explain why St Brigid's resonates across the generations, 6 June 2009.

^ March down Liebig Street, Warrnambool, 17 July 2009

What would Saint Brigid say?

church built with an emphasis on compassion appears to be shattering a community, reports **MARY ALEXANDER**

We'll fight on, vow supporters

Friends rejoice
Church sale a testament to effort

Stars back Crossley
Luhrmann, Black and Brown join in

Friends raise $30,000

Loan plan for church

Church sale put on hold
Community hopes to buy St Brigid's

An act of betrayal

AR BIKIES, NCY A URCH?

Morale boost for organ...

By EVERARD HIMMELREICH

ORGANISERS of a campaign to save St Brigid's church and hall at Crossley for community use received a big morale boost from a strong response to a fundraising concert last week.
Friends of St Brigid's spokeswoman Teresa O'Brien said more than 400 people turned up at the concert at the Killarney camping ground on the...

The Standard SATURDAY

CROSSLEY: Rebels offered St Brigid's as new clubhouse

A passionate community is refusing to let its church go

For many people, St...

Group vows to bid Church to go on market

By MARY ALEXANDER

A THREE-YEAR campaign to save Crossley's historic St Brigid's Church is expected to come to an end this month when the building is finally placed on the market.
Warrnambool real estate agency LJ Hooker is due to call for tenders for the 95-year-old church, hall and surrounding land.
The Friends of St Brigid's group, set up to raise money and keep the property in community hands, has vowed to make a bid.
It has called its members to an urgent meeting at the Crossley hall next Monday night to discuss the tender.
"The time is now to pull together as a community and save these culturally important buildings..."

"If we don't, it will just sit there and rot."
He said funds from the sale of the property would stay in the parish and be used to refurbish other church buildings.
LJ Hooker director Paul Harris said the sale campaign would be finalised at a meeting with parish representatives this week.
Koroit's Felix Meagher, who helped compose the music for last year's epic film Australia, is a strong supporter of the campaign to save St Brigid's for the community.
"These are inspirational buildings to people of Irish-Australian background," Mr Meagher said. "They are much beloved buildings and I hope every..."

...ol chapter of the Rebels motorcycle club would have enjoyed a commanding view fr... Hooker's offer.
Digital image: SHERILL

St Brigid's ... shaky ground

By CHAMON VOGELS

THE future of Crossley's St Brigid's church is certain with a local community group need serious financial assistance to stop the prop... falling into private investors' hands.
The community's historic Catholic church, and tennis courts sit on a two-hectare (five-a... block that is earmarked for sale.
The Friends of St Brigid's group wants to re... the property to keep it in public hands.
FOSB secretary Teresa O'Brien said the g...

HOLY FIGH HITS SNA

LETTER OF THE WEEK

Sale a 'moral outrage'

THERE has been much justifiable controversy and division regarding the rushed sale of St Brigid's Catholic Church, hall complex and land — situated at Crossley since the 1870s — against the wishes of the local community who want to return and develop the complex together with local support, Moyne Shire and government grants.
As is well known our ancestors donated, built and maintained this magnificent complex. They were the survivors of the Great Famine in Ireland and after tyrannical persecution, property confiscation and religious persecution, came and pioneered this area.
With much dedication and sacrifice they built St Brigid's, which was dedicated by the Archbishop of Melbourne or Mannix for its blessings (The Standard, June 28, 1914) with the expectation the gathering would remain for centuries to come.
Clearly as rushed sale is a total and complete violation and breach of trust by the hierarchy and finance committee of the Ballarat diocese.
It is a moral outrage to let it...

In the gun: St Brigid's historic church at Crossley.

...aware and informed in detail of the community's needs and plans for its future, knowing it is not theirs.
To say we will refurbish Koroit church with some of the sale proceeds is tantamount to saying it is OK to rob Peter to pay Paul — not acceptable in this recognised Irish capital of Australia.
Furthermore there is a profound total lack of vision by the hierarchy in selling St Brigid's with the pro-jected explosion of population in this area. With $6 billion infrastructure plans in place and many projects under way, this area is expected to become the energy capital of Victoria.
The Crossley-Killarney area could well become a satellite city of Warrnambool within the next 30 years because of its location, scenic beauty and close proximity to the Prince Highway.

With this analysis would the future hierarchy expect this generation and future ones to build another new St Brigid's at far greater cost, knowing the past history and our present needs decision — I doubt it.
The hierarchy and finance committee of the Ballarat diocese must show some sense and co-operate with the Save St Brigid's committee rather than expect the 30 pieces of silver for its sale and hierarchy what may ask that we hierarchy what would Christ say on this moral decision? Needless to know what St Brigid's opinion would be as it was built in memory of her, for us to carry on the great work and charity of this great patron saint of Ireland.
Let the Catholic hierarchy today take particular heed of the community feelings of division over this sale and return St Brigid's to its rightful owners as a trust of St Brigid's for the whole community's benefit. Stop the sale now and negotiate sensibly while the opportunity still exists — do not sell St Brigid's, hand it back.

Jim McCarthy, Rooneys Road, Warrnambool

ARY ALEXANDER

CROSSLEY: Church does a deal with Friends

IT'S THEIRS!

CROSSLEY CONCERT

By ALEX JOHNSON

AFTER a three-year battle to save St Brigid's church and hall the Crossley community yesterday claimed victory — believing their offer for the property had been accepted.
Celebrations were tinged with uncertainty as Friends of St Brigid's secretary Teresa O'Brien, who had the documents were yet to be signed.
"Apparently our bid has..."

for the property. Mr Harris declined to comment yesterday.
The Koroit parish finance committee rejected three tenders for the property two weeks ago and placed it on the open market for $429,000.
"This figure was reduced to an undisclosed "compromised" figure during a meeting between the Friends of St Brigid's and the finance committee last week.
Ms O'Brien said on Sunday that the group had to raise another $100,000 by Thursday to be able to offer the...

available in coming days. Ms O'Brien said the group was "ecstatic and overwhelmed" that there has been a change of heart" among the finance committee members.
"It's great news, it's fantastic and everything but until we have got the document signed we are feeling a little bit of shock."
Father Bill Van de Camp, of the Koroit parish, refused to confirm the sale yesterday.
He said the finance committee had always been prepared to sell the property to the group if it could raise the asking price.

nite but we presume (the documents) will be signed.".
Ms O'Brien said the group held an eight-hour meeting which ended at midnight on Sunday to find enough funds to make yesterday's bid.
"We have put forward the absolute best possible bid that we can.
"We will now work really hard to keep the buildings and be able to do them up but we have got a strategy.
"When those papers are signed the doors will be opened to everyone to come and help us celebrate this great..."

FATHER BILL VAN DE...

Nobody kno... will go aho... nothing is s... but we pre... (the docum... will be s...

^ Archie Roach and Ruby Hunter sing for St Brigid's, June 2009.

^ 'When Irish Eyes Are Smiling': The Friends of St Brigid's take to the stage, June 2009.

^ An Irish session in full swing

^ Time to celebrate, September 2009

^ The Friends of St Brigid's examine hundred-year-old titles, (left to right) Gerry O'Brien, Elise Gillin (standing), Liz Lane, Mick Lane, Teresa O'Brien, with Grenville Skewes in the background, September 2009.

^ A piece of 'our' history – St Brigid's on the market

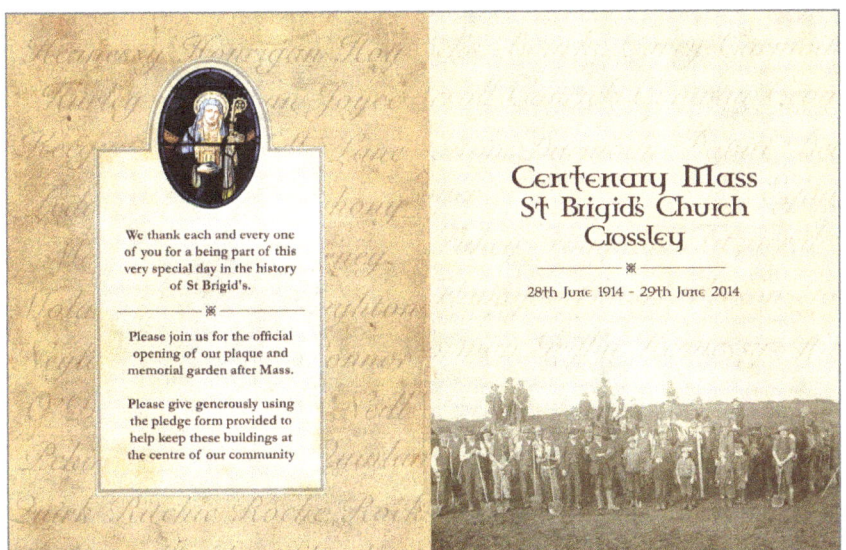

^ The Centenary Mass booklet. The photo depicts our forefathers on the cleared site of St Brigid's, Crossley in 1913.

^ The congregation at St Brigid's Centenary Mass

^ 'Take this, all of you and eat': the 100th birthday cake, along with a challis loaned from the O'Brien family

^ Nearly 70 years after they sat side by side at St Brigid's making their first Holy Communion Dad and Gerry O'Brien receive the Eucharist from Fr Bill Van de Camp.

^ Friends of St Brigid's Chair and member of the centenary committee, Dennis Bushell, opens celebrations in the hall as three elders prepare to cut the cake.

^ Helen Doyle receives praise for researching and recording 100 of our local family histories in her book, *The Church on the Hill*.

^ Standing on the paved impression of St Brigid's Cross, Bishop Paul Bird and Fr Van de Camp bless our Well of Healing and Peace.

^ My heroes

CHAPTER SIXTEEN

A black day

Whenever there is Irish music playing at Crossley, any music really, the night doesn't finish before 3 am. Once they get going with their fiddles and their banjos and their drums, they go some place, and to watch them is to have a deeply meditative experience. Of course, there is lots of chatting and laughter and tea too. Forever the caretakers, Mum and Dad always stay faithfully to the end, to make sure all is well before the lights are turned out.

Our Sunday meeting was the most relaxed yet. We all rolled back to Crossley at 10 am, someone fired up a barbie and we stepped into a familiar routine. Dismantling photos and memorabilia, washing dishes and mopping floors, scouring the yard for beer bottles and packing up lights and the last of the hay bales – a good clean up at Crossley can sometimes be as much fun as the night itself. The sun was shining; children ran around, the *7:30 Report* camera crew interviewed people and an Irish fiddle played loud on the stereo.

'We raised $10,000 last night,' Gerry reported. He'd spent half the night counting and recounting out every last 5 cent piece. Gerry hates to be 5 cents out. He was looking very pleased with himself. Teresa read out the correspondence. I looked forward to this part of the meeting. It was like our dose of positivity, that no matter the outcome, all this wouldn't be in vain.

Saving St Brigid's

Teresa read out a letter from Sister Clare Griffen, from the Brigidine Congregational Leadership Team in Ireland.

I write on behalf of the Brigidine Congregational Leadership Team with a message of support for your dreams and vision for St Brigid's. Our prayers are very much with you as negotiations continue over these weeks. May you continue to sense St Brigid's cloak of compassion and hope around you and your little community. While St Brigid's fire burns quietly in Kildare, we too will be carrying her flame of hope and prayer in our hearts and homes as you work to rekindle life in St Brigid's and your community.

Every blessing, Clare.

Teresa gave us another shot to our arm. 'PILCH have found us a barrister, a QC specialising in property and trusts, to investigate the case.' Ripples of excitement flowed through the atmosphere of content.

Helen Doyle, the historian, was putting together a nomination to amend the Moyne Shire Heritage Overlay so St Brigid's would be protected before the tender closed, to ensure that even if we lost, a developer couldn't come in and knock the place down.

Archie and Ruby and all the musicians had agreed to do another concert in just over two weeks' time. It was Shane's idea to capture the Melbourne communities' imagination and turn on a great old country hall night in the big smoke. As we sat there, exhausted but elated, the day after the night before, Teresa tried to firm up the details to take our road show to the Thornbury Theatre in Melbourne. We had ten days to do it all over again. Could we muster the energy?

Of course we could, and if not St Brigid would help us along.

Anything felt possible now.

Our elation was short-lived. Our early bid had been rejected. Father Van de Camp had knocked us back with the puzzling rejoinder that 'I'm not necessarily selling to the highest bidder'. But the canon lawyer, and the Bishop for that matter, had said that the priest must sell to the highest bidder. Why was nothing straightforward with these men? What game was he playing?

Bad news was followed by potentially good news. Councillor Colin Ryan was set to move a motion at the Moyne Shire council meeting to request a heritage overlay from the Minister for Planning. Colin Ryan assumed, and therefore so did we, that the motion would be passed. Then, any new owner would have to apply to council to have any changes made on the exterior and interior of the building. As the close of tender drew closer, this was *some* consolation that the buildings would be protected, if the worst happened on July 17 and the buildings were sold off to a developer.

But the motion was rejected with a 4-3 vote against us. The councillors believed that they might be compromised by agreeing to such an overlay halfway through the tender process and would be seen by others to reduce the potential for a higher bid via tender. They didn't want to be seen to be actively influencing the outcome of the tender process. We'd now become accustomed to the idea that we couldn't really rely on the Church to take care of the communities' interests, but the idea that elected councillors seemed to be putting the Church ahead of the citizens felt like complete hypocrisy.

Again we were hit with the reality that in less than three weeks, our beloved St Brigid's could possibly be knocked over, or slapped into the shape of a three-storey motel or stripped back to become a set of sleek apartments.

Not that any of these options appeared to concern Father Van de Camp.

The eighth of July was my twenty-ninth birthday. For days now, we'd all sat glued to the *7:30 Report* in case our story went to air without forewarning. I'd only just rung around a few friends to see if they wanted to share a birthday dinner, and was on my way from St Andrews to the pub in Fitzroy, when Liz rang to say tonight was the night. I couldn't get off the train quick enough. I politely asked the barman could he switch the channel to the ABC please? He looked at the old blokes at the bar watching the sports channel and shook his head.

'There's a black-and-white TV out the back,' he offered.

I played with the rabbit ears until the fuzz was gone then sat down expectantly waiting for Kerry to come on the telly. I'd hardly seen my friends in weeks, months even. Some of them, not even since I'd come home from overseas. A couple of friends randomly turned up who I hadn't seen in years.

'Shhh,' was my first word when they walked in the door. They patiently sat and waited while the segment was on, and then I breathlessly filled them in on the month that was.

Our eight minutes of fame on the ABC was a beautifully shot portrayal of the green fields and meandering cattle and old-fashioned dairies that I called home. I could barely wait to hear what they had to say.

Thousands of kilometres from Dublin, four hours' drive from Melbourne sits a little piece of Ireland. And alongside these green paddocks and potato farms between the local villages of Killarney and Crossley sits a church atop a hill. For the Irish settlers who arrived here 150 years ago this was the place to celebrate their strong Catholic faith. For many of their descendants, Saint Brigid's now represents the last remaining link to the past and it's a link they're not willing to part with.

There was Jim McCarthy being interviewed sitting among the Celtic crosses of the cemetery, talking about his family motto: 'To be brave and faithful, nothing is impossible'. And there was Teresa in the foreground of the looming red-brick church, telling the world that these buildings were more than bricks and mortar. And there was Father Van de Camp, telling the reporter that 'We can't live on the laurels of the past. We have to move on.'

Father Van de Camp went on to report that 'the Church is not into selling churches. It's into building churches and maybe if they were church attenders and supporting the church financially, it might still be going.'

It was infuriating listening to him. We'd offered financial support, probably more than anyone else in the parish ever had, and he'd rejected it.

And there was Bill Dwyer, Mary O'Brien's brother, who farms up the road from Crossley, two generations after his forefathers donated the land for our church and hall.

'We still think of it as a church. But it's really a shed now.'

And there was Father Van de Camp again, insulting our modest efforts at rebuilding a community. 'It is an emotional campaign and therefore it ceases to be logical.'

The reporter asked him what he would do if a commercial entity

A BLACK DAY

outbid us.

'If somebody comes in with $700 000 we would be stupid to say we're not accepting that.'

'So an art gallery or a B&B or a restaurant?' the reporter enquired.

'That would be wonderful, yes,' he said, not realising the corner he was painting himself into. Why would he be so welcoming of a commercial enterprise; and not find it in himself to support the efforts of a group of people to set up our own community, cultural and heritage centre? The answer was anywhere upwards of $400 000, it was plain to see.

The segment finished with Kerry O'Brien's boyish grin. 'Saint Brigid herself might have the last word.'

They say that if you pray to St Brigid, she will lead you on a merry dance before granting the miracle. It felt anything but a merry dance, feeling like you were always ten steps behind, dancing the waltz to techno music, trying not to step on toes, bumping into those around you, while keeping a smile on your face and reminding yourself that this might just be the time of your life. All of us had moments when it was all too much and we simply wanted to get off the dance floor. But the music hadn't finished and you hardly wanted to be a wallflower, wondering if you were missing the moment. So we kept our feet in motion and hoped soon we might dance to the tune of our own music.

As the emails of support flowed in afterwards from around the country, there was a flurry of cheques thrown our way, but none of them put us anywhere near the ballpark $700 000 that was now being bandied around. 'Thanks for igniting our imaginations' came one response. 'I am not Catholic and I am not Irish and I have never been to Crossley, but I think that Church building should stay in your community.' 'Your ancestors would be proud' came another. 'How do we learn from the messages of our ancestral traditions? Your battle is a wonderful example', 'I want your buildings and your spirituality and your heritage to belong to you (and to me too)', and then simply 'Where does one donate?' It was a huge boost to hear the response of people we'd never met, who in eight minutes understood at the deepest level what it was that we were fighting for.

While the weight of public opinion was on our side, it was never going to be enough to win the day. Hundreds of thousands of people came out onto the streets to rally against war in Iraq, and it didn't stop the government from making an unpopular decision. Until now, our fight had largely taken place within the internal structures of the Church, because of the deep respect and corresponding expectation we placed in it as a moral institution. Now it was clear that through deliberate policies and practices of the Catholic Church – silencing victims, behind-closed-doors negotiation, a lack of obligation or commitment to community consultation and protecting their brotherhood and their wealth at all costs – they were causing and perpetuating an ongoing conflict that might have been avoided with a few good men and an open door. Now that a light had been shone on the problem and the wider public had become aware, the Church's actions were suddenly violating more widely held societal values, beyond our mere Catholic ones. We wondered, as our barrister prepared her preliminary advice, if the Church's actions might also violate the civil law of this nation.

Unfortunately, civil law didn't work in our favour either. The break in the chain business – the irregularities in the titles didn't amount to much, as predicted. Nor did the question of a breach of trust. The advice we had from the QC stated what we'd already assumed to be true. Gifts to churches and religious institutions are presumed to be made for religious purposes and not to be gifts to the present members of the congregation. This legal argument nicely complemented the conservative religious right, who were vehemently arguing in the newspaper and in derogatory emails to our secretary that the church was built as a church, and not for social or cultural purposes. The thing is, no matter the legal precedence on this question, those people are our grandparents. We know what their intentions were when they built this church. It was on the written record, and enough people in our community, including my father, held living memory of them and an intimate understanding of their intention to build a church as 'a legacy to their children'. We saw our community as a living embodiment of their hopes and wishes and their living, continuing faith, and simply believed that as descendants of those who had gifted these buildings, we should have certain privileges in the decision-making to sell it.

A BLACK DAY

The notion that if the buildings couldn't be used for religious purposes then they may as well become one man's castle, argued by the religious right and supported by this legal clause, absolutely dumbfounded me. To me, and now even my religious mother was beginning to agree, a community working together in solidarity towards the common good is as much an act of faith as a community sitting bowed in prayer. This is not a new revelation. Jesus Christ challenged the high priests and Pharisees of the Jewish hierarchy and made it absolutely clear that dogma without real action in the world is meaningless. This was the revelation of the New Testament.

Even overlooking the idea that the church and hall were donated for only religious purposes – a highly contestable notion – then surely, now once the gift our grandparents had given could be no longer used for express 'religious purposes' (itself an idea that could be challenged on at least two grounds – firstly, that there are plenty of people who, then and now, wanted to participate in the religious ceremonies of marriage, funerals and christening at St Brigid's but were denied that right, and secondly that before its closure St Brigid's had enjoyed a higher mass attendance rate than the Koroit church), surely the gift should be held in trust for purposes as close as possible to the spirit of the original donation. In other words, if the trust could no longer be carried out or upheld precisely as the donors intended, the donation should revert to the donors, or their descendants. Yet, in legal terms this is no small request. There is no precedent of a religious trust changing its nature and becoming secular. To pursue this line of reasoning would be not only to challenge the Catholic Church, but also to create a new legal precedent in Australia. There were all manner of legal possibilities and question marks and grey areas, that with time up our sleeves could be investigated and might potentially swing things in our favour, but given that time was not our friend, it was not surprising therefore, that the barrister formed the opinion that it would be difficult for The Friends of St Brigid's to oppose the sale on the grounds of a trust or proprietary interest.

It is the Supreme Court that oversees the jurisdiction of trusts, and only the Attorney General can legally bring a court application to seek a declaration regarding a charitable trust. We were three weeks away from the close of tender, so pursuing further action was nigh impossible, and given the heavily weighted factors against us, it was unlikely the Attorney General would spend public money bringing any proceeding. The QC's advice amounted to what we already knew: we must continue fundraising to purchase the buildings back.

The advice wasn't surprising, so we could hardly be deflated, especially when our questions provoked keen interest and great scrutiny. It was affirming to realise that our questions weren't of mere local interest, but had broader implications across the country. Given the significant role of the Catholic Church in contributing to social and cultural life and welfare in Australia, the fall in church attendance does not necessarily mean that the buildings and the institution that oversees them are not required by the communities that depend on them. For me, it poses a massive challenge to the Catholic Church to re-imagine itself and its role in society. The questions we raised aren't going to go away anytime soon.

There wasn't much time to dwell on the aborted legal challenge, for there was still much work to be done. Our 'Saving St Brigid's' show went on the road, and we held another successful fundraising concert in Melbourne, to the delight of a city audience. But we were exhausted, and no doubt our morale suffered under the legal and heritage setbacks and our early bid rejection, as predictable as they might have been. Another personal setback came for Shane, when his father had a severe stroke a few days before Shane flew out to Ireland for a tour with the Black Arm Band. We all felt for him and ourselves, too, for he would be sorely missed in the tough weeks ahead.

As chair, Liz had written to the Minister for Planning, Justin Madden (who incidentally is Shane's cousin, not that that fact proved helpful), requesting that he assist us in protecting the buildings before close of tender on the seventeenth of July. She got a letter back acknowledging that the vote of Moyne council was lost, and therefore no request had been made by council to the minister. And then they issued a statement we found hard to agree with. 'The sale of the property does not necessarily threaten either the church or the hall and does not warrant the intervention of the minister to apply heritage overlay controls.' The merry dance

A BLACK DAY

continued.

A faint feeling had begun to nag at some of us. Were we losing our grip on this campaign? No matter the logic of the Moyne Shire decision, the coverage it created cast another seed of doubt in the minds of people who wanted to believe that St Brigid's was old and empty, and we who wanted to save it were wishful-thinking stargazers. Some people looked further afield for support and sent through their ideas, 'Kevin Rudd is meeting with the Pope this week – perhaps we could get him to bat on our behalf?' It was suggested that we shine a light on the Pontifical Commission on the Cultural Heritage of the Church, to force Church leaders to abide by their own protocol. It was mind boggling and exhausting.

I tried to remind myself of Bill Moyer's 'eight stages of a social movement'. The perception of failure generally occurs just when a social movement is becoming outrageously successful, he says. We could only hope that the reluctance of the Shire to intervene merely highlighted the strength of our campaign. Surely success was just around the corner, I told myself.

For weeks, Liz had struggled to get quotes on insurance and was constantly told that the age of the buildings made them difficult to value and insure. As if deciding what cost we could mortgage a community's future wasn't difficult enough, but when those in the business failed to come up with a price, we were left wondering where on earth the Church got its figures from. A week before the tender closed, Mary-Ellen rang the Ballarat Diocese and found out the actual truth behind a familiar refrain.

'Churches cost a lot to maintain' we'd been constantly told in person and in public by the Church. They weren't telling us anything we didn't already know: it was our families who'd provided the total finances to fund such maintenance at St Brigid's for the last forty years. But the question of insurance costs was one that we couldn't answer. The parish of Koroit bore those costs, and the way the priests spoke, we figured they didn't come cheap.

'Guess what I found out about St Brigid's today?'

'It's been sold?' I wouldn't be surprised. Anything was possible.

'You know how they keep going on about the insurance? They make it sound like it costs an arm and a leg? Well, today I learned that

Saving St Brigid's

St Brigid's church is insured for $27 000 and the hall is insured for the same. The lady I spoke to at Catholic Church Insurance commented that the buildings mustn't be worth very much if that's all they're insured for. Clearly not in Father Van de Camp's eyes. And there he is last week on national television asking for seven bloody hundred thousand dollars!'

'They're insured to pay for a bulldozer to come in and clean up if the place burned down. Clearly they haven't placed any real value on St Brigid's for a long time. It just makes you so *mad* to think that all these years they've been talking up the high costs of insurance as if we have no comprehension, and they've been paying a pittance for it. I can't believe what they get away with!'

Four days before the tender closed, and we still hadn't secured a loan. Liz, Teresa and Gerry were spending endless hours on the phone and in the offices of bank managers trying to get the best deal they could. They were the ones required to sign off on the loan, and Liz was very much feeling the heat of having her details on the application, even though she was making the application on behalf of an Association. Still, not the kind of financial risks you entertain when you've just bought your own home and had a baby and are trying to establish yourself. By this time, Shane was in Ireland. He steadied Lizzie's nerves from the other end of the email.

Hi Liz,

I would love you to pass on my best wishes to everyone. I'm sorry I won't be here when the tender is announced, but I'll spread the word in Ireland. I may well be at St Brigid's well in Kildare, when the decision is announced, praying for good news from home.

You have all fought the good fight, faithfully and honourably, for the right reasons and you should hold your head high.

In the process, you have sent a message out across Australia about the values that are cherished here in this community and lit a fire in the heads of many more.

What a group. What a community! What a fighting spirit.

The moral choice will now fall on Father Bill (Van de Camp) and the finance committee.

A light still shines from that Church up on the hill.

Have no fear, St Brigid's cloak is over us all.

A BLACK DAY

Beannachtai,
Shane

My last pitch to the media was timed for the day the tender closed. I'd collected messages of support from some of our more high-profile supporters. I went to school with Jonathan Brown, the Brisbane Lions captain, whose parents had married at St Brigid's, and whose grandmother, Val Mugavin, always sat in the row behind us at Sunday mass. Archie Roach sent through a few words and Mary Black in Ireland sent her love along with Ted Egan AO from the Northern Territory. Film director Baz Lurhmann had even been to St Brigid's, and we had a great photo of him outside the church. I rounded up all their quotes and sent them out to the press.

The morning of the seventeenth of July, Teresa woke up with no voice. Six weeks of nonstop phone calls and endless meetings; early-morning radio interviews and late nights had taken their toll. For someone normally so vocal, it was pretty funny to hear only a squeak when she opened her mouth. So I was handballed the 7 am ABC interview. The host clearly hadn't picked up the day's paper, because when I acknowledged the support we'd received from near and far, and some unlikely quarters, he was audibly impressed when he read out the names of our all-star support crew. It was a feelgood start to the day.

We'd agreed that since we'd gone about our work quietly, the only proper way to submit our tender was to invite the community to share in the moment with us. Some worried that this was an antagonistic move; most of us just felt the need to mark the moment. We arranged to gather at the civic square in Warrnambool, and wearing our tshirts and armed with our placards and stickers and flags, we marched down Liebig Street, singing over and over 'The Church up on the Hill'. It would have been one of those cringeworthy moments, except that there were too many of us to let your individual ego be affected, and the claps and cheers and tooting horns we received along the way told us that we had the wider community's support right behind us. Paul Harris from LJ Hooker thought all his Christmases had come at once, to open the door of the real-estate agency to see fifty-flag bearing people wearing green singing in choir and the media hustling in the door to get a shot. We spent the afternoon sitting in the pub, reflecting on the rollercoaster the past six weeks had been and allowing ourselves, for the moment at least, to savour the taste of success. While we were yet to win the buildings, we knew we'd won the community's support, or at least enough of it to know that we were doing the right thing.

The Koroit parish finance committee met on the Monday night. We know, because my brother Patrick is on it, just another twist in the tale. He attends mass in Koroit and sends his children to St Patrick's primary across the road. When he stepped down as chair of The Friends of St Brigid's in 2008, he believed he could represent the Crossley community and his own wife and children's interests from inside the club, rather than hanging around the outside. I think by this stage he was probably wishing he hadn't, such was the pressure within our family, and the community.

Pat rang our house just after 10 pm. He sounded agitated and nervous. It was a difficult situation – his position on the Finance Committee required confidentiality, and yet he knew he had a responsibility to his family and the Crossley community who were desperate for news that night, fearing the worst: that some developer had slapped a million dollars on the table. He gave me nothing, so I handed the phone over to Dad, and slipped into the study, where I quietly picked up the phone. He didn't even spill any beans to Dad and so they played this game of Dad asking one-word questions like 'Was our bid competitive?' and Pat answering with a small yes. It was clear that the finance committee hadn't received the deluge of tenders from 'Melbourne' they were expecting. So we were in the game, I had to suppose, but the sound of Pat's voice gave me little confidence.

I woke up the next morning with a tummy bug. Mum had it too. Perhaps it was just the nerves, but I felt washed out and yukky and after I drove Michael to work at 6 am, I fell into a deep sleep until 11 am. At lunch time, Pat dropped in to pick up the mower and I pried a few words out of him. He didn't talk money, just said that all tenders were below expectations. It didn't sound to me like we were out of the game, but nor was it what I wanted to hear. Fired up as I was, wishing I could just walk into that meeting and give them my two cents and make them all see what

A BLACK DAY

we stood to lose, I didn't envy the position Pat was in. I knew it wasn't that easy. These people were friends from our childhood, the mums and dads that had been on the 'Parents and Friends' at St Pats, who worked on the school canteen, whose kids we went to school with. I don't think it was an easy time for any of them. Least of all Pat. Because of his previous involvement with The Friends of St Brigid's, he felt he was perceived to be pushing a purely St Brigid's agenda, when in fact he actually truly did believe that keeping St Brigid's in the community was in the best interests of the entire parish. But it appeared that others didn't see it that way.

The committee were to reconvene that night.

Liz, Teresa and I spent Tuesday writing up notes for Pat to present to the finance committee on our behalf – a list of positives and negatives for the choice in front of them. The list of positives for FOSB was long, of course; so was the list of negatives as to why they shouldn't reject all offers and put the buildings on the open market. Given all the press the community had in its favour, and with heritage applications pending, rural zoning and a clear position from the Council Mayor, who'd want to buy them now? I went home just after 4 pm and tidied up the notes perfectly for Pat. When I rang to deliver them, I found out that he'd just left. The meeting started at 5 pm, not 7 pm as I thought. Bugger.

I spent the next two hours lying in front of the fire, paralysed in suspense. When Mum sat down after dinner, St Brigid's prayer card in hand, the candle burning that the Brigidine nuns in Ireland had given her beneath the picture of St Brigid's well in Kildare, I watched her in prayer and suddenly felt the urge to join her. Agitated and unable to focus on anything, not even packing my clothes for my imminent move to Sydney, I took the prayer card and read along with her, praying for St Brigid to grant the miracle we'd been waiting for. I hadn't prayed with my parents since the last time they made me say the rosary with them around the fire at home, when I was about thirteen. Then, I squirmed in my chair and hated them for being so embarrassing as they yelled at me for forgetting the words, or more likely, stubbornly refusing to say them, convinced I was the last thirteen-year-old in the world whose parents made them say the rosary at home. Now things felt like they'd come full circle, and when all the letters had been written and all the lobbying had taken place, there didn't feel like there was anything left to do, except pray.

Eventually I rang Pat's to get an answer, even as Mum and Dad insisted I shouldn't. Again he was coy and wouldn't let anything slip. The bottom line was that still no decision had been reached. In fact, unable to make a decision, the finance committee handed over control of the buildings to LJ Hooker.

'What does that mean?' I said shaking my head at the idea of Paul Harris smacking his lips together in glee with dollar signs in his eyes.
The finance committee were clearly expecting more than what any of the received tenders had offered. 'The tenders were less than market price,' Pat told me.

'What the fuck does that mean? What *is* market price? You tell us.' Not one real-estate agent or insurance agent had given us the same price – most avoided the question altogether. They were only wild guesses that bounced somewhere between $300 000 and a million dollars. Basically nobody had any idea. Even the bloody business manager of the Ballarat diocese suggested to Father Van de Camp that if $200 000 was all that had been offered in the tender process, then that *was* the market price. Market price is what the market is willing to pay. All of a sudden, we the community had become consumers in a market, and to my mind, our offer was already far above what we should have had to go to. On the rates notice, the place was valued at $230 000 which was about as certain a figure as we could find. Pat couldn't say when, but said we'd be informed and given a price for which we should match, if we wanted to stay in the game.

I could have choked. How dare they? 'I can't believe you didn't walk out,' I said, feeling about as angry with him in that moment as I did the Catholic Church.

The next day I revisited my own life and made a typical rushed trip to Melbourne to get my fingers stamped for a bloody UK visa that I hardly wanted, but being so close to finalised it gave me five years to keep my options open. I felt like I could hardly throw it away. I submitted the thing on the dot of five o'clock and hoped the British High Commission had more mercy and compassion than the Catholic Church. I caught up with a friend for coffee naïvely hoping that some kind of resolution had been found at home. And then Liz rang.

'I just got a phone call from Dennis Bushell.' Dennis Bushell grew up in Killarney and joined our campaign after reading the full page of letters to the editor six weeks earlier. 'Paul Harris just rang him and told him we weren't successful.'

'Dennis Bushell? Why on earth is the real estate ringing Dennis Bushell?' Dennis was a great asset to our committee, but he was neither president, secretary nor treasurer. Why was the real estate ringing a bloke he happened to know around town, to pass on that kind of news?

'So we've got our price. It's in the high $300 000's. We've got 24 hours to come up with a new offer, or the property will be put on an open market for $425 000.'

'$425 000. You're joking?! That's $200 000 above the rated price! That's about fifteen times what the buggers have got the place insured for.' In fact, today was the very first time in three years, after *all* our years of attempts at seeking negotiation, that the Catholic Church had given us a figure. Their style left a lot to be desired.

'I'm not joking. Where are you?'

I was standing in the rain on Elizabeth Street, watching the commuters rush by towards their train home.

'What should I do?'

'Maybe you should pay our QC friend a visit.' Liz was in Gerry's kitchen and, together with Teresa, was clutching at straws.

I looked like a drowned rat and was hardly about to bowl up to the door of a Collins Street law firm, so I went to the university library and pumped out a media release, entitled 'Thieves in the Temple', a critical, but also bewildered piece based on the fact that the Catholic Church could hold a community to ransom like this, who'd worked so hard and seemed to be behaving more like Christ than the Church itself. I got on the night train back to Warrnambool, my phone stuck to my ear, to listen in as the committee congregated at the hall and expressed their feelings in words I wouldn't print. After four hours they agreed to bump up the offer by $10 000 but no more, simply the most we could realistically stretch ourselves given the loan we'd been approved for.

The next morning Liz and I were straight out to 'the Shed' in

Killarney. Despite my pre-prepared media release we weren't ready to share our disappointment with the media, but Paul Harris, bless him, couldn't wait to let them know that St Brigid's was about to hit the open market. So much for our 24-hour negotiating 'grace' period. Not content with just being a real-estate agent, suddenly Paul Harris was behaving like a public-relations consultant for the Catholic Church and was milking it for all it was worth. In between radio interviews, somebody dropped off his business card to the bikie gang in Warrnambool with a handwritten note saying 'thought this might make a good club house'. The next day the front-page newspaper article ran the headline 'Dear bikies, fancy a church?' with a picture of the church and the bikie flag at its mast, a moment of comic relief in an otherwise pretty devastating few days. The letters and the 'SMS your view' pages of the paper summed up the bleakness: 'Bikie gang shows more respect than Catholic Church and Paul Harris put together. Thank you Mr Hooker.'

The newspaper rang on the hour, every hour, and every hour we felt more and more incensed, but too scared to open our mouths lest the bottled-up anger explode. We scoured our phone lists, and googled our hearts out, looking for anyone, anyone at all, who appeared to have money and we had no shame in picking up the phone and asking them. It wasn't exactly strategic thinking, it was merely operating under the pump. At one point, Teresa hung up the phone and said 'That was a $30 000 phone call.' Heartened by the response, we kept going.

Overwhelmed and claustrophobic from too many hours sitting in Shane and Teresa's shed, I got in the car and drove down to the beach, just to breathe in the fresh air and get my feet wet. Dad was driving around the countryside collecting letters of disapproval from parishioners to submit to Father Van de Camp. Just before 5 pm, Gerry put forward the motion that FOSB put in a renewed bid of $205 000, which we all unanimously supported. At 4:47 pm, Teresa picked up the phone to Paul Harris, with everybody sitting around her, and made the offer. At 5 pm, we checked LJ Hooker's website again and saw that St Brigid's was now being advertised on the open market with a $425 000 price tag attached. What happened to the 24-hours grace period? Who was in charge here? Did Mr Harris even consult Father Van de Camp? No, we learned later, he hadn't, just rejected our bid off his own back. I guess that's to be expected when the Church hands over control to a real-estate agent.

The newspaper kept ringing. For the first time, we were at a loss to know what to say publicly, feeling bound by contractual processes, and bizarrely, after all that had happened, we still felt silenced by the Catholic hierarchy, in whose hands lay the power to decide upon our community's fate.

Liz and I drove home, so drained and bewildered and at a loss to know what to do, it felt like we we'd been at a bedside vigil, on the brink of an irreplaceable loss. As is the way in times of distress and grief, we stopped in at the pub and drowned our sorrows over a glass of red. Back at her house, I fell into bed and had drifted off to into a restless sleep, where my phone kept ringing, loud and irritating. The phone often rang in my dreams these days. But when I opened my eyes in the pitch black, I saw the illuminate light flashing on the floor beside me.

'Hello,' I said groggily. It was ABC radio. 'What time is it?'

'We'd like to do an interview with you about St Brigid's.'

Why were they ringing me in the middle of the night? I told them Teresa O'Brien is our spokesperson and they hung up.

In that moment before real wakefulness, the reality of the day not yet sunk in, I wondered why they were calling me. Then it hit me, as I sat up in bed. St Brigid's. It's gone.

I scrambled for the 'recent' button on my phone. Teresa was top of my list. It was engaged.

I swung my legs over the bed and stumbled out into the loungeroom. Liz was lying on the couch, cuddled up with Stella; *Sunrise* on TV. She looked as wrung-out as I felt.

'That was the ABC', I said as the phone rang in my hand.

'Gina, ABC want to do an interview. What should I say?', said Teresa breathlessly at the other end of the phone.

'God, Teresa, I don't know. It's 6:15 in the morning. Have you been to bed? You sound wide awake,' I said, eying the clock on the mantelpiece.

'Yes, but Dennis Bushell rang me fifteen minutes ago. He'd just got the paper. We're on the front page.' Her voice was hoarse, deadened by fatigue.

'I didn't think they'd do that. They said they wouldn't go to the papers. I don't know what to do anymore, Gina. What do we say?', Teresa O'Brien, always so strong, so poised, so confident, was crying, like *really* crying.

'Fuck, Teresa, I don't know. We lost. Say whatever you fucking like. We've played their game for so long; we hardly know how to tell it as it is. They've treated us like dirt all the way through this thing. What have we got to hide now?' I said angrily.

'We've worked so bloody hard, none of us have slept in weeks. Why are they doing this to us?' she said, her voice choked up.

Liz and Stella lay on the couch and watched me pacing the floor, tears streaming down my own face.

'Teresa,' I said quietly and slowly. 'You get on the radio, and tell them what you just told me. Tell them how hard we've worked, what this means to us. Tell them how exhausted you are. This is not fair, and you don't need to pretend anymore.'

It was hardly professional media advice, but I no longer cared. I was exhausted, and sick of playing this game. We'd worked so hard to play by the rules, to keep our mouths shut and say only nice things about the Church. We stuck to our main messages about protecting and preserving heritage and culture, and the need for a community gathering space. I was so sick of writing those lines over and over again, Teresa as spokesperson must have felt like a broken record.

For the first time in three years, she let go of the script.

I boiled the kettle and tried to wake up, flicking the radio on and the familiar ring of the ABC news bulletin sounded through the house. 'Today is a black day for our community and rural communities everywhere.' I was stunned to hear Teresa's normally strong voice, broken and teary, the first words to boom from the ABC news bulletin.

I turned the radio up full bore.

'If the Catholic Church can't sit down and negotiate with the people in their own communities, it's a sad day for all of us. It's disgusting.' Her words fell out in bitterness.

'We've fought this for nearly four years now. We've lost a lot of

A BLACK DAY

sleep over the last six weeks. We've tried to do the right thing. We offered what we could afford. We're on our knees, and literally begging for mercy.

'Father Van de Camp arrived in our community just over 12 months ago. Yet his decision could wash away 130 years of our history, and spell the end of our community.'

She was brilliant. Liz and I stood glued to the floor, tears streaming down our faces, while Stella whinged for her breakfast.

'An emotional Teresa O'Brien, secretary of The Friends of St Brigid's, whose bid to buy back their community church has just been rejected,' the news presenter read.

When the news update was finished, the ABC presenter reintroduced his first guest, Teresa O'Brien. 'You can hear by the exhaustion in her voice, how hard this community have worked,' he said.

And Teresa was back on line. 'Steve, we've been working for nearly four years on this case. We're bewildered by the price the Catholic Church have put forward. We put in a fair price, but we haven't got endless amounts of money. We're a small rural community.'

The presenter hardly had to ask questions. This was Teresa's moment, and she took it, in a way she'd never done before. All her frustrations, her sense of injustice, poured out. But not in an incoherent, accusing or offensive way. It was incredibly raw, and deeply traumatic to listen to.

We weren't the only ones to think so. The presenter was clearly moved, and so were the listeners who rang in to support.

As soon as it was over I rang Teresa. It took me a couple of goes to get through to her, I wasn't the only local listening to ABC radio at 7 am obviously.

'Geez, Teresa, I know I told you to say whatever you liked, but you really went for it!'

'Yeah, I think Steve got a bit more than he bargained for there.' We had a laugh, the tension released somewhat. I could hear Teresa's kids beginning the morning routine before school, so let her go.

'We'll be out soon,' I promised.

By the time 8 am came around, we were tuned into 774 ABC Melbourne's airwaves. It was amazing to hear Teresa O'Brien's teary voice, immediately after that news jingle, before the ABC flagship programme, AM, telling the world 'Today is a black day for rural communities everywhere'. Our pain and exhaustion and loss had made prime-time news.

We picked up the paper on the way to Killarney. LJ Hooker and the parish priest had got pride of place on the front page. 'They thought we were just going to give it away,' said Father Van de Camp, patronisingly. 'This is definitely the most interest I've ever had in a property I've sold,' said Paul Harris.

Lucky for Paul Harris and LJ Hooker. Not so lucky for the community. We spent another day in the Shed making phone calls and conducting interviews, uselessly, because St Brigid's now sat on an open market with a $425 000 price tag on it. It was well beyond our reach.

We might rise to fight another day, but that Friday afternoon, as people began to congregate at Shane and Teresa's, we patted each other on the back for our efforts, like footballers who've just lost the grand final, lamenting the fact that the Catholic Church had simply got the better of us, putting St Brigid's well and truly, perhaps deliberately, out of our reach.

I drove home to Mum and Dad's and sat down on the couch, directly facing them sitting in arm chairs across from me. A candle was burning, as usual, alongside Mother Mary, a crucifix, the Bible and an assortment of prayer cards and rosary beads. An empty fish-and-chip paper lay on the floor.

'There's none left,' I observed pointlessly. My voice was leaden, it sounded like it was coming out of a mouth far away from here.

'There's ham in the fridge,' Mum said in the same tone.

'I'm not hungry.'

'We lost, Mum,' I pointed out, as if she hadn't heard.

My mum is normally so good in a crisis. People go to her to share their woes. She holds their hands and looks into their eyes with deep concern and always, *always* knows the right thing to say. I know that because they tell her. They tell me. I've seen my mum hold up half the sky in a crisis.

Tonight, she looked straight through me, like she hadn't heard. I started to cry.

'It's gone, Mum.'

A BLACK DAY

No response.

Dad, sitting alongside her, stared at the six o'clock news blaring beside me. I wanted to switch off the TV and scream at them, but I just sat there, sobbing like a child.

'The bastards!' I swore with all the anger I could muster.

Mum and Dad said nothing. Nothing. There was nothing to say. It must have been twenty years since I'd cried like that in front of my parents, as if they could do something to make it better. I was an inconsolable child. But there was no consolation to be had.

I went to bed, and slept not a wink.

SAVING ST BRIGID'S

Chapter Seventeen

The race to the finish line

At the end of that black day, I sat in the kitchen drinking brandy and thinking about Nana. I can imagine what she'd have to say about this. Poor Nana didn't know half the story; Mum and Dad would never have done that to her, and still she knew. It wasn't right. You hardly needed your wits about you to see that.

At 2 am, I told the world on Facebook that I was devastated. Friends and colleagues from London and New York, who knew not why, wrote sympathetic comments on my wall as if I'd just had a death in the family. Is this what it felt like?

At 4 am, I wrote to every nun and brother I could remember that I used to work with. Wasn't there something, anything, anybody could do? I wrote to Frank Brennan, a Jesuit priest and human-rights lawyer – Shane's friend. Funnily enough, he wrote straight back. A new idea, a sliver of hope, maybe.

I went back to bed, tossing and turning until dawn. 'We lost. I'm leaving. It's gone. I have to go now. We lost. I'm leaving. Sydney. Job. Monday. We lost.' My brain was malfunctioning, incapable of coherent thought. Or any thought at all. It was stuck, like a needle on a record player, on one note: 'We lost and I'm leaving again.'

At 7 am, I rang Mary-Ellen. I knew she had a shift at the hospital today.

Desperate, I asked her if she could get me some sleeping tablets. I knew what the response would be.

'No, Gina.' Only Mary-Ellen can say no like that and still sound compassionate and caring.

'You need to see a doctor. Do you think it's wise to be going to Sydney today? Can you renegotiate your start date?'

I probably could have. But even thinking about it felt too hard.

'Where would I find a doctor?' I didn't even live in this town, I thought bitterly, but I didn't dwell too long on that point in case I cracked.

All I wanted in life now was sleep, and sleep wouldn't come.

At 9 am, my eyes dry and salty, my brain pounding inside my skull, saliva collecting in my mouth like I might vomit, Elise, my new friend in Tower Hill, knocked on the door. She'd organised a surprise for my leaving day. She drove me to Warrnambool and delivered me to a hairdresser. I badly needed a haircut, but simply didn't have the money. It was her shout. Six weeks earlier, I didn't know the girl. Now, she was like my best friend. I spent an hour with my head melting into the hands of the hairdresser, avoiding her inane conversation, wishing I could just crawl under a rock and run away from the world. Elise took me op shopping and I bought a new outfit for my first day at work. I was ready to go, I guess.

At home, I did my ritual goodbye. I climbed to the top of the volcanic crater at Tower Hill, huffing and puffing all 200 steps of it. I stood at the top and looked out at the land, at the sea, and wondered what would become of this place. Our story might be etched into the soil here, but who would remember it? In that farmhouse down before the sea, my parents sat, bereft and beaten. To the north side of the crater wall, sat a man in a big white presbytery all on his own, a man who had the power to change all this. I wondered if Saint Brigid was still looking down on us. At Killarney beach, I took my shoes off and walked in the chilly shallows, just to feel alive again. Though I had cursed God in the night, today, as my heart softened with the waves that crashed on the shore, I thanked the Creator for at least giving us a place where we could find solace. I guess we were lucky in that way.

Liz drove me to the airport with a suitcase of clothes and a doona in a garbage bag. Nothing had changed since Monica drove me to

THE RACE TO THE FINISH LINE

Melbourne the very first time I 'went away', aged eighteen, with an old pot and pan and cup and plate that Mum cleaned out of the cupboards. When was I going to grow up and get serious about life?

In the car, Stella talked about the animals at the Werribee zoo. I fielded phone calls from journalists. 'Yes, I'd love to do a story, but I'm actually moving to Sydney.'

'Sydney?'

It sounded ridiculous. I'd just spent six weeks on the phone to these journalists, imparting my passion for my community. They probably thought I was a fraud.

In Sydney, I tried to put together my bed, bought from a friend of a friend, packaged in plastic and bags of screws and nails. I failed and went out to get a curry. When I returned, I lay on the mattress on the floor, wondering about sleep. I pulled my doona over me, no care for sheets or pillowcases, and this time sleep came. Waking up to the warm Sydney sun streaming in the window was the sweetest feeling. I'd actually slept for the first time in weeks it seemed, and I felt human again.

Back at home, they hadn't given up. The executive of The Friends of St Brigid's wrote to express their 'extreme disappointment by your decision to reject the tender', and to request a meeting to negotiate with the finance committee. The request was accepted and on the following Tuesday night, Teresa, Milton, Dad, Liz and Mary-Ellen met with the finance committee. The Friends were given thirty minutes to outline our arguments once again and set the record straight on a whole lot of misconceptions and misunderstandings (the finance committee didn't seem to understand the concept of an incorporated association and were under the impression, thanks to our national media coverage and support, that we had bucketloads of money hidden away somewhere), before being told they would receive a response to our request for a negotiated figure, as a matter of urgency. Two days later Teresa received a phone call to say that if we offered $305 000 then our offer would be accepted. Teresa requested seven days to come up with the money, which was agreed. On Friday, Father Van de Camp rang Teresa and told her another party was ready to sign on the dotted line. He stressed the urgency of the Friends putting in an offer, and Teresa pleaded with him to understand that she couldn't make such a decision on her own, that it would need to go to a vote. The Friends of St Brigid's would meet again in two days, on Sunday afternoon.

On Sunday afternoon, the crew met at 3 pm as usual. Options were laid on the table as to how the group might come up with the $305 000. There was talk of a staged acquisition, re-alignment of boundaries, putting in an injunction. There were phone calls to solicitors and real-estate agents and people with money in Warrnambool, Port Fairy, Melbourne. Phones rang, people came and went, and came back again. The meeting was adjourned so people could discuss and ponder the options, and then a motion was put forward to offer $305 000 as a staged acquisition over twelve months. It was accepted and the meeting broke again while Teresa awaited an expected phone call from Father Van de Camp. I participated in this marathon meeting over the phone, in snippets, sitting in my bed in Sydney, filing our media clippings. There was the sound of jubilation, jokes and laughter. They sounded strong and confident, like they might just pull this thing off.

At around 6 pm, Father Van de Camp rang and dismissed the offer, because earlier that day he'd already verbally accepted an offer from another party.

Teresa fell to the floor in the kitchen, crippled in pain and shock. Doubled over on the ground, the reality sank in.

'It's gone,' she cried. 'We've lost it.'

All I could hear was the gasping and cries of people in distress. The feeling of elation had just plummeted in a single moment into complete despair.

There was the sound of phones ringing and people talking in hurried, panicked voices. Questions were being thrown back and forth between lawyers and journalists and church leaders whose numbers we had and who we could trust and then out among the group again. It was chaotic and crazy and I wished like anything I could click my fingers and be there. There was serious talk of squatting in the church, as Teresa and Kate shared a cigarette outside, wondering how they'd get through the freezing winter in that big old church. They bet that Gina, the homeless one among us, would welcome the opportunity. It was nice to feel included

The Race to the Finish Line

from a thousand miles away.

At 9 pm, Sister Adele Howard, a Mercy Sister from Melbourne, drove out to Crossley to see if she could help. Along with all the Howard children, she too had grown up singing at St Brigid's church as a child. Like her brother and sister, Shane and Marcia, she too must have felt the impending loss deeply.

Driving down the mad mile, in the howling wind and rain, past the Celtic crosses of the cemetery, she threw her hands in the air and summoned up the spirits of the old people.

'Come on, you old ones, come with me to Crossley, we need your help.'

A poised, well-groomed woman, she breathed fresh air into the chaos in the hall. The group were running out of options and asked her if she would go, on their behalf, to see Father Van de Camp. And so with their blessing, she drove a lonely road around the rim of Tower Hill Lake, the wind nearly whipping the car off the road. Standing at the presbytery door, on that wild August winter's night, with only one light shining from an upstairs window, Father Van de Camp didn't answer her knock. Carrying the full weight of expectation and suffering of a community, she dialled his number. Eventually he came to the door in dressing gown and slippers. He welcomed her in, boiled the kettle, and arranged some Anzac biscuits on a plate.

What was said, we will never really know, but we do know Sister Adele described the distress she had just witnessed and appealed to his better nature. All that now matters, is that in that eleventh hour, Father Van de Camp had a change of heart.

She returned to Crossley a half-hour later.

'It's yours.'

There was so much shrieking and cheering and noise, I couldn't figure out what had just happened.

'What???'

'Get your offer into LJ Hooker at 9 o'clock in the morning. Father Van de Camp will contact Paul Harris to accept the offer.'

'But Father Van de Camp told us that the other party are meant to be signing on the dotted line at 9 am.'

'Get there at eight-thirty then,' she said with a grin.

Kate had started knitting a scarf when she arrived. By the end of the meeting, the scarf complete, and Liz was asking if she could buy it. Their epic meeting had lasted nine hours.

I spent the next morning, second week at my new job in Sydney, hanging out of the toilet window, looking across a Sydney skyline, as I tried to soak up the excitement and adrenalin of my community, talking in whispers as they met for coffee across the road, waiting for the real-estate agent to open its doors, wondering if the other party were sitting alongside them in the busy café, with their own plans to sign on the dotted line. It sounded like some kind of crazy 'amazing race'. It certainly had been an epic finish. The bid was made, the phone call went through, and finally, finally, our offer was accepted. The merry dance was over. The miracle had been granted.

It was barely 9 am and my sisters and parents and friends were popping champagne in the main street of Warrnambool. I was more homesick than I've ever been. When I eventually hung up the phone, I went and found my boss.

'I need to go home.'

'Not feeling well?'

'No, I need to go home-home. I need to go home to Tower Hill. They just saved St Brigid's. I need to be there.'

It wasn't a request. He could sack me if he wanted to. I was exhausted and burnt out and needed to be with my mob to see what victory felt like.

Thankfully, he got the point.

The music played long and loud in the Crossley hall that cold August night in 2009. It was the usual no-fuss affair, everyone arrived with their picnic baskets and eskys, to share around the table, as the musicians ramped up their instruments, the piano accordion and violin and guitars in full swing, and as usual 'St Brigid's Wishing Well' welcomed the generosity of those who cared to donate.

As usual it was Teresa who summed up our sentiment.

'It's been quite a battle,' she said with a sigh of relief. 'It was

THE RACE TO THE FINISH LINE

October 2005 when Shane first sat down and wrote a three-page letter to Father Bryant explaining the significance of the buildings, and first mooted the idea that St Brigid's could be the first Australian-Irish cultural heritage centre. That's almost four years ago now.'

She talked about the challenges, the low times and the price people had paid for Saving St Brigid's. But it was the collective spirit, she said, the knowledge that 'we can do this', that kept us going.

'We had no idea, when we started out, the long journey that was ahead of us.'

She paid tribute to each of us around the room, from Liz, the reluctant chairperson who couldn't control a meeting, to Jim for his handwritten letter to Kerry O'Brien that took us to a national audience, to those who transcribed titles and archival material, those who made cakes and sandwiches and those who brought new ideas and whose advice helped us keep our heads through the insanity.

Like most people in the area, Teresa had gone away and come back here, and for her, saving St Brigid's was the means to know people beyond names in a phone book.

'In the last three and a half years my tapestry has been all the richer and all the greater, and I now have an enormous blanket of connections brought together in this community. For that alone, that was the St Brigid's miracle for me.'

She saved her most heartfelt tribute for our elders.

'Our elders are the glue which holds our community together. They have our history, they've carried our story, they've lived it. We've got to protect that story. They've bought us this far, now its up to us, to take our community forward into the future.'

In a little speech to the old ones, she told them: 'Do not lose heart, because your children and your grandchildren will continue your legacy. It's simple, and perhaps it goes without saying, look after each other, respect your elders, don't let each other down – it was these basic values that you learned in that church, that you've passed down in this community. Half of us don't go to mass, some of us aren't even Catholic – but those principles are universal. It's about being a community.'

'But man, it was hard work. They put a capital value on our

community, and dollar after dollar they kept raising the bar, and we had to keep going out there to find more money. In the end, we took an enormous debt on our shoulders. But the Irish did it for themselves, they built this hall, they built their own church. They didn't have an education, or the income or the infrastructure or the resources that we have. If they can do it, surely we can.'

And this, she told us, was not a story that finished here in South-West Victoria. In Ireland, Shane would be celebrating. Teresa had broken the good news to Seamus Begely a musician in Ireland, who told a packed house in Dingle, Ireland that they'd better come out to Crossley, Australia to find what they've lost in Ireland.

'We got caught up with the money and we forgot what it was all about. When I sat among your families at Crossley, I felt like I was part of a real living community. It was a beautiful thing, and I'll never forget it.' Teresa choked up when she thanked us all. 'It's been an honour to be a part of this.'

'Three cheers for The Friends of St Brigid's,' someone piped up. When the cheering and whistling died down, it was Dad's voice that cut across the crowd.

'I'd like to say a few words,' he said quietly. 'I'd like to raise a glass to those who are no longer with us. The people whose presence I feel every time I step into this hall.'

'To Des Gleeson and Frank O'Brien who locked the church door every week. To Mr Farley and Johnny Nagel and Joe Harrington, the blokes who took the tickets at the door on those cold wintery nights. To my mum…and to all the other women who made the sandwiches, this one's for you,' he said, his voice cracking with emotion.

'They were great times we had in this hall, and it's the old ones we have to thank that we're even here.'

I watched my 70 year-old father, and I could see in his misty eyes that in this place, he was an obedient God-fearing five-year-old, he was a brave young lad of fourteen leaving school, and he was a shy young man of sixteen falling in love.

'I met my wife in this hall,' Dad continued on, bringing tears to the eyes of everyone in the hall as Mum and Dad's eyes met across the room.

THE RACE TO THE FINISH LINE

'Times were tough back then, but the Sunday night dances were the highlight of our lives.'

Dad didn't need to tell us kids, we'd heard it often enough. 'We've been married almost fifty years, and we've never had it easy, but our memories of Crossley were what kept us going.'

'No one has worked as hard at this place, than Loretta. We could have let it go a long time ago, but Loretta was always saying, "The old ones did it for us. It's our job to pass it on."'

'I think it's been worth it, Love,' Dad said with real admiration in his voice for my mum, his companion of more than half a century. Mum stepped over and took his hand. We were all brimming with tears, as Dad borrowed from the Fureys song that I'll forever associate with the love my parents share.

'Loretta, I love you, as I loved you when you were sweet sixteen.'

With tears streaming down our faces, my sisters and I joined Mum and Dad for a group hug. And then the sound of the harmonica signalled the tune of another song we'd come to think of as ours. The Friends gathered around, and Myra Howard led us in our happiest rendition of 'Church up on the Hill'. We lingered in chorus over the last lyric, relishing that finally, finally, our dream had become a reality.

'Fade away, not fade away, survive and live another day, a light still shines from that church up on the hill, a light still shines from that church up on the hill.'

Somebody once said to me 'You're lucky, you know', when standing at the top of Tower Hill, pointing out my ancestral ground, that long stretch of land that runs by the sea. In our globalised, fast moving, mobile world, few people knew what it was to grow up in the place where both sides of their family came from. It was a rare thing, they said, to stand on the land where your ancestors first arrived and feel that you belong there, in every sense of the word.

In the car on the way back to Melbourne, a flight to Sydney to catch, I craned my neck around to take one last long look over those potato fields that I call home. The view had always taken my breath away. It's simply beautiful. But now, its meaning resonated with something much deeper inside me. In the past few months, it was like I'd come to fully realise who I was, where I belonged in this world. In that church up on the hill, I'd learned how to believe, to have faith. In the fields below, I learned how to stand up for what I believed in. We'd fought in good faith, and the victory was ours.

'You're lucky, you know,' I whispered to myself, as I went back out into the world, the south-west coastline slipping from view.

Epilogue

On a warm day in the summer that followed, we sat on the floor in the hall listening to Irish tunes, learning how to weave St Brigid's cross from the rushes we brought up from the Killarney swamp. It was the first of February, St Brigid's day, the first day of the northern spring. To celebrate the saint who is patroness of just about everything – dairy maids, infants, midwives, blacksmiths, poets, nuns, students, poultry farmers, sailors, scholars and travellers – we held a family fun day out and asked the kids to dress up in her honour. Little girls walked around wearing peasant skirts, a scarf over their heads; one carried a chicken. Another dressed like a Josephite in a brown habit, boys in waistcoats came as scholars, the babies came as well, infants in swaddling cloth. Phil and Helen Keegan organised games that harked back to my childhood; potato sack, egg and spoon and tunnel ball with a spud, a race around the church.

    We all took home a cross and hung it above our doors, to ward off evil spirits and keep us safe. Saving St Brigid's has been such an education for all of us, reconnecting us to long-forgotten traditions, even in Ireland. 'You people are more Irish than the Irish,' laughed the new school principal at St Patrick's primary, just moved here from Ireland.

    It wasn't the first time we'd heard that. I guess that's the story of migration, the world over. When love of the homeland binds people together, through music, dance and tradition, with a passion that leaves them holding it strong, long after it's left behind at home. The funny thing was, that for most of us, we hadn't realised we had been holding onto it – that the everyday things we took for granted, like big families, endless cups of teas, and lively wakes that went long into the night, the way things were, was in fact a unique culture.

That summer, our community mourned the passing of a great friend. When John Amor, an environmentalist and community worker, discovered he had cancer, he said he wanted his funeral at St Brigid's. He'd grown up Catholic, but had long given it away. He hadn't lost his respect for his religious tradition, and a building as sacred as St Brigid's was a fitting place for a farewell. But it was more than that. John was a volunteer in every community organisation imaginable. St Brigid's embodied the way he'd chosen to live his life. The altar was decorated with flags and pictures, and a dozen caps were lined up, each representing a group or club he was a part of – the CFA, his wildlife rescue, community radio. I've been to a lot of big funerals, it's what we Irish Catholics do, but this was something else. Speakers had to be hooked up so that the crowd outside could hear the heartfelt speeches. The people there were from all walks of life; many had no relation to St Brigid's, but all shared their gratitude for what we'd saved. Afterwards, a tree was planted in John's honour at the front gate. After the soup and sandwiches were over and the crowd had gone home, a few of us stood around that young sapling and talked about what the day had meant.

'Today was the beginning of a "post Church" community,' said Shane. 'This was about church in the broadest sense of the word.'

This felt like how church was meant to be – warm, welcoming, inclusive; people sharing a deep sense of respect and connection. St Brigid's is no longer a Catholic church. It's not consecrated as such, but that doesn't seem to worry too many people. St Brigid's has played host to its fair share of weddings and funerals in the past few years. We simply ask that they treat our sacred church with the respect and honour it deserves. We haven't yet been let down. People come from near and far to celebrate their major life moments at St Brigid's. Some, no doubt, simply because it's hard to find a more beautiful building, others because their Catholic upbringing demands it of them; and then there are some who travel back

EPILOGUE

to Crossley for their big day, because their parents or their grandparents did it before them. St Brigid's has a remarkable reach.

St Brigid's has also played host to some amazing public events. In the winter of that first year we owned St Brigid's, Donna Dixon organised a dinner in partnership with Port Fairy Consolidated School, Stephanie Alexander Kitchen Garden Program. The dinner was called 'Shared Hands', a celebration of the pioneers who built St Brigid's, the community who fought to save them, the farmers, young and old, who grew the food, the businesses that donated it, the chefs who volunteered their time to prepare it, and the little hands who served it.

It was the first function we've ever held in the church. People sat, ten to a pew, at candlelit tables. The O'Brien girls went to town on the flowers; the children made lavender posies and hand drew pictures as name settings. With their drawings of tractors, potatoes and pumpkins, Donna screenprinted chef's hats and aprons for the kids, who waited on tables and served up the delicious local fare, made by some of Port Fairy's top chefs. The food was topnotch, the children were adorable, and the atmosphere was warm and cosy, in the unique setting of the hundred-year-old Romanesque church. It was a rare treat, and an unforgettable night.

Nights like these are hard work, taking teams of volunteers months and months to organise, which is fine if that's the thing you do each year for your community. The thing about The Friends of St Brigid's is that we are saddled with an enormous debt, and we have to pull off fundraisers like this month after month, to cover the bare minimum of $25,000 of mortgage repayments and insurance for the year. And that's before we even think about utilities or maintenance or upgrades. We've had more sausage sizzles than we care to remember, sold soup and soda scones, held garage sales and catered at dozens of weddings, funerals and parties, just to keep the mortgage payments up. On the upside, with the grant-writing skills of Mary-Ellen on the team, we've been quite successful in obtaining grants, from the local shire, to state government; even the Irish government have given us money. We've got grants for everything from a ride-on mower to hosting a Men's Shed, replacing the roof on the old hall, and for a new, commercial kitchen. All this is a tremendous asset for the community. However, each grant comes with its own need for volunteer hands on deck and project management skills, responsibilities and reporting lines that are a big ask for a small community organisation. And grant funding still doesn't pay the mortgage. The work is never ending, and at times I wonder if it's beyond us. We've all had our moments where we've wondered if we did the right thing in saving St Brigid's and saddling ourselves with such a financial burden. I ring home to hear that Mum's been up at the crack of dawn, making scones and sandwiches, and had her hands in the sink at Crossley for the past four hours and Dad and Gerry, aged seventy-something, have just got their white cards, and are climbing the scaffolds to help build the new roof. My parents are working as physically hard as they did when they first opened the doors to the hall, back in 1990, for the 'Back to Crossley'. I worry about them, of course. It's not what you want for your parents in their retirement, to be cleaning toilets and pulling weeds at the local hall.

But then again, I know very few people in their seventies with as much sense of purpose and drive as my mum and dad. There's no doubt that St Brigid's gives them great fulfilment in their autumn years. Their energy is infectious – a phone call home always broadens my perspective, lifts me out of a rut and reminds me again of why we're put on this planet.

No, it's definitely not easy, although nothing worthwhile ever is. I learned that a long time ago.

And I'm obviously not the only one to think so. There can't be many community groups who work as hard as ours; there are even fewer who carry the burden of a 25-year mortgage, just to keep their community alive. But this is no ordinary community. The Friends of St Brigid's are remarkable people, strong and wise and witty. A monthly meeting at Crossley is a comic affair, from the business of cake making to mowing lawns and mortgage repayments it's funny to watch people grapple in that space both within and well outside their comfort zones. But there's always a certain spirit in that room that keeps people coming back. It's the spirit of a group of people who have been tried and tested and found strength in their adversity, and in each other.

And through it all, they still know how to have a good laugh. There are always lots of laughs at St Brigid's.

Then there are those who come out of the woodwork, just when

Epilogue

we feel we are on our last legs. Countless volunteers have quietly joined us along the way, and some have moved on, but all share the sense that we are a part of something, something that matters for the world. St Brigid's is still hanging in there on a knife-edge. There are no guarantees that we'll make it. When interest rates rise, we hold our breath. When a booking is made, there's always a mad scramble to find enough volunteers to make sandwiches and wait tables. And somehow, it comes together.

St Brigid smiles down on us, as we continue to dance the merry jig.

The St Brigid's session, on the Monday after the Port Fairy Folk Festival, has gone from strength to strength. Since that first one seven years ago, jammed in at the Killarney Recreation Reserve, the crowd gets bigger every year. The faces are now familiar, people who came that first time were so moved they came back and keep coming back after all these years, because they say it makes them feel a part of something, something larger than themselves. That's the thing about St Brigid's, it satisfies something deep within, and you don't have to be Irish or Catholic or from Killarney to understand that. On that Monday night after folkie, I've often heard people say that though they live hours away, they feel that St Brigid's is their community too. They feel at home here.

The music is in a class all of its own, drawing more and more musicians to the table, some local, some not, some with thick Irish accents and steeped deep in the tradition; others from different parts of the world, who bring foreign instruments and new sounds to the session. This year, an eccentric Irish chap with a twinkle in his eye leapt to his feet and held the room captive with the most impassioned recital of his poem, 'The day that love won', a poem about the day they laid down their arms in Northern Ireland, a day he prayed would come for conflicts the world over. We've played host to the Pigram Brothers from the Kimberley, Noriana Kennedy and the Beoga Brothers, Seamus Begley, and in 2012 Mary Black returned to Port Fairy and popped into Crossley before her national tour. She heaped praise on our community for holding onto the spirit of Ireland, and when she sang 'When Irish eyes are Smiling', there wasn't a person in the room who didn't join in.

Every year, the Lakes School of Irish Music and Dance, led by Felix Meagher, welcomes some 200 people from around the country to our district, who come to celebrate their Irish culture and heritage. There are music lessons and Gaelic language classes, writing workshops and dance classes – there's something for everyone. From the shy little ones that bravely face the crowds in Irish dance costume, to the old owls who share their wisdom in their poetry, it is the most wonderful celebration of Irish culture and heritage. Most years, St Brigid's hosts the 'The Spud Poets' night, which wouldn't be the same without Mary Fitoussi Bourke and her theatrical recital of her loveable poem, 'The Humble Potato'. This year gone by, we hosted the Ceili Dance. Twirling barefoot around the dance-floor by grey-haired men with smiling eyes, I caught a glimpse out the windows, raised on a hot summer's night. Black-and-white cows dotted the countryside; sprinklers fanned the potato fields. Not a whole lot had changed in a hundred years, I thought as I smiled to myself, thanking our ancestors for the legacy they had left us.

When I was a kid, Crossley was the place to be on Christmas Eve. I remember playing in the yard, with the sky glowing pink and red with the setting sun, 'Away in a Manger' ringing in my head, the magic of Christmas in the air. They are good memories. Even when Christmas Eve became the night of the year to hit the pub in Warrnambool, I still went to Mass at Crossley first, just to get into the spirit. All those years that St Brigid's fell silent, under the lock and key of the parish priest, Christmas was never quite the same. Once St Brigid's was ours once again, Christmas Carols was one of the first events to be locked in on the annual calendar. It's always a huge night. That first year, opera singer Peter Brocklehurst raised the roof of the church. Musicians come from everywhere, and for many budding young artists, the Christmas Carols is their first real live audience. The church is packed to capacity; 150 kids squash in cross-legged on the floor, dressed as angels and shepherds, waiting expectantly for Santa to arrive. One year, I stood there in a pew, alongside Mum and Dad and Marcia Howard, singing 'Gloria', their soaring voices lifting mine higher and higher into the vaulted ceiling above, just as our ancestors did at the opening mass now almost 100 years ago. Tears pricked my eyes as the emotion surged through me and I savoured the moment that made our battle so worthwhile.

I wonder what Father Van de Camp thinks as he drives past St

Epilogue

Brigid's these days, watching a community come alive in a dormant parish. Our community had been divided; alienated from the Church that had sowed the seed on which we had saved St Brigid's. But things didn't have to be this way. We have saved so much, yet there was pain and hurt in doing so, and now the two will be forever entwined.

But the battle is not yet over. It takes a lot of time and energy to protect and conserve heritage, and time and energy are in drastic short supply at Crossley. In 2010, we received a state government grant to conduct a business plan and an architectural design for St Brigid's Cultural and Heritage Centre. We commissioned one of Victoria's most respected museum curators with a very clear brief: we want our story told, but ours is a living culture, we don't want a static exhibition gathering dust under glass. Secondly, please do not interfere with the integrity of the building, and thirdly, our community will always need access to these buildings, for events like the Christmas Carols. John Challis was true to his word and produced an exceptional set of architectural drawings that depict floating display boards, discreet screens that drop from the ceiling, the confessionals as audio booths, a moveable dance floor and sound system, for our young dancers and musicians to perform the vibrant, living culture we are proud to share. All of this can always be packed away when St Brigid's is needed for a wedding or funeral. The plans are brilliant, the concept both innovative and respectful. But the truth is bringing it to life will cost hundreds of thousands of dollars. And our community has a mortgage to pay. Whilst some of us would give our right arm to sink our teeth into a project like this, the fact is, most of us are all-consumed by the monthly fundraising effort, and don't have the time or energy to prioritise heritage conservation. And it's pretty hard to argue with that.

Still, when I sat in the church at the launch of our architectural plans, Shane singing 'The Church on the Hill', as we toasted our work with an Irish whiskey, I had to believe that one day my grandchildren *will* come to St Brigid's and be proud of the legacy that was left to them. Our story will carry on. St Brigid's will survive.

Mum and Dad celebrated their fiftieth wedding anniversary at St Brigid's in May 2012. We celebrated in style; the ten of us children surprised them in a limousine and rolled out the red carpet, with a veil and bouquet for Mum and a flower for Dad's suit lapel. We drove down the back roads of Killarney and Dennington, listening to our parents reminisce about their wedding day, before we watched them renew their vows in a special fiftieth anniversary mass just for the bridal couple and their children.

Hundreds packed into the Crossley hall – their ten children and thirty grandchildren, and their brothers and sisters and nieces and nephews galore, their wedding party reunited, old-timers from the dances, Nestle's workers and retired farmers, Crossley churchgoers past and parishioners from Koroit, and of course, our Friends of St Brigid's. It was a joyful moment when my parents stood on that stage with their heads held high before an adoring crowd, who cheered their life and their love, and the contribution they have made over fifty years in our community. We all knew full well, that if it wasn't for Loretta and Mick Lane, we would not be standing in that special place.

Watching them, I could see that they were living proof of what Mum always used to say, 'you only ever get out of your community what you put into it'.

Though I didn't understand when I was young, it was good advice, I realise now.

Afterword

In the months since my book was first published in March 2014, I have often quoted my great-grandfather Dan Lane, who said at the opening mass at St Brigid's on June 28, 1914, that they wanted to leave their children a legacy. So it was quite moving to find myself, 100 years later to the day, standing in his footprint on the altar of St Brigid's church, welcoming people to the St Brigid's centenary celebrations. As Gerry O'Brien said in his speech, quoting from Martin Luther King, 'We, The Friends of St Brigid's, had a dream…and I think we got there today'.

It was an emotional moment for all of us who had fought so hard for so many years to keep St Brigid's in community hands.

As with the Last Mass in Chapter 1 of this book, people came from all over Australia to celebrate St Brigid's 100th birthday. As the weekend kicked off, people threw their arms around old school mates and dance partners they hadn't seen in fifty years. It was a joy to watch.

On the Saturday, we ran bus tours of the local area, down the narrow lanes of Crossley, by the sand dunes of Killarney and around that old volcano at Tower Hill. We invited the people on the bus to share their stories and for a moment there, I felt I had stepped back in time. Gazing across the stone fences and whitewashed dairies at those green fields, I saw through the lens of those wisecracking, tweed capped elders and it didn't take much to imagine myself back there, in a slower paced, bygone era – because somehow, against all the odds, this wonderful community had managed to retain the best of it.

Amidst the celebrations, I had the pleasure of launching another book, *The Church on the Hill: a Centenary History of St Brigid's, Crossley and its Irish-Australian community*, authored by Dr Helen Doyle[1].

Saving St Brigid's

While my book tells a mostly modern day story, Helen's tells the story of our forebears, their Irish origins and how they stamped their influence on this little corner of South West Victoria. Remarkably, Helen has captured more than 100 short family histories of our families who settled at Crossley, Killarney and Tower Hill.

And finally, the day we thought might never happen. On Sunday June 29, 2014, the new bishop of Ballarat, Bishop Paul Bird, joined Fr Bill Van de Camp to preside over the first Catholic Mass at St Brigid's since its closure in 2006. The pews were again packed end to end, and the clergy acknowledged the incredible efforts of our forebears in building St Brigid's. Unfortunately our incredible efforts at saving St Brigid's went unmentioned; the elephant in the room.

For many people however, it was a day of healing and reconciliation. All those familiar faces under the one roof again, joined in both prayer and a proud past that prevails, despite it all. One parishioner of old said to Mum and Dad that he 'hadn't felt right about St Brigid's' ever since that abrupt Last Mass, and yet he felt the centenary Mass had really helped to heal old wounds.

Well aware of those wounds inflicted during our battle, but also in relation to other abuses of Church power, The Friends of St Brigid's unveiled a memorial plaque and a 'Well of Healing and Peace'. This beautiful and serene garden overlooking the Southern Ocean welcomes all of those who seek refuge, peace and healing, in the true tradition of Christ. Families are invited to buy a paver, to mark our generation's legacy in the soil, just as our ancestors did a hundred years before.

---

1. "The Church on the Hill: a Centenary History of St Brigid's, Crossley and its Irish-Australian community" is available at www.bridinbooks.com.au

If you have enjoyed our story, we welcome your support to help us keep St Brigid's in community hands.

Tax deductible donations can be made through The Foundation of Rural and Regional Renewal, at www.frrr.org.au or directly to The Friends of St Brigid's at www.stbrigidscrossley.org.au

SAVING ST BRIGID'S

ACKNOWLEDGEMENTS

I might never have written this book if not for Bernadette Walters of One Day Hill publishing, who believed in the story and my ability to tell it, from the very start.

Shane Howard, it was your music that stirred my consciousness; it was your cultural knowledge, both Irish and Indigenous, that informed parts of my book; and it was your wisdom that I looked to at crucial stages during the journey. Your eloquent words in the opening of the book are a gift for which I will always be grateful.

To Mary Black for your generous support to our community; to you and Daniel O'Leary for your warm and encouraging words in this book.

To Colleen Hughson for filming my family and the Friends of St Brigid's while they told their story – I will be forever indebted for those precious hours of footage. Thanks must go to Monica O'Brien, Sue Elms, George Dummet, Ange Runci, Jenny Hughson and James Russell, who spent countless hours transcribing the interviews.

During the campaign Dr Helen Doyle spent long nights researching and writing a heritage assessment for Heritage Victoria. Your encouragement and generosity with your work enabled me to extend the scope of my story beyond whatever I initially thought I could.

Authors Brigid Delaney and Chrissie Foster: through the journey, in different ways your stories gave me the confidence to share my own.

To my sisters, Angela, Monica, Catherine, Mary-Ellen and Liz for taking turns to provide 'the writer retreat', for seeing me through the years required to complete this book; for a willingness to drop everything to discuss anything from the 'big picture' to the smallest detail.

To my brothers, Robert, Bernie, Patrick and Michael for being there, in a way that sometimes only brothers can.

To Sari Baird, Andrew See, Gren Skewes and Anthony Palmer, for your advice and wise counsel. To Andy Hamilton and Helene Clarke – for being the kind of readers that all writers should have.

Without Teresa O'Brien, we might never have saved St Brigid's, and I may not have this story to tell. Your confidence has long been my inspiration, and your strength so often a source of my self-belief. With special thanks for putting up with months of my indecision about the front cover! I love it!

To my proofreaders, Ian Sibley, Alex Kolasinki and layout designer, Mike Chanter. Thanks to photographer Wes Pryor, digital advisor Haydn Thompson and film producers Jary Nemo and Lucinda Horrocks from Wind & Sky Productions for your genuine interest in my story and generosity of spirit in giving me your best and asking for little in return.

To photographers Daniel Bickers, Chris Vaughan, Robin Sharrock, Andrew McCrae, Wes Pryor and Teresa O'Brien; Rob Gunstone, Aaron Sawall and Damian White of *The Warrnambool Standard* and Greg Carey and the Koroit Historical Society for permission to publish photos.

To the Warrnambool Art Gallery for permission to reproduce Eugène von Guàrard's Tower Hill. For permission to reproduce lyrics, thanks to Shane Howard and Mushroom Music, 'Solid Rock', 'Rise Up', 'Silvermines', 'Church Up On The Hill', Marcia Howard 'Wild and Free', and Kev Carmody 'Cannot Buy My Soul'.

To my aunties Katy Bray (nee Maloney) and Helen McGrath (nee Lane) for so carefully documenting our (ever-growing!) family tree – a wonderful gift for the generations to come. Thank you also to Ray Lane, whose research guided me to my ancestral ground in County Clare.

Acknowledgements

To the 189 people who contributed to my crowdfunding campaign on Pozible: thank you for helping to make this book possible.

To my mates who supported me through the fundraising drive – Andrew Bell, Liz Billings, Haydn Thompson and Ros Nairn – I couldn't have done it without you.

To those who endured living and working with me: after all these years, I hope the read is worth it!

To my friends at Gokula House, Anna and Chris, Shannon, Jez, Geva, Rob and Renita for the nourishment of body and soul every Sunday – both a world away, and yet in essence much the same as the Sunday ritual of my childhood. I am humbled by your selfless service to our community.

To all those I met along the way who gave me a hand and my friends who gave me their ear I thank you from the bottom of my heart.

To the Friends of St Brigid's – to think that many of you were unknown to me only a handful of years ago, but every time I wanted to give up writing, there you were, turning up, 'turning' sausages, selling raffle tickets – giving me the motivation to stick with it. This is *your* story too.

And finally, to Mum and Dad, Loretta and Michael Lane, for giving me the gift of this story to share.

SAVING ST BRIGID'S

Regina Lane was raised in the heartland of Irish Catholic Victoria, if not Australia. One of ten children, she grew up on a potato and dairy farm, nestled in the shadows of an ancient volcano, called Tower Hill, in southwest Victoria.

She was named Regina, in the Latin tradition, after the queen of heaven, and Brigid, after the patron saint of their local church, St Brigid's, in Crossley, where she attended mass every Sunday as a child.

She began her professional life as a social-justice worker, firstly for the Brigidine Sisters and then the Catholic Archdiocese of Melbourne, advocating on rights for refugees, reconciliation with Indigenous Australia, and anti-global-poverty campaigns, among other issues. She pursued her passion for social justice in the UK, working on the Make Poverty History campaign for CAFOD (the Catholic Agency for Overseas Development), the United Nations in New York and GetUp in Sydney, before joining the Australian Conservation Foundation in Melbourne, before becoming a publisher at Garratt Publishing.

Saving St Brigid's is her first book.

www.ingramcontent.com/pod-product-compliance
Lightning Source LLC
Chambersburg PA
CBHW050529300426
44113CB00012B/2013